St. Joseph County

Interim Report

This interim report is designed to be utilized as a working document by government agencies, local organizations, and private citizens as the basis for a wide variety of projects.

3rd Edition, Published June 2006

Left: Visitors enter and exit the Spring Brook Park.
Courtesy of Historic Preservation Commission of South Bend and St. Joseph County.

Left: Man poses in front of the Philadelphia Grill, circa 1920. *Courtesy of Historic Preservation Commission of South Bend and St. Joseph County.*

Cover: An 1875 drawing of the Jacob Whitmer/ Miller Farm (10006) in German Township. *Courtesy of Historic Preservation Commission of South Bend and St. Joseph County.*

Acknowledgments

Indiana Department of Natural Resources

Kyle J. Hupfer, Director,
Department of Natural Resources;
State Historic Preservation Officer

Jon C. Smith, Director,
Division of Historic Preservation and Archaeology;
Deputy State Historic Preservation Officer

Frank D. Hurdis, Jr.,
Chief of Registration and Survey,
Division of Historic Preservation and Archaeology

Steven D. Kennedy,
Chief of Grants and Administration,
Division of Historic Preservation and Archaeology

Published by:

Historic Preservation Commission of South Bend & St. Joseph County

Staff:
Catherine D. Hostetler, Director
Julie Schutte, Assistant Director
Wayne Doolittle, Preservation Specialist

Board Members:

Lynn A. Patrick, President
Todd Zeiger, Vice President
Mary Jane Chase, Secretary
Timothy S. Klusczinski, Treasurer
Catherine D. Hostetler
Martha J. Choitz
Gerald Udjak
Diane Wrobel-Illes
Joann Sporleder, Architectural Historian

St. Joseph County Board of Commissioners:

Cynthia A. Bodle
Mark A. Dobson
Steven Ross

Westerly Group, Inc.

Historic Landmarks Foundation of Indiana

Pat Wachtel, Interim President

Suzanne Stanis,
Director of Heritage Education and Information

Todd Zeiger, Northern Regional Director

Credits

Shannon Hill, Survey Coordinator, Layout and Typesetting

Amanda Jones, Layout and Design

Scott Brown and Jennifer Eblin, 2005 Field Surveyors

Candy Hudziak, Data Coordinator and Editorial Assistant

Nancy Connor, Publication Maps
Base maps were prepared in ArcView GIS from TIGER data provided by the United States Bureau of the Census.

Catherine Compton, Line Drawings

Priority Press was responsible for the printing of this interim report.

Histories adapted from the 2000 *St. Joseph County Interim Report* and the 1993 *City of South Bend Summary Report.*

In Appreciation

This project was funded in part by a U.S. Department of the Interior, National Park Service Historic Preservation Fund grant administered by the Indiana Department of Natural Resources, Division of Historic Preservation and Archaeology.

The Historic Preservation Commission of South Bend & St. Joseph County wishes to thank the following, whose support and sponsorship made this project possible:

St. Joseph County Commissioners

St. Joseph County Council

Introduction

History

The Indiana Division of Historic Preservation and Archaeology (DHPA) has conducted the Indiana Historic Sites and Structures Inventory as a continuing program since 1975. Historic Landmarks Foundation of Indiana (HLFI) assisted in developing the program and has surveyed 76 of the 82 counties surveyed to date in cooperation with the DHPA.

The major impetus for a comprehensive inventory of Indiana's cultural resources came from the National Historic Preservation Act of 1966. The Act declared it the role of the federal government to foster the preservation of our cultural resources in partnership with state and local governments and the private sector. In order to implement this policy, the Act created the National Register of Historic Places, comprised of buildings, sites, structures, objects, and districts significant in American history, architecture, archaeology, engineering, and culture (see Fig. 2, p. 9 for more information). It also established a partnership between the federal government and the states, whereby each state developed a state historic preservation program to be approved by the U.S. Secretary of the Interior. To gain approval, the governor of the state must appoint a State Historic Preservation Officer (SHPO) and a State Review Board. One of the responsibilities of the SHPO is to conduct a comprehensive statewide survey of historic properties and maintain inventories of such properties for the purpose of locating, identifying, and evaluating cultural resources. Another responsibility is to ensure that historic properties are taken into consideration in planning and development through the environmental review process, known as Section 106.

Left: An idyllic setting at Blake Garden. *Courtesy of Historic Preservation Commission of South Bend and St. Joseph*

Uses of the Survey

Upon completion of any county inventory, all original survey forms, maps, and photographs are filed with the DHPA. The DHPA uses the inventory to administer state and federal programs for historic preservation, particularly the environmental review process. By examining the inventory data, DHPA staff can determine whether any historically significant properties fall within the area to be affected by a proposed project, and take steps to mitigate that impact.

The DHPA also uses the inventory in the nomination process for the National Register of Historic Places. The survey forms indicate which properties are likely to be eligible for the National Register and provide information useful in preparing nominations. When owners or other interested citizens prepare National Register applications, the DHPA uses the survey data to evaluate the property's significance relative to others that have also been recorded in the inventory and to check the completeness of the information provided.

The survey data is also used by other governmental agencies and organizations involved in project planning and development to determine if historic properties will be affected by their projects. The inventory and its summary report also boost private citizens' awareness of the cultural heritage present in their communities. Finally, the inventory provides a permanent historical record of a county's resources at a particular point in time.

Ultimately, all counties in Indiana will be surveyed to locate, identify, and evaluate cultural resources. Like historic sites and structures, archaeological sites are also being surveyed under a similar program. Together, the two programs will provide an overall view of what cultural resources are present in the state. The survey will not end with the last county, however. The DHPA will continuously supplement and update existing data as the resources grow older and change and as later structures acquire significance with time.

St. Joseph County Inventory and Interim Report

Using monies from the U.S. Department of the Interior, National Park Service, the Indiana Department of Natural Resources, Division of Historic Preservation and Archaeology, awarded a grant for the republication of the 2000 St. Joseph County survey to the Historic Preservation Commission of South Bend and St. Joseph County (HPC). The HPC contracted with HLFI to produce the new publication.

Initial work on the survey began in 1999. During 2005, a fieldcheck was made to verify the 1999 data and add sites that now meet the inventory criteria. As a result of the initial survey and subsequent fieldcheck, which covered 402 square miles, the surveyors entered a total of 1,244 sites and structures into the final inventory. The original inventory forms are on file at the Division of Historic Preservation and Archaeology, 402 W. Washington Street, Room W274, Indianapolis, Ind. 46204.

Unfortunately, 25 of the structures documented in the 2000 *St. Joseph County Interim Report* have been demolished. Their entries remain with a note updating their status. Conversely, 131 new sites were added to the inventory during the 2005 fieldcheck.

This report reflects information available at a specific point in time. DHPA calls these reports "interim" because it expects that further research will result in additions and corrections to the inventory. Those with corrections or additional information to contribute should contact the DHPA at the above address.

The evaluations and ratings expressed in this interim report represent the opinions of the surveyors and consultants involved in this survey project. The Indiana Department of Natural Resources, the Indiana State Review Board and the U.S. Department of the Interior make final decisions on the eligibility of properties for the Indiana Register of Historic Sites and Structures and the National Register of Historic Places.

Methodology

Selection of Counties

The Division of Historic Preservation and Archaeology take many criteria into consideration when deciding which counties will be surveyed. It gives preference to counties in areas that have seen little or no survey activity and about which little is known. If it is known that development, particularly state- or federally-assisted activities, will soon affect a particular region, then a county will receive priority.

The DHPA also gives special consideration to counties that are thought to have a greater-than-average number of historic resources, particularly if they are threatened. The DHPA annually assesses survey priorities, which the State Review Board changes if necessary.

Preliminary Research

Before field documentation began in St. Joseph County, preliminary research and interviews with local historians provided the surveyors with a basic orientation to the county's development. Early maps and historical accounts revealed dates of settlement, early major industries, historical transportation routes, agricultural evolution, and original town boundaries. Evaluation of this information indicated areas of the county that might contain concentrations of historic sites and structures. Surveyors drove all county roads to obtain a general assessment of existing cultural resources. They noted any building types or styles unique to the area and conducted additional research using public records, county histories, newspapers, and other historical publications. They also consulted historical photographs.

Identification and Inventory

In inventorying St. Joseph County, surveyors looked for buildings, bridges, markers, outbuildings, and anything that might meet the criteria of the National Register of Historic Places (Fig. 2, p. 9). In general, they examined most structures built in or before 1965. They excluded buildings constructed after 1965 unless they were within a historic district or had outstanding architectural or historical importance. Alterations or additions obliterating the historical and architectural integrity of a building may have kept it from being included in the inventory. Buildings were not, however, excluded solely on the basis of their physical condition if their historic integrity remained intact.

Surveyors used the Indiana Historic Sites and Structures Inventory form (Fig. 1, p. 8) to record information on each structure, often speaking to the current occupant. They also took black and white photographs.

Surveyors inventoried most properties as individual entries. In instances where several structures were architecturally or historically related, surveyors recorded them together on a single form. Thus a farmhouse and its barns, or a house and its landscaped grounds, were recorded as a single entry.

In cities and towns with high densities of significant structures, surveyors defined boundaries and inventoried some areas as historic districts. Surveyors determined general boundaries by historic and/or geographic factors as well as the historic and architectural cohesiveness of the area. The DHPA considers these boundaries advisory, however, until it receives more detailed research and an applicant prepares actual nomination forms for the National Register.

Surveyors collected information on each building within a historic district's working boundaries, including those evaluated as non-contributing, on a street-by-street basis. They compiled additional research with the assistance of experts in local history, and prepared short narratives on the historical and architectural development of these areas. After the surveyors completed and verified the field work, they assigned ratings to each site.

Criteria and Evaluation

Professional architectural historians at the Westerly Group, DHPA, and HLFI evaluated the significance of each inventory entry by measuring it against the National Register criteria for evaluation (Fig. 2, p. 9). They assessed properties in terms of their historical significance, architectural merit, environment, and integrity before assigning one of the rating categories (O, N, C, or NC, explained on p. 8-9).

To explain the significance of the historic sites and why they appear in the inventory, surveyors chose from a list of 29 historical themes or areas of significance that establish a context for evaluating the resources (see Fig. 1, p. 8). Surveyors checked one or more areas of significance for each resource with the exception of entries in historic districts, in which case surveyors evaluated the significance of the entire district.

Left: This Italianate Cube (00025), built by Amos Irwin in 1875, features a cupola. *Courtesy of Historic Preservation Commission of South Bend and St. Joseph County.*

Ratings

In assessing integrity, surveyors attempted to determine how much of the original architectural fabric remained. They may have lowered a property's rating if it experienced extensive alterations, such as the application of artificial siding, removal of trim or porches, later additions, changes to windows, or structural modifications. The relocation of a building from its original site often lowered its rating. After consideration of these factors, DHPA and HLFI assigned one of the following ratings to each property.

Outstanding (O)

The "O" rating means that the property has enough historic or architectural significance that it is already listed, or may be eligible for listing, in the National Register of Historic Places. "Outstanding" resources can be of local, state, or national importance.

Notable (N)

The "N" rating means that the property did not quite merit an "outstanding" rating but still is above average in its importance. Further research may reveal that the property is eligible for National Register listing.

Contributing (C)

A "C" rating means that the property met the basic inventory criterion of being pre-1966, but that it is not important enough to stand on its own as individually "outstanding" or "notable." Such resources are important to the density or continuity of an area's historic fabric. "Contributing" properties may appear in the National Register if they are part of a historic district but do not usually qualify individually.

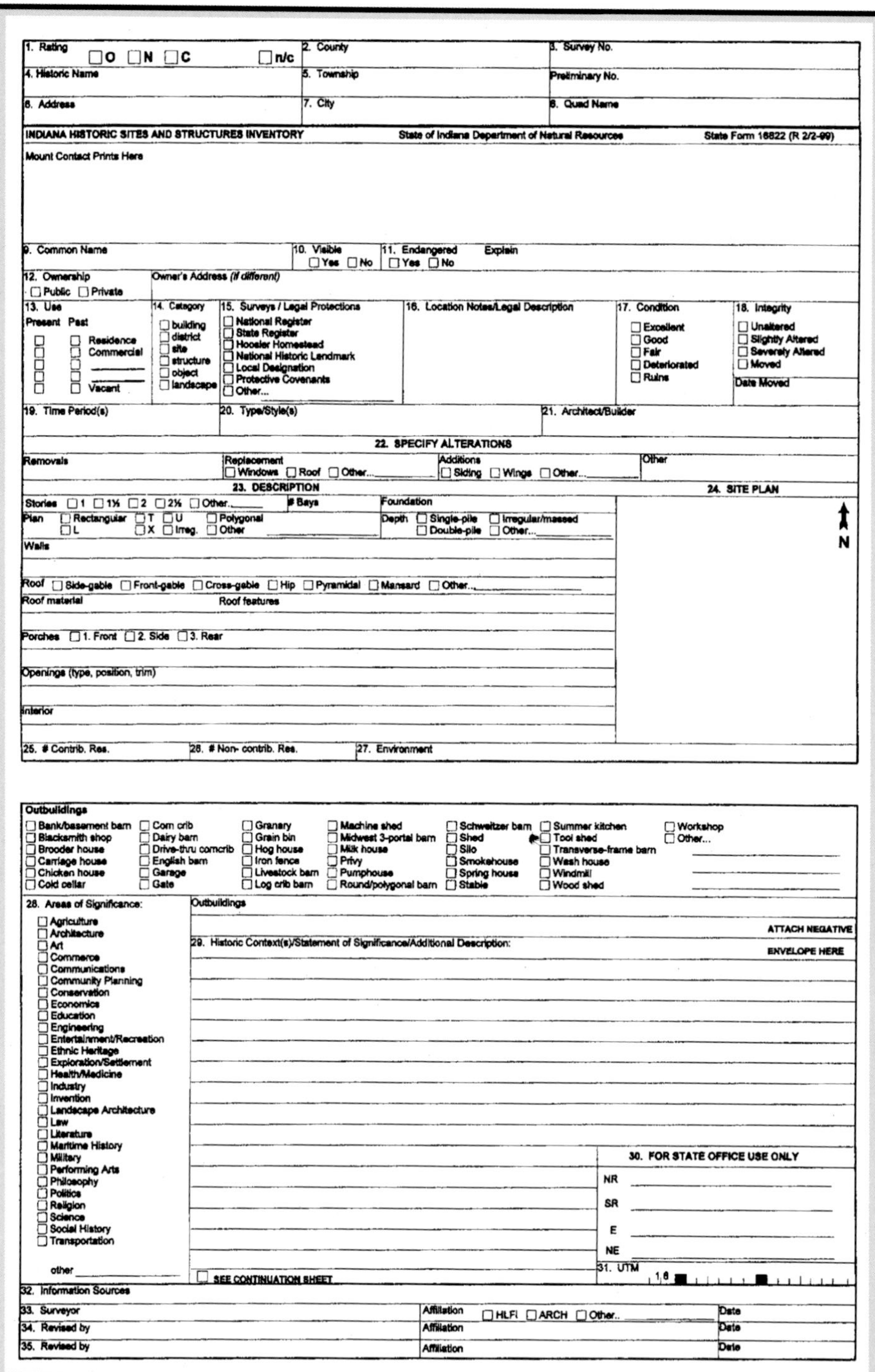

1. Rating ☐O ☐N ☐C ☐n/c
2. County
3. Survey No.
4. Historic Name
5. Township
Preliminary No.
6. Address
7. City
8. Quad Name

INDIANA HISTORIC SITES AND STRUCTURES INVENTORY — State of Indiana Department of Natural Resources — State Form 16822 (R 2/2-99)

Mount Contact Prints Here

9. Common Name
10. Visible ☐Yes ☐No
11. Endangered ☐Yes ☐No
Explain

12. Ownership ☐Public ☐Private
Owner's Address *(if different)*

13. Use — Present / Past: ☐ ☐ Residence; ☐ ☐ Commercial; ☐ ☐ ______; ☐ ☐ ______; ☐ ☐ Vacant
14. Category: ☐building ☐district ☐site ☐structure ☐object ☐landscape
15. Surveys / Legal Protections: ☐National Register ☐State Register ☐Hoosier Homestead ☐National Historic Landmark ☐Local Designation ☐Protective Covenants ☐Other...
16. Location Notes/Legal Description
17. Condition: ☐Excellent ☐Good ☐Fair ☐Deteriorated ☐Ruins
18. Integrity: ☐Unaltered ☐Slightly Altered ☐Severely Altered ☐Moved
Date Moved

19. Time Period(s)
20. Type/Style(s)
21. Architect/Builder

22. SPECIFY ALTERATIONS
Removals
Replacement ☐Windows ☐Roof ☐Other...
Additions ☐Siding ☐Wings ☐Other...
Other

23. DESCRIPTION
24. SITE PLAN
Stories ☐1 ☐1½ ☐2 ☐2½ ☐Other.____ # Bays
Foundation
Plan ☐Rectangular ☐T ☐U ☐Polygonal ☐L ☐X ☐Irreg. ☐Other
Depth ☐Single-pile ☐Irregular/massed ☐Double-pile ☐Other...
Walls
Roof ☐Side-gable ☐Front-gable ☐Cross-gable ☐Hip ☐Pyramidal ☐Mansard ☐Other...
Roof material
Roof features
Porches ☐1. Front ☐2. Side ☐3. Rear
Openings (type, position, trim)
Interior
N

25. # Contrib. Res.
26. # Non- contrib. Res.
27. Environment

Outbuildings
☐Bank/basement barn ☐Blacksmith shop ☐Brooder house ☐Carriage house ☐Chicken house ☐Cold cellar
☐Corn crib ☐Dairy barn ☐Drive-thru corncrib ☐English barn ☐Garage ☐Gate
☐Granary ☐Grain bin ☐Hog house ☐Iron fence ☐Livestock barn ☐Log crib barn
☐Machine shed ☐Midwest 3-portal barn ☐Milk house ☐Privy ☐Pumphouse ☐Round/polygonal barn
☐Schweitzer barn ☐Shed ☐Silo ☐Smokehouse ☐Spring house ☐Stable
☐Summer kitchen ☐Tool shed ☐Transverse-frame barn ☐Wash house ☐Windmill ☐Wood shed
☐Workshop ☐Other...

28. Areas of Significance:
☐Agriculture ☐Architecture ☐Art ☐Commerce ☐Communications ☐Community Planning ☐Conservation ☐Economics ☐Education ☐Engineering ☐Entertainment/Recreation ☐Ethnic Heritage ☐Exploration/Settlement ☐Health/Medicine ☐Industry ☐Invention ☐Landscape Architecture ☐Law ☐Literature ☐Maritime History ☐Military ☐Performing Arts ☐Philosophy ☐Politics ☐Religion ☐Science ☐Social History ☐Transportation
other

Outbuildings
ATTACH NEGATIVE
29. Historic Context(s)/Statement of Significance/Additional Description:
ENVELOPE HERE

30. FOR STATE OFFICE USE ONLY
NR
SR
E
NE
31. UTM 1,6

☐ SEE CONTINUATION SHEET

32. Information Sources
33. Surveyor — Affiliation ☐HLFI ☐ARCH ☐Other.. — Date
34. Revised by — Affiliation — Date
35. Revised by — Affiliation — Date

Fig. 1

Non-Contributing (NC)

Properties rated "NC" are not included in the inventory unless they are located within a historic district. Such properties are usually built after 1965, are older structures that have undergone bad alterations and lost historic character, or are otherwise incompatible with their historical surroundings. These properties are not eligible for the National Register.

Of the 1,244 entries made in the *St. Joseph County Interim Report*, DHPA rated 113 "outstanding" and 346 "notable." Again, readers should view these ratings as advisory recommendations based on the information available to the surveyor at the time of the survey. Change in location, sensitive restoration, additional research, extensive physical damage, or inappropriate remodeling could affect the entry's significance and rating at a later date.

Mapping and Numbering

Mapping

HLFI recorded all inventory entries on United States Geological Survey (USGS) 7.5 Minute Series topographical maps. The United States Department of the Interior also uses this quadrangle map series for the National Register program. Each USGS map has its own name and assigned three-digit number that is included in the survey number (see Fig. 3 for the USGS map overlay for St. Joseph County). Surveyors record the map coordinates of each entry on the inventory forms so that people can precisely locate the property on any copy of the USGS map.

A graphic artist created the smaller maps used in this publication based on TIGER data from the U.S Bureau of the Census, adding street names and locating entries with a site dot and three-digit number. For districts or scattered sites within a community, she created more detailed maps to indicate the location of historic resources within the area.

Fig. 2

National Register Criteria for Evaluation

The following criteria are the National Register standards for evaluating the significance of properties. The National Park Service designed these criteria to guide states, federal agencies, the Secretary of the Interior, and others in evaluating potential entries. The quality of significance in American history, architecture, archaeology, engineering, and culture is present in districts, sites, buildings, structures, and objects that possess integrity of location, design, setting, materials, workmanship, feeling, and association, and:

A. that are associated with events that have made a significant contribution to the broad patterns of our history; or

B. that are associated with the lives of persons significant in our past; or

C. that embody the distinctive characteristics of a type, period, or method of construction, or that represent the work of a master, or that possess high artistic values, or that represent a significant and distinguishable entity whose components may lack individual distinction; or

D. that have yielded, or may be likely to yield, information important in prehistory or history.

Criteria Considerations

Ordinarily, cemeteries, birthplaces or graves of historical figures, properties owned by religious institutions or used for religious purposes, structures that have been moved from their original locations, reconstructed historical buildings, properties primarily commemorative in nature, and properties that have achieved significance within the past 50 years shall not be considered eligible for the National Register. However, such properties will qualify if they are integral parts of districts that do meet the criteria or if they fall within the following categories:

A. a religious property deriving primary significance from architectural or artistic distinction or historical importance; or

B. a building or structure removed from its original location but that is significant primarily for architectural value, or is the surviving structure most importantly associated with an historic person or event; or

C. a birthplace or grave of an historical figure of outstanding importance if there is no other appropriate site or building directly associated with his productive life; or

D. a cemetery that derives its primary significance from graves of transcendent importance, from age, from distinctive design features, or from association with historic events; or

E. a reconstructed building when accurately executed in a suitable environment and presented in a dignified manner as part of a restoration master plan, and when no other building or structure with the same association has survived; or

F. a property primarily commemorative in intent if design, age, tradition, or symbolic value has invested it with its own historical significance; or

G. a property achieving significance within the past 50 years if it is of exceptional importance.

Inventory Number

HLFI assigns a site number to each inventory entry for filing purposes. Three orders of site location information have been incorporated into the 11-digit numbers, as seen in the example below.

COUNTY	QUAD MAP	SITE
141	339	66030

County Number: The first block of three digits identifies the county. The National Park Service assigned this number to identify the county for National Register nominations. The number for St. Joseph County is 141.

Quad Map Number: The second block of three digits identifies the USGS quadrangle map on which the resource is located. Based on Fig. 3, the 339 in the example refers to the Lakeville quadrangle map.

Site Number: The last block of five digits forms a discrete site number. The first two digits refer to the site's township and the final three digits are its actual number.

DHPA and the Westerly Group assigned two-digit numbers to each township (see Fig. 4). For example, Harris Township, the northeastern-most township, begins with site 00001. Clay, the next township, is 05000, German is 10000, and so on. For example, the site number 66030 refers to the 30th site in Greene Township. Because St. Joseph County is so large, the increment between townships is sometimes less than five; additionally, the numbering skips a large range reserved for the cities of South Bend and Mishawaka.

Surveyors number areas of scattered sites or historic districts according to the township in which they are located; scattered sites and districts take the next number up from the township number. For example, the city of New Carlisle has a historic district and its own area of scattered sites. Since New Carlisle is located in Olive Township (whose

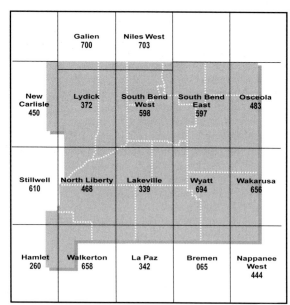

Fig. 3 USGS Quad map overlay

first two digits are 62), the district takes the number 63 and the scattered sites take the number 64. DHPA always lists the courthouse square or commercial historic district first, followed by residential or industrial districts, then the scattered sites.

St. Joseph County Road Numbering and Address System

In 1933 County Surveyor Earl Feldman and the St. Joseph County Commissioners developed a new county road naming system that still is used today. Last names of statesmen, authors, pioneers, and county officials were chosen for the east/west county roads. They are ordered alphabetically from north to south with the exception of Roosevelt Road, which honors President Franklin D. Roosevelt. The north/south county roads were named alphabetically from east (Elkhart County line) to west (LaPorte County line).

In 1955 the current county road numbering system was adopted. Each mile of county road was given 1,000 possible addresses. The east/west roads are

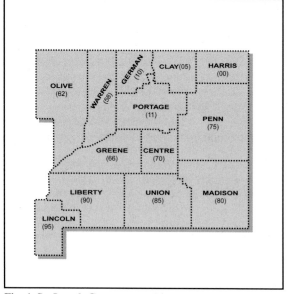

Fig. 4 St. Joseph County township numbering

numbered from 10,000 to 34,000 between Ash and County Line Road and the north/south roads are numbered from 50,500 to 73,000 between State Line Road and Tyler Road.

Even numbers are usually on the south side of east/west roads and on the west side of north/south roads. Conversely, odd numbers are usually on the north side of east/west roads and on the east side on north/south roads.

Right: The Studebaker Tree Sign (62031) is a familiar landmark in St. Joseph County. *Courtesy of Historic Preservation of South Bend and St. Joseph County.*

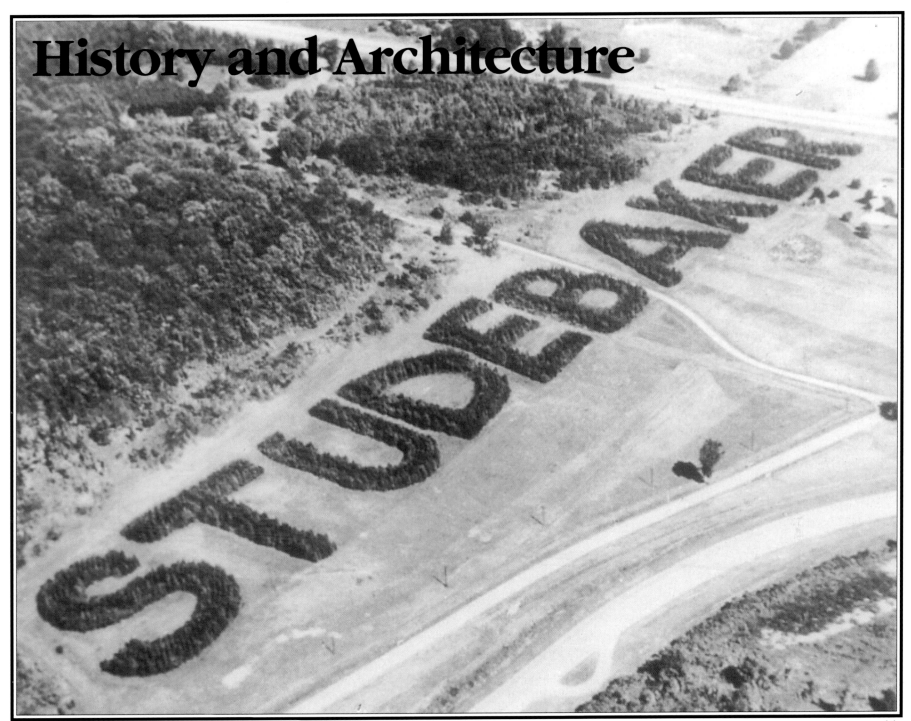

St. Joseph County History

St. Joseph County lies in the north-central portion of Indiana. It is bordered to the west by LaPorte County, to the south by Marshall County, to the east by Elkhart County, and to the north by the state of Michigan. The county's terrain is characterized by fertile prairies and low, swampy marshes. The St. Joseph and Kankakee Rivers traverse the land. Native Americans forged a portage between the two rivers that was later used by European settlers and other travelers between Michigan and Illinois.

Local Native American tribes, including the Potawatomis, Ottawas, and Chippewas, established trails that were later used by European settlers. Some of these trails have become part of the county's contemporary street and highway systems. Crumstown Highway in South Bend roughly follows the Potawatomi Trail. The Chicago Road and Dragoon Trail also roughly follow former tribal trails.

Pioneers began to settle the county early, despite its harsh and sometimes hazardous conditions. The earliest settlers were from French Canada and the Detroit area, followed by immigrants from New England and some of the middle and southern states. They sought the driest routes and avoided marshes when they began constructing roads in the county.

Pierre F. Navarre is generally recognized as the first permanent white settler. Coming as a representative of the American Fur Company of Detroit, Navarre made his home on the south bend of the St. Joseph River in 1820. He was followed by colleague Alexis Coquillard in 1823 and by Lathrop M. Taylor, an agent of Samuel Hanna and Company of Fort Wayne, in 1827. By 1830, 287 people resided in the county. That year, the Indiana legislature passed an act to form St. Joseph County. Its original boundaries covered an area of thirty square miles and encompassed portions of the present-day LaPorte, Marshall, and Starke Counties. It had only four townships: Michigan, Deschemin, German, and Portage. The county boundaries changed several times before taking its current perimeters in 1839. The current division of townships was not finalized until 1866.

In the late 1820s, a treaty with the Potawatomi Nation and an act of the Indiana General Assembly provided for the planning of a road from Lake Michigan to Indianapolis. The plan was soon abandoned because it would have traveled through the swamps of the Kankakee Valley, land many believed to be worthless. However, a second planned route for the Michigan Road was completed by the late-1830s. It extended from Michigan City on Lincolnway West to South Bend, then south on what is today Michigan Street and US 31 South. The Michigan Road reached all the way to the Ohio River in Madison, Indiana and brought many travelers and settlers to St. Joseph County, especially where the road passed in Union Township, an area of favorable agricultural land. Despite these

efforts, road travel remained primitive and uncomfortable in the county as late as 1875.

Settlement in most of the county began in the 1830s. However, the vast marshes or heavy forests of Clay, Madison, Lincoln, and Union Townships made farming difficult, resulting in those areas being settled later. German Township was home to the first county seat, St. Joseph, in 1830. St. Joseph was located just northwest of South Bend on farmland owned by William Brookfield, which was later called McCartney Farm. However, less than a year later the seat was relocated to South Bend. In 1831, the Indiana General Assembly dissolved the Board of the Justices of the Peace, which had governed the county, replacing it with a Board of County Commissioners. The first commissioners were David Miller, Joseph Rorer, and Aaron Stanton.

By 1840, the county's population had grown to more than 6,000 and many villages dotted the landscape, including South Bend, Mishawaka,

An 1875 view of the former Theodore Rittinger farm and residence in Olive Township. *Courtesy of Historic Preservation Commission of South Bend and Saint Joseph County.*

This 1903 image depicts the dredging of the Kankakee River. *Courtesy of Historic Preservation Commission of South Bend and Saint Joseph County.*

New Carlisle, North Liberty, Osceola, Terre Coupee, Plainfield, and Lakeville.

As the terrain influenced settlement patterns in St. Joseph County, it also influenced the type of industries that developed within its boundaries. The lumbering of native trees such as walnut, ash, oak, and hickory became a primary occupation of county residents. Because of this, the Singer Manufacturing Company moved its cabinet works to South Bend in 1868. Other prominent occupations included milling and agriculture.

The St. Joseph River served as both a mode of transportation and a power generator for local industry. The first ferry license was issued by 1831 and Nehemiah B. Griffeth began his ferry operation at the foot of Water Street (currently LaSalle) in South Bend. He was followed by Coquillard, who established another ferry at Market Street (today's Colfax) in 1835. That year, the first dam in the county was constructed at St. Joseph Iron Works, the original name of Mishawaka. Another dam was begun in South Bend the following year and completed in 1844.

Technological advances resulted in the construction of several bridges, which eliminated the need for ferries. The first bridge was built in Mishawaka in 1837, followed by bridges in South Bend at Market Street (now Colfax), Jefferson Boulevard, Michigan Street (Leeper Bridge site), and Mosquito Glen (Darden Bridge site). The first bridges were of wood construction; they were replaced by iron bridges in the late-nineteenth century followed by concrete bridges in the twentieth century.

Unlike the St. Joseph River, the Kankakee River seemed to offer more problems than benefits to area residents during the nineteenth century. As early as 1850, an act was passed to reclaim swampland around the Kankakee by constructing levees and through draining, but attempts failed. In 1881, the Indiana General Assembly authorized a survey to determine the best method of drainage for the area. Finally, in about

1890, progress was made when a rock ledge in Momence, Illinois was removed from the river to allow an outlet for it. The rich loam and sand soil land was finally dry and fertile. Many laws that had been enacted to deal with the problems of the Kankakee were effectively applied to regulate drainage in other marshy areas of the county, promoting both settlement and agricultural pursuits.

The coming of the railroad in the mid-nineteenth century ushered in prosperity and a new era of St. Joseph County's transportation heritage. The first locomotive of the Michigan Southern and Northern Indiana Railroad (later the Lake Shore and Michigan) reached South Bend in 1851. The line cut through the northern half of the county linking it to Toledo, Ohio and Chicago. A branch of the Michigan Central Railroad reached the area by 1880, comprised of a ten-mile stretch of tracks from South Bend to Niles, Michigan. Within that decade another line was completed that extended from Port Huron, Michigan, through Lansing to Mishawaka and South Bend, then on to Valparaiso and Chicago. For a time it was called the Chicago and Lake Huron Railroad, but it later became part of the Grand Trunk system. The Indianapolis, Peru, and Chicago Railroad serviced the southern part of the county,

extending from Michigan City to Indianapolis through Walkerton in the 1850s. In 1873, the Baltimore and Ohio Railroad also cut through Walkerton connecting Baltimore with Chicago. In 1849, the Indiana, Illinois, and Iowa line, often called the "Three I's" was laid out linking Walkerton, North Liberty, Lakeville, and Chicago. In 1884, the Wabash line connected Lake Maxinkuckee to South Bend passing through Lakeville. The Vandalia line was constructed in 1893 and extended from Toledo to Chicago, passing through Wyatt, Lakeville, and North Liberty.

By 1880, the county's population was 30,000. 3,000 workers were employed in factories. Prominent manufacturers of the time included the Studebaker, Oliver, Singer, and Birdsell companies in South Bend; Milburn's Wagon Manufacturing Company, Perkins Wind Mill Company, Kamm Brewery, and the Mishawaka Wollen Manufacturing Company in Mishawaka; and the North Liberty Manufacturing Company and the North Liberty Home Manufacturing Company in North Liberty. Despite the impact of the industrial age, agriculture remained the primary occupation of three-quarters of the area's

An 1875 drawing of the former John Main farm and residence in Warren Township. *Courtesy of Historic Preservation Commission of South Bend and St. Joseph County.*

workers. Primary crops included wheat, corn, oats, potatoes, and fruits.

In 1899, local entrepreneurs formed the South Bend, Mishawaka, Elkhart, and Goshen Interurban Railway, having powerhouses in South Bend, Osceola, and Dunlap. It later became the Chicago, South Bend and Northern Indiana Railway Company. By 1903, an interurban ran between South Bend and Niles, Michigan, reaching Berrien Springs, Michigan three years later. In 1905, the east-west line extended to LaPorte and Michigan City. The interurban was an important means of travel for those who lived in the country, even after the introduction of the automobile. Rural dwellers could hop on an interurban to take them to town for social activities such as dances, athletic events, circuses, and fairs. However, by the mid- to late-1920s, the success of automobiles and buses hurt the interurbans and companies began experiencing financial difficulties, eventually causing them to go out of business. Today, the

country's only interurban still in existence from that heyday is the Chicago, South Shore and South Bend, commonly known as the "South Shore," which runs from South Bend to Chicago daily.

The shift in transportation modes paralleled a shift in occupation. By 1940, less than 2% of the county's population were engaged in agricultural pursuits. The manufacturing of automobile-related products gradually overtook agriculture-related products. Studebaker, which had manufactured wagons for half a century, converted to automobile production in 1920, while other companies, such as Birdsell, who made clover hullers and farm wagons, went out of business altogether. Because of the rise in popularity of the automobile, there was an emphasis on building and improving roads during the 1920s. New roads and automobiles allowed people to live farther from their workplace and the movement to the suburbs, which had begun with the interurbans,

The Italianate-style Witmer/Miller House (10006) reveals decorative paired brackets, ornate window hoods, and a second-story balconette. *Courtesy of Historic Preservation Commission of South Bend and Saint Joseph County.*

continued. Roseland, Indian Village, and Osceola were far enough away from the larger towns that they became havens for people looking to "get away" from the city.

Suburban growth continued throughout the twentieth century. Areas in Clay, Penn, and Harris Townships are still seeing that growth today. However, the preservation movement is making citizens aware of St. Joseph County's cultural and architectural heritage and the potential that exists in reusing historic structures. The revitalization of town centers and rural farmsteads is being accomplished by a generation of new pioneers who are returning to rehabilitate structures that were long left to deteriorate. This report includes a listing of historic sites and structures in St. Joseph County that are worthy of preservation. For similar information for South Bend and Mishawaka, see *The City of South Bend Summary Report* and *The City of Mishawaka Summary Report.*

Left: Two men pose outside of Globe Clothiers in the summer of 1928. *Courtesy of Historic Preservation Commission of South Bend and Saint Joseph County.*

Designated Properties

National Register of Historic Places

Lakeville High School, 1929
601 North Michigan Street, Lakeville (86001)

Mishawaka Reservoir Caretaker's Residence, 1938
16581 Chandler Boulevard (75093)

New Carlisle Historic District, 1835-1940
Roughly bounded by the north side of Front Street, the west side of Arch Street, the south side of Chestnut Street, and the east side of Bray Street, New Carlisle (63001-091)

Franklin & Martha R. Rupel Farm/Evergreen Hill, 1839-1919
59449 Keria Trail (70002)

Jeremiah Service House/Old Republic, 1861
302 East Michigan Street, New Carlisle (64003)

Studebaker Clubhouse and Tree Sign, 1926, 1938
32132 SR 2 (62031)

University of Notre Dame Main and South Quadrangles, 1913-1938
Notre Dame (13001-066)

Wertz-Bestle Farm, c.1872-1949
51387 Portage Road (10004)

Indiana Register of Historic Sites and Structures

Daniel Ward House, 1865
16021 Cleveland Road, Granger (05027)

St. Joseph County Historic Preservatioin Commission Local Landmarks

Auker Log House
54335 Rose Road DESTROYED BY FIRE

Gerry Battles Farm, 1869
60649 Hickory (75076)

George S. Bickel/Geyer Log House, c.1850
66251 Cedar Road (80077)

Andrew J. Brenneman Farm, c.1890
66963 Cedar Road (80080)-

Cook School, 1880
12768 Dragoon Trail (75032)

Fredrick Cowles House, 1875
19701 Cowles (05016)

Henry Crofoot Farm, c.1875
61601 State Road 331 (75071)

Willard Crofoot Farm, 1901
60500 State Road 331 (75055)

Alfred Curtis Farm, c.1875
59101 Apple Road (75024)

Darden Road Bridge/St. Joseph County Bridge No. 5, 1885/1906
21000 Darden Road (05037)

Francis & Rosanne H. Donaghue House, 1861
63049 Turkey Trail (70038)

Thomas Ehlers House
63907 Bremen Highway

Phoebe & George Fisher House
51177 Lilac Road

John Follmer/Milliken/Kownover Farm, c.1838
12594 Adams Road (00011)

German Township School, c.1890
53117 Olive Road (10011)

Grabowski Barn, c.1880
16977 Adams Road (05001)

Seth Hammond Farm, 1885
61723 Oak Road (66021)

James & Mary Ann Harris House, 1843
52407 Grape Road (05026)

Harris Township District No. 1 Schoolhouse, 1892
14912 Brick Road (00021)

Stanza & Warren Irvin House, 1875
13546 Brick Road (00025)

Emil & Anna J. Johnson House, 1914
60717 Locust Road (70005)

William C. Kownover Farm, 1877
50106 Bittersweet Trail (00006)

James Leach House, c.1860
18075 Roosevelt Road (70025)

The outstanding Metzger House (00014) is a locally-designated landmark. *Courtesy of Historic Preservation Commission of South Bend and Saint Joseph County.*

Levi & Sara W. Mangus House, 1878
65150 Redwood (90021)

Metzger House, 1847
14309 Adams Road (00014)

John B. & Henriette F. Metzger House, c.1889
14297 SR 23 (00024)

Allen McEndarfer Farm, c.1850/1890
25618 Quinn Road (90030)

McEndarfer/Liberty Township District No. 7 School, 1901
66984 Pine Road (90028)

Aaron N. Miller House, c.1855
24888 Cleveland Road (10012)

Mishawaka Reservoir Caretaker's Residence, 1938
16581 Chandler Road (75093)

Olive Township District No. 12 School
30750 Inwood Road

Pleasant View/Union Township District No. 2 School, 1903
65014 US 31 (85026)

Rosebaugh/Solomon J. Knepp House, 1869
66441 Walnut Road (90011)

John J. & Lydia Rupel House, 1859
24845 SR 23 (66010)

Jacob & Elizabeth H. Russel Farm
59375 Myrtle Road (66060)

Robert Savidge House, 1868
16327 Cleveland Road (05028)

George F. Schafer Farmhouse, 1908
19251 Roosevelt Road (70029)

George & Elizabeth Schafer House, 1908
62290 Miami Road (70027)

Augustus Schalliol Farm, c.1914
63012 Beech Road (80003)

George Seifer House, c.1890
68286 Miami Road (85071)

Zachariah & Sarah L. Sheneman House
68437 Pine Road (90044)

Jacob Smith House, c.1870
11518 Adams Road (00005)

Joseph & Julie Ann Snyder Farm, 1871
13271 Adams Road (00012)

James Stuckey House, 1840
53597 Ironwood Road (05039)

Studebaker Clubhouse/Bendix Woods Nature Center, 1926/1938
32132 SR 2 (62031)

Catherine & John Smith House, c.1870
51991 Ash Road (00003)

George & Elizabeth Sumption House, 1832
60413 Sumption Trail (66016)

Alfred Talley House, 1856
53190 Juniper Road (05031)

William Thornton/Samuel Heiss House, 1875
10708 Edison Road (75009)

Topper/Hay Farm, c.1900
19109 Johnson Road (70013)

Ullery/Joseph Farneman House, c.1870
61191 US 31 (70018)

James Q.C. & Mary Jane Vandenbosch House, 1876
61955 Locust Road (70032)

Daniel Ward House, 1865
16021 Cleveland Road (05027)

Werzt-Bestle Farm, 1883
51387 Portage Road (10004)

Jacob Whitmer/Miller Farm, c.1872
50705 Orange Road (10006)

Samuel H. & Elizabeth Zaehnle House, 1883
16479 Brick Road (05025)

Historical Themes in St. Joseph County

This inventory contains 1,244 listings for historic resources including sites, buildings, landscape features, and structures. Surveyors evaluated each resource according to the 29 areas of significance that appear on the survey form (see p. 8). In St. Joseph County, seven areas of significance emerged as dominant themes: transportation, architecture (both high-style and vernacular), agriculture, commerce, industry, religion, and education.

This report presents these themes in order of historical development. Transportation, which is usually the earliest element to appear during an area's settlement period, appears first, followed by a discussion of the county's vernacular and high style architecture, and then agricultural development. Subsequent themes describe major institutions that appeared as the county was settled. The report develops each theme, placing St. Joseph County resources within the historical context of local, state, and national trends.

Transportation

The evolution of transportation is a key component in any region's historical development. The earliest routes followed Indian trails or waterways to gain access to uninhabited lands. As an area was settled, crude roads, often following the routes of the old Indian trails, were cut out of the wilderness. Turnpikes or toll roads soon appeared, serving private interests.

The Land Ordinance Act of 1785 greatly affected transportation in Indiana. The Act called for land surveys to be made according to a square grid, and roads generally followed the section lines of the grid. The grid system is more evident in northern Indiana because of its even terrain. In southern Indiana, where the earliest transportation routes developed, the irregular terrain did not lend itself as readily to the grid system.

After achieving statehood in 1816, Indiana devoted its formative years to infrastructure improvements. Workers completed the Michigan Road, which linked Madison with Michigan City in 1826. The National Road, which linked Cumberland, Md., to Vandalia, Ill., reached Richmond, Ind., in 1828 and arrived in Terre Haute by 1832. The government-funded roadway opened the frontiers of Ohio, Indiana and Illinois to settlement.

Indiana's 1836 Internal Improvement Bill provided for the construction of a network of canals. The legislation eventually bankrupted the state, but not before completion of the Indiana stretch of the Wabash and Erie Canal, linking Evansville to Lake Erie. However, even as the canals reached completion, they were already becoming obsolete. The state's first railroad line was completed from Madison to Indianapolis in 1847, ushering in a century that would be dominated by the railroad.

Many historic resources associated with St. Joseph County's numerous forms of

76013 The Lakeshore & Michigan Southern Railroad Depot in Osceola was once a bustling center of activity, but now sits vacant and boarded.

transportation remain. The impact of the railroad on both the urban and rural areas of St. Joseph County was substantial. Rail lines through the county provided outlets for the area's farmers to the larger markets in Indianapolis and Chicago. By the close of the 19th century, many towns could trace their beginnings to the construction of the rail lines, including Lydick and Roseland. One of the most visible resources associated with the railroad is, of course, the depot (76013). Railroad bridges, though less distinctive, are more commonly found.

An outgrowth of the railroad was the development in many cities of interurban railroad systems. A rival to the soot-spewing steam engines, electric railroad engines began to make their appearance in the closing years of the 19th century. Initially developed as street railways in urban centers, the electric railroads provided clean and quiet, if not always reliable, transportation. Improvements in technology allowed for larger cars that could go longer distances. The interurban railway dates from 1888, when Lafayette had the first city-wide electric intraurban line, to 1893, when the tracks moved beyond the limits of the city of Brazil, eventually reaching as far as Knightstown.

Steel rails laid down by small companies tied cities and towns together. Consolidation of these lines led to larger, more efficient lines connecting more distant parts of the state. Large networks of lines owned by companies such as the Union Traction Company; the Terre Haute, Indianapolis and Eastern Traction Company; the Fort Wayne and Northern Traction Company; and the Chicago, South Shore and South Bend Railroad soon tied most of Indiana's major towns and cities together. By 1920, one could travel from any part of the state to the Union Traction terminal in Indianapolis.

05037 The Darden Road Bridge spans the St. Joseph River in Clay Township and dates to 1885/1906. The pratt through truss bridge is listed in the National Register of Historic Places.

Increased pressure from newer, more efficient railroad engines and the automobile signaled the end of the electric interurban system. One by one, the tracks closed during the Depression, and after World War II, the trains became a thing of the past. Only the South Shore Line from South Bend to Chicago was left to serve the northern populace. It still runs, carrying commuters across the industrial region of Northwest Indiana.

Just as the railroad replaced the canals as a major mode of transportation during the 19th century, the advent of the automobile during the early 20th century would forever change the face of Indiana. St. Joseph County's road system improved greatly. Roads went from narrow dirt paths to gravel and macadam on more heavily traveled routes. These improvements and expansion of the road system affected the country's economic and social systems. With the establishment of the State Highway Commission in 1919, the state began construction of a 3,200-mile network of roads, linking county seats and communities with populations of more than 5,000 and connecting Indiana with adjoining states. The Lincoln Highway, the nation's first coast-to-coast route, ran east-west through northern Indiana.

With these developments came the replacement of wooden bridges, first with the more durable and stronger metal-truss bridges and later with concrete. New bridges are replacing early metal-truss and concrete bridges at an alarming rate; St.

Joseph County retains examples of Pratt truss (05037) and concrete arch (75103) bridges.

Just as important to auto travel as roads and bridges are facilities to maintain the automobile and its passengers. Gas stations, service garages, roadside diners, and tourist cabins sprang up along Indiana's roads to serve the motoring public. St. Joseph County boasts an example of the small house-with-canopy-style gas station (75018).

Because early automobiles were usually not completely enclosed, they were particularly vulnerable to the weather. Some owners kept their cars in large public garages, while others used existing barns or carriage houses. Soon, the private garage or "automobile house" began to appear. At first, homeowners built garages away from the house due to the fear of fire from gasoline, which drivers often stored in large tanks in or near the garage. With the proliferation of gas stations in the 1920s, it was no longer necessary to store gasoline at home, and the garage moved closer to the house, eventually becoming part of the house as attached garages gained popularity.

Vernacular Architecture

Many houses in both the rural and urban areas of our country fall into easily identifiable forms or house types. These house types had their origins in Europe, came to North America with the colonists, and subsequently moved westward with the settling of the frontier. Often, builders adapted these traditional house types to a particular locale and combined them with popular trends in architecture to produce what is referred to as vernacular architecture.

The people who settled in Indiana came from widely diverse backgrounds, bringing with them a variety of building traditions. Because Indiana settlers generally came north from the Ohio River, many originated from southern states such as Kentucky, Virginia, and North Carolina. It is no wonder then that housing types popular in

the south appear in abundance in the southern one-third of the state. Across the northern section of Indiana, settlers from the New England states as well as various ethnic groups brought building types familiar to them. As the state became increasingly homogeneous, these regional housing types grew in popularity and eventually spread throughout Indiana.

The following are some of the vernacular building types found in St. Joseph County.

Log-Construction/Single Pen

The earliest permanent buildings constructed after the European settlement of the frontier were of hewn-log construction. While not of a particular architectural style, hewn-log buildings and especially log houses are of diverse origin. Generally, they combine various building and house types of British tradition with horizontal hewn-log construction techniques. The precise origins, if such exist, of hewn-log construction as manifested in Indiana are not known. Similar, though not identical, construction techniques appear in the heavily forested regions of northern and central Europe and in Scandinavia. Some theorists attribute the dissemination of horizontal log construction in America to German and Scandinavian immigrants, though this is not certain. In any case, hewn-log construction flourished in the hardwood forests of the American frontier. Americans adopted the log building, usually referred to as a "cabin," as a

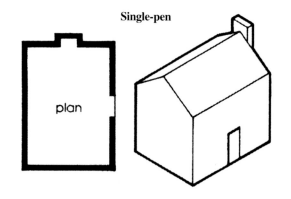

Single-pen

plan

80077 The c.1853 George S. Bickell Log House is an example of the single-pen type, most common in early log structures, and is significant for its contribution to Indiana's settlement period.

favorite symbol, if not an icon, which represents the self-reliant and honest virtues of the frontier.

Today, the apparent simplicity of log buildings often belies the sophistication of the flush corner notching systems by which builders joined the logs as well as the high level of craftsmanship invested in the hewing of logs. Please note that hewn-log buildings differ from the so-called log cabins, which were of round-log construction and were in most cases crude, temporary buildings that have not survived to the present.

Usually, settlers replaced their hewn-log buildings with larger buildings of frame or brick construction and quite often relegated them to less prominent locations where they served as outbuildings or became abandoned. In other cases, log buildings were incorporated into newer structures so that their form and construction are virtually unrecognizable. Most log buildings date to the early years of European settlement. However, construction of hewn-log buildings was not uncommon throughout the first half of the 19th century and even later in some places.

The single-pen house was normally a one-room rectangular-plan structure with a sleeping loft above. The gable-end chimney, built of fieldstone, could be either on the interior or

exterior of the structure. The windows were small, and because of the scarcity and impracticality of glass on the frontier, were covered with oilcloth or wooden shutters. St. Joseph County retains several single-pen log houses (05049, 80014, 80075).

Double-Pen

One of the most common methods of expanding the single-pen log house, a frequent occurrence as settlers' spatial needs increased, was simply to add another similar or identical pen to one of the gable ends of the existing pen. In many such cases, builders left the gable-end wall, now the shared interior wall of the two pens, intact. With the pens thus not being connected by a passage through the interior wall, an exterior door for each pen was needed. This resulted in the double-pen house (75001).

Though the two front doors on double-pen houses were most common in log construction, the double-pen form also appears in houses not built of logs. Stone, brick, and frame houses may also have two doors on the facade. Some historians explain this as the continuation of the Upland South building tradition, but this theory does not explain why double-entry houses occur in areas far removed from southern influences.

A more likely theory is that the double-entry house developed from the tradition of keeping private, family space separate from that used for formal entertaining. Visitors would use the

"formal" door that led directly into the formal parlor, while family would use the other door that gave access to the more comfortable (and probably less well-furnished) family space. Families with many children would also find two doors more convenient than one. Occasionally, one will find that one of the two doors is more ornate or of more expensive construction, which suggests the idea of "public" space. If this theory is correct, many of the double-entry houses are more closely related to the hall-and-parlor than to the double-pen type. Since field surveyors were not always able to determine the internal arrangement of rooms, most double-entry houses are classified as "double-pen" for the purpose of this survey.

Hall-and-Parlor

The hall-and-parlor house, like the double-pen house, is composed of two rooms arranged side by side, though with only one exterior door. The hall-and-parlor house, as it exists in St. Joseph County, is related to the medieval English house type of the same name. In this case, the hall is not a passageway but a large, multi-purpose room, while the parlor is the more private of the two rooms and is often smaller. Door placement is usually off-center. In the earlier examples, chimneys were located at one or both gable ends; later examples have interior chimneys. Like the double-pen houses and other linear-plan house types, the hall-and-parlor usually had a rear extension forming an L- or T-plan, and in

Double-pen

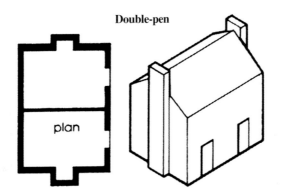

plan

Hall-and-parlor

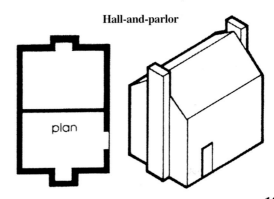

plan

10010 This hall-and-parlor house in German Township displays small, clerestory windows.

many cases, these extensions, along with the front portion of the house, are original. Examples of the hall-and-parlor house remain throughout St. Joseph County (10010, 75002, 80022).

Central-Passage

The central-passage house is similar to the hall-and-parlor and double-pen houses in its two-room, linear plan. It differs in that it has a passage between the two rooms (00011, 06001, 58004). This gives the main portion of the house a greater sense of formality and symmetry than found in the preceding house types. The centrally located doorway and balanced fenestration lent themselves well to the Greek Revival style, which often embellishes central-passage houses. As in the preceding house types, the central-passage house is of British origin. Settlers with roots in the middle and southern

states of America's eastern seaboard commonly built them.

I-House

The natural progression of housing types from the simple one-and-one-half-story hall-and-parlor house to a full two-story structure culminated with the development of the I-house. Like the hall-and-parlor house, the I-house evolved from the English one-room house with an end chimney. The addition of a second story onto the basic floor plan of the hall-and-parlor or central-passage house reflected the growing prosperity of an agrarian economy. Therefore, it is little wonder that the I-house was the predominant housing type in rural areas.

Geographically, the I-house can be found from the Middle Atlantic region, south to Maryland and Virginia, and then west. First identified as a distinct building type during the 1930s, the I-house was most pervasive in Indiana, Illinois, and Iowa, hence the name I-house. Its basic form made it easily adaptable to a variety of architectural styles so that the I-house persisted from the late-18th to the early-20th centuries. Despite the diversity of floor plans utilized in the I-house, its basic form is constant. The house is two stories, one room deep, and at least two rooms wide. Typically, the facade is symmetrical with a central entry in a three- or a five-bay

90063 This 1½-I-house in Liberty Township dates to the mid-19th century and displays rectangular clerestory windows above an enclosed porch.

configuration. Sometimes, a four-bay I-house will feature two entries. Besides these shared characteristics, the I-house took a variety of forms. Building materials included brick, clapboard, or stone. Placement of chimneys varied; they might be found at each gable end flush with the wall, on the house's exterior, or paired at the center of the structure. Demands for additional space necessitated the building of ells or wings at the rear of the house as well as the addition of porches. However, despite these modifications, the basic form of the I-house remained unchanged. Because of its simplicity of form, builders could freely apply decorative details representing diverse architectural styles. As a result, Greek Revival details such as corner posts and cornice returns, or Italianate-style brackets and elaborate porches, were common additions to the I-house. These reactions to popular architectural styles bridged the gap between rural, folk-derived building types and the academic, architect-designed structures of urban areas.

A variety of I-houses remain in St. Joseph County, including 1 1/2 (90063) and three-bay (00012) examples.

Central-passage

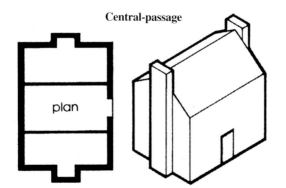

plan

I-house

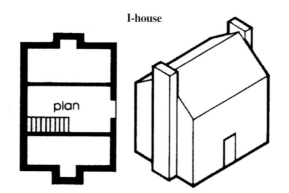

plan

Double-pile

Another massed-plan type, the double-pile house, is rectangular in plan, two or two-and-one-half-stories in height, two rooms wide, and two rooms deep with a central passage running from front to rear. Builders frequently employed this form of house during the 18th century in the United States, and it is often referred to as a "Georgian" plan house, though, as we see in St. Joseph County, builders continued to build the double-pile house throughout the 19th century, transcending stylistic classification (80045, 90045).

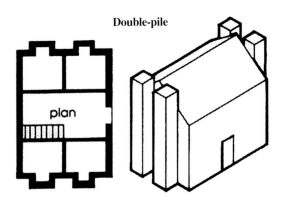

Double-pile

90045 Although altered with the addition of vinyl siding, the John Long House is still a nice example of a double-pile house with Greek Revival elements and is also significant for its association with the early settlement of Liberty Township.

Gable-front

Architectural historians distinguish gable-front houses by their front-facing, gabled roof above the façade possessing the main entrance (70012, 75072, 80020). These are found in all parts of the county dating from the mid-19th to well into the 20th century.

The gable-front house is rectangular in plan and most commonly one-and-one-half stories in height. Gable-front houses developed into a popular house type during the Greek Revival era, when architects designed American buildings to be reminiscent of Greek temples. They achieved the effect of a classical pediment by placing the principal facade beneath a gable end, which forms a triangle. Architectural historians call gable-fronts "temple-front" houses when they are fully attired in Greek Revival dress. While the temple-front variety was common in New England and upstate New York, Midwestern examples appear mainly in northern Indiana and southern Michigan.

Rural areas as well as towns boast gable-front houses. The type's suitability to narrow-fronted lots in expanding urban areas made it a popular house type, as did its adaptability to a variety of styles, including Greek Revival, Italianate, Queen Anne, and Craftsman.

Gable-front

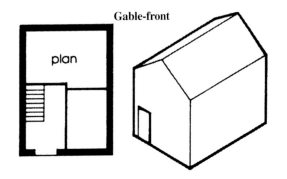

Several sub-types of the gable-front house appear with great frequency in St. Joseph County and warrant mention. The **gabled-ell** is a gable-front house with a side extension, which forms an L-shaped plan. Gabled-ell houses can be one, one-and-one-half, or two stories in height, and in all cases, the ell (or side extension) is the same height as the gable-front portion of the house (10001, 75076).

Gabled-ell

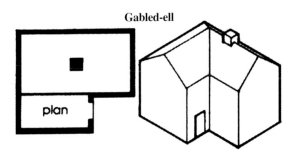

75076 The Gerry Battles Farm in Penn Township is home to this gabled-ell house that has Stick style detailing. The house retains a front porch with turned posts, original windows, and a two-story bay window with scrolled brackets.

Similarly, a gable-front house having a perpendicular front projection that forms a T is referred to as a **T-plan** house. These are also found in a variety of heights, with both front and rear portions of the same height (80078, 85013, 92039). A T-plan house whose wing extends to the side instead of the front is known as a "**lazy T.**" Most of these T-plan houses are one or one-and-one-half stories tall (00003, 58010, 97029), while the similar "**upright-and-wing**" house has a two-story main portion and a lower wing (58011, 62017, 81012).

21

T-plan

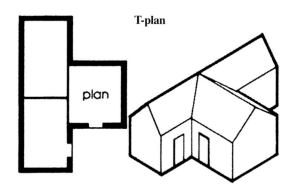

92039 **The Levi Yonser House in North Liberty is an 1887 T-plan, seen here in 2000. The house features Stick-style details including fishscale shingles.**

Upright-and-wing

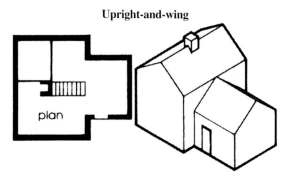

58011 **This Upright-and-wing house in Warren Township has brick walls, window openings with stone heads and narrow sills, and a wide cornice.**

An interesting variation of the gable-front house occurs in St. Joseph County: the **cross-gable square** house usually dates from 1860 to 1885 and has a square footprint with a large gable on each side (66032).

66032 **This house in Greene Township is a good example of a cross-gable square plan. The house features a full-width porch and dates to c.1905.**

Pyramidal-roof Cottage

Identifiable by its roof shape, the pyramidal-roof house is a one-story building commonly of frame construction. Its square plan allows for a simple, informal massing of rooms. The exterior of the

Pyramidal-roof cottage

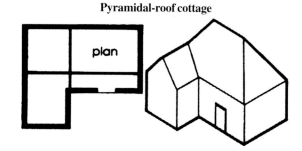

pyramidal-roof house is generally plain, though additions such as ells, porches, corner towers and applied ornamentation lend variety to some examples. Door and window placement varies according to the interior arrangement of rooms. Chimneys, centrally located within the house, usually appear at the apex of the steeply pitched roof (75106, 76002, 91005).

The origins of the pyramidal-roof house are not clear. It appeared in the late 19th century and remained popular into the early decades of the 20th century. Some pyramidal-roof houses in the lower Mississippi Valley may have developed out of French colonial house types; however, in the Ohio River Valley, the folk origin of the pyramidal-roof is less certain. What is clear is that it was a popular house type in many industrial areas, where it was often mass-produced as inexpensive workers' housing.

76002 **This c.1940 house in Osceola is an unaltered example of a pyramidal-roof cottage whose roof peak does not come to a point.**

Bungalow

Shortly after the turn of the century, the bungalow type emerged. By the 1930s, it had become the dominant house form in American domestic architecture. The term "bungalow" comes from India, where it refers to a low house surrounded by galleries or porches. The American bungalow originated in California and spread nationwide largely through the work of Charles and Henry Greene and by way of pattern books and architectural magazines. The inexpensive, fashionable, and generally modest scaled bungalow was particularly suitable to the burgeoning middle class in America's urban and suburban areas. Rooted in the Arts and Crafts movement, which stressed the importance of "honest" materials and construction, the bungalow type featured simplicity of detail and massing, roofs with exposed rafters and knee braces, and facade surfaces of stucco, wood or rubble stone. Porches, normally under an extension of the main roof, were essential components of the bungalow.

Bungalows are typically small buildings, one or one-and-one-half stories tall. However, they were so popular that architects incorporated many elements of the bungalow style, such as knee braces, ribbon windows, large porches, and overhanging eaves, into larger buildings.

05040 This California bungalow in Clay Township has a prominent front porch with round-arched openings.

05044 This dormer-front bungalow in Clay Township retains original clapboard siding, double-hung windows, and a full-width, integral porch with tapered piers.

Architectural historians often categorize these bungalow-style architectural and decorative elements as Craftsman.

Bungalows usually appear in three basic types: the **California bungalow**, which has a gable front, with a gable-front or hipped porch (05040, 07003, 58034); the **dormer-front bungalow**, which has a facade dominated by a single central dormer (05044, 80080, 82004); and the **western bungalow**, which has a hipped roof, often with dormers (11022, 70014, 82007). In its later stages, the bungalow form often appeared with Colonial Revival details or no stylistic details at all.

11022 This Portage Township house is a good example of a western bungalow having Craftsman elements. The c.1920 house exhibits a hipped roof with hipped front-facing dormer and an integral porch supported by tapered square posts.

American foursquare

Similar to bungalows in style and widespread popularity is the American foursquare house. Like the bungalow, its relative simplicity and practicality made it enormously popular. Sometimes classified as **vernacular Prairie**, **cornbelt cube**, or **Midwest box**, the standard two-story American foursquare house has a low-pitch, hipped roof with hipped attic dormers; wide, enclosed eaves; and a one-story porch spanning the width of the front facade. American foursquares are frequently seen with Craftsman elements such as tile roofs, knee braces, and ribbon windows; some have no decoration at all, while others may have Colonial Revival details on entries, windows, and porches.

Builders prefabricated many American foursquares and bungalows and marketed them through catalogs. St. Joseph County has many American foursquares (58040, 75028, 76003).

80017 This brick American foursquare on the Derkson Farm in Madison Township features the typical low hipped roof and front dormer.

Minimal Traditional

Appearing in the 1930s through the 1950s, minimal traditional houses may appear similar to older vernacular types. Usually side-gabled, the roof often has a front-facing cross-gable. The porch is usually very small, and may be integral to the house or have its own separate roof (00008, 07004, 64020).

Postwar Houses

The Second World War halted all non-essential building; this, coupled with the pre-war slowdown in house construction due to the Depression, caused a huge demand for single family housing after the war. Returning servicemen, armed with the GI Bill of Rights and wanting to start families, began pursuing the "American Dream": a family, job, and home of their own.

The housing of the postwar era showed a dramatic change in style and taste from even those houses built just before the war. Gone entirely were the European-influenced period revival styles; the Colonial Revival endured due to its broad appeal, but began to lose its distinctiveness. New forms and trends began to make inroads into the popular tastes. Cheap transportation, new construction methods, and the availability of land all impacted the types of houses built in the years between 1946 and 1959. Chief among the new, popular houses was the ranch. An outgrowth of a style rooted in California and other western states, the ranch flourished in the land-rich suburban housing boom.

Three distinct subtypes based on the footprint or massing of ranch houses may be found in Indiana. Within the subtypes, builders could add different stylistic elements, changing the appearance externally. In the 1930s, West Coast architects adapted the one-story **traditional ranch,** characterized by its linear plan and defined organization of living space. Its footprint varies, with L- and U-shape plans being most common. Roofs of traditional ranches are usually low-pitched and hipped with wide, boxed eaves. Native stone, brick, or a combination of the two are the most typical wall materials. Though usually hidden, garages are an integral part of the plan (63047, 63080, 92042).

The **massed ranch** subtype, as its name suggests, has a massed rather than a linear plan. It shares some characteristics with traditional

05041 The Robert Kollar House in Clay Township was built between 1952-53 by its owner. The concrete walls have extra reinforcing rods and there is a large, boulder-clad chimney.

ranches, including a low-pitched, hipped roof (often with multiple planes) and wide, boxed eaves. What sets it apart is the width and depth of its footprint, which has less frontage to the street and extends deeper into the lot upon which it is built. The massed ranch typically features an attached garage, but it is not integral to the plan (12006, 81014).

As the ranch began to grow in popularity, attention to detail, by necessity, began to wane. The mass construction practices perfected during the war and the rapid expansion of the suburbs led to an explosion of the ranch house's popularity. The **minimal ranch** house was an outgrowth of this popularity. Architects designed these inexpensive homes as scaled-down versions of the traditional ranch. Characteristics of minimal ranches include side-gabled roofs, a strict linear plan and footprint, and minimal use of masonry. Many of these homes lacked garages, though builders might attach a carport to a gable-end (05041).

High-style Architecture

For the most part, architectural styles in Indiana, especially in the areas outside the urban centers, were expressed in a popular rather than a pure academic fashion. They reached the state first not through trained architects but by way of carpenters' guides and builders' manuals. In the pre-railroad era, builders applied stylistic motifs

derived from these books to otherwise vernacular building forms. After the arrival of the railroads, the range of stylistic possibilities broadened as new building products and technologies became available and as communication in general improved. Also, the post-Civil War era witnessed the rise of the architectural profession in America, which resulted in an increase in the number of "high-style" buildings.

The following are some of the most common architectural styles in Indiana:

Federal

The first architectural style to appear in St. Joseph County was the Federal style, popular during the first four decades of the 19th century, which coincided with the first wave of settlement. It is essentially an extension of the late Georgian style and is sometimes referred to as the Adam style for Scottish architect and designer Robert Adam (1728-92). Adam's work had a tremendous impact on British architecture during the late 18th century and on American architecture in the years between the War for Independence and the War of 1812. The continued reliance upon Britain as a cultural model is reflected in Federal architecture, which takes its name from the Federalists, a

66016 The 1832 George & Elizabeth Sumption House in Greene Township, with its flat stone window sills and lintels, is a rare example of the Federal style in St. Joseph County.

conservative American political party during the nation's early years. Federalists favored maintaining close ties with Britain during the late 18th and early 19th centuries. The style remained popular long after America's relations with Britain had soured, especially in areas of westward expansion.

The Federal house is characterized by sparse ornamentation, such as narrow cornice moldings and simple door surrounds, if any. Windows tend to be large, evenly spaced, and multi-paned. Doors have transoms, sometimes of a semi-elliptical shape in the more refined homes. Chimneys are located at the narrow ends of the building and the roof usually is low-pitched and side-gabled. The Federal style is rare in St. Joseph County (00017, 05039, 66016).

Greek Revival

The next style to appear, Greek Revival, was the first and most popular of several romantic revivals, which dominated 19th-century American architecture. After the War of 1812, Americans desired to sever their strong cultural bonds with Britain. As a result, the American people sought an architectural style that reflected their increasingly democratic values and aspirations, and for this they turned to the architecture of ancient Greece.

Several important factors account for the Greek "mania," which swept across America in the early 19th century. Archeological discoveries in Greece, and later the Greek War for Independence (1821-30), aroused much interest and sympathy among Americans. Also, the Greek Revival style, remotely patterned after the temples of ancient Greece, was a bolder and more vigorous style than the refined and delicate Federal style and thus better suited to the American landscape and mentality.

It is no accident that the style's popularity was at its height during a period of increased male suffrage and general political liberalization. Americans viewed themselves as successors to

Athenian Democracy, and by the time the Greek Revival had run its course, it appeared in all settled areas of the United States, applied to buildings of virtually every function.

The chief features of the style are the often minimal references to ancient Greek temples found in such elements as wide entablature moldings, cornice returns, doors with paneled jambs, and classical surrounds. Less common, though present in many high-style examples, are classical porticos.

As typical with the Federal style, most of the county's examples of the Greek Revival style are vernacular house types with applied architectural details referring to the style (66025, 75013, 90045).

80065 This c. 1850 Greek Revival house in Madison Township features a simple entry porch and narrow transoms surrounding the front door.

Gothic Revival

Even more romantic than the Greek Revival is the Gothic Revival, popular in Indiana domestic architecture from the 1840s through the 1860s and in ecclesiastical architecture from the 1840s well into the 20th century. For this style, much of the inspiration came from Britain, though the American expression is quite different and came a generation or more later. Increased industrialization, evidence of political corruption, and various other anxiety-producing factors of the mid-19th century evoked a yearning for a simpler and purer way of life. This was reflected in all areas of culture—painting, music, and most notably, literature. For instance, the writings of Scottish novelist Sir Walter Scott, which portrayed the medieval era in glowing terms, were enormously popular. Architecture also responded to the romantic sentiments of the mid-19th century by incorporating Gothic forms based on

92015 The Gothic Revival North Liberty Church of the Brethren on east Market Street displays an assymetrical gable accented with a multi-paned pointed arch window.

models from the 12th through the 15th centuries into building designs.

Most people connect the Gothic style with religious architecture; it is an emotional, upward-soaring style usually associated with the great stone cathedrals of Western Europe. American builders, using native materials such as wood and brick (stone was reserved for elaborate buildings), translated elements of the Gothic style into a purely American expression, which was at its most charming in domestic architecture.

The most characteristic element of the Gothic style is the pointed arch. Used by medieval builders to span widths and scale heights of ever greater dimensions, the pointed arch in the hands of American builders became a primarily decorative device, faintly echoing its structural origins. Another converted component of the Gothic style is the ornate tracery that American builders executed in wood with the aid of the newly invented steam-powered scroll saw. This tracery was applied to the eaves at gable ends and appeared in ornate porches. Steep-pitched gable roofs, often with finials at the apex, expressed the Gothic verticality and caused the Gothic Revival to be dubbed the "pointed style" in the 19th century. Eared drip moldings were placed above doors and windows, and some Gothic Revival buildings had parapets resembling medieval fortresses. The preferred facade material was board-and-batten siding, which reinforced the verticality. Brick and clapboard were also common (75051, 76019, 92027).

The Gothic Revival style remained popular in ecclesiastical and funerary structures until approximately 1930. Gothic churches, tombstones, and mausoleums appeared at various levels of sophistication, and by the 20th century, there was a greater concern for accuracy in the display of Gothic elements.

Italianate

The Italianate style appeared in St. Joseph County a few years after the Gothic Revival, gaining widespread acceptance in both rural and urban areas and in commercial and domestic architecture. Its extraordinary popularity lasted as late as the 1890s, particularly in commercial buildings. Based on the domestic architecture of the Italian Renaissance, the Italianate style tended to emphasize the picturesque qualities of rural Italian villas, though, as in the preceding styles, the American expression was quite distinct from its historical inspiration (00003, 05025, 10004).

Important features of the domestic Italianate style are the wide, projecting eaves with ornate brackets and tall, narrow windows with round or segmental-arch heads. The roof is often hipped and has a low pitch. Italianate ornamentation was often applied to I-houses; other common house types are the four-over-four variety, sometimes called "Italianate cube," (62003, 64003, 75029) and the L-plan house, sometimes with a tower. More elaborate Italianate houses may have a belvedere, ornate window-hood moldings, and quoins at the corners. Builders equipped most homes with ornate wooden

66037 The Ephraim Rupel House in Greene Township is a notable example of the Italianate style. It exhibits wide eaves supported by paired, scrolled brackets, and original double-doors.

63035 This 1895 Italianate building in New Carlisle formerly housed the E.H. Harris Grocery. The two-story commercial building displays a bracketed cornice, double-hung sash windows on the second floor, and a cast-iron storefront.

porches. They used both brick and frame construction, with the less expensive balloon-frame construction prevailing after the economic panic of 1873.

The Italianate style was also immensely popular in late-19th-century commercial buildings (63035, 91004, 96015). These were rectangular commercial blocks, two or three stories in height, with flat roofs and large storefront windows. Cast-iron vertical members supported the storefront windows. Italianate detail appeared in the often elaborate cornices, round or segmental-head upper-story windows and moldings, and sometimes in additional ornamentation such as ashlar block veneer and quoins. While cornice detail and window-hood moldings were first executed in wood and stone, they were later manufactured in prefabricated stamped metal. This allowed for lavish ornamentation at an economical price. Metal cornices and window hoods appear on some Italianate homes as well.

The Italianate style was quite popular in St. Joseph County, coinciding with the growth of the railroad and the ensuing prosperity.

Second Empire

During the 1860s and 70s, a new style enjoyed brief and intense popularity. American architects modeled the Second Empire style, sometimes called the French Mansard style, after contemporary French architecture. During Louis Napoleon's reign over France's Second Empire (1851-1870), French architects revived the mansard roof, a 17th-century design associated with the work of architect François Mansart. The French Second Empire was a period of highly-charged nationalism and to the French people, the mansard roof was a distinctly French innovation whose 19th-century revival evoked the glories of their country's late-Renaissance era. To Americans who increasingly looked to Paris for the latest in fashion, the Second Empire style was a strikingly modern and sumptuous form of architecture.

62009 This Second Empire carriage house is part of the Hubbard Farm (62010) in Olive Township. The c.1880 structure displays a mansard roof, two large round-arched door openings, and round-arched window openings.

The mansard roof, the Second Empire style's major defining element, is a dual-pitched, hipped roof. Its lower slope is steep with a concave, convex, or straight surface, while the upper slope has a low pitch and is often concealed. In addition, the Second Empire style is characterized by lavish ornamentation and boldness of form. Second Empire homes and public buildings are generally imposing structures, often boasting towers. Roof ridges might be topped with cast iron crestings, while decorative eave brackets support overhanging eaves. Quoins accent corners while window and door openings are embellished with highly-decorative surrounds. The style was well suited to the flamboyant post-Civil War and post-railroad era when ostentation and excessiveness of taste were not discouraged.

St. Joseph County retains several examples of the Second Empire style (13051, 62009, 70032).

Romanesque Revival

Architects used the Romanesque Revival style, appearing in various phases from the 1880s through the first decade of the 20th century, less in houses than in large public and commercial buildings. The Romanesque Revival style looked to the 10th through 13th centuries when builders in Europe rediscovered ancient Roman forms. The most prominent elements of the Romanesque style and its 19th-century counterpart are the round arch and the heavy masonry facades. Romanesque Revival buildings tend to have massive hipped roofs, many with wall gables and conical or pyramidal-roof towers or belfries. They are generally ponderous and fortress-like, conveying an impression of defiance (63019, 85026, 97024).

The most influential proponent of the style, Henry Hobson Richardson (1838-1886), developed his own Romanesque vocabulary, which became known as the **Richardsonian Romanesque** style. Architects of large public buildings to which the style was well suited

97024 Architect W. H. Bost designed the 1903 United Brethren in Christ Church in Walkerton, which was built by Ernest Liebole. The Romanesque Revival place of worship features a cobblestone foundation and a massive octagonal tower.

often imitated it, though not always successfully. In Indiana, several courthouses, churches and schools approximate the Richardsonian Romanesque style.

Stick

Stick style houses feature exterior walls of wood clapboard or shingles. Decorative boards raised above the wall surface and placed vertically, horizontally, or diagonally give the style its name. The style arose from ideals popularized by Andrew Jackson Downing in his successful pattern books of the mid-1800s. Medieval half-timbered houses provided the style its inspiration, as the stickwork mimics the varied surface patterns of the past. The style was most popular from 1860 to 1890, as architects and carpenters applied Stick ornamentation to houses and other buildings (63078, 75076, 92019).

Other decorative elements of the Stick style include trusses under gable eaves, exposed rafter tails, and braces on porch supports. Stick style

63078 The 1887 Augustine/Brown house is the only Stick Style, balloon-framed house in New Carlisle.

97014 This c. 1900 Queen Anne style house on Roosevelt Road in Walkerton exhibits an extensive assymetrical front porch with Ionic columns.

houses are relatively rare when compared to other styles of the period, such as the Italianate and Romanesque Revival styles. Many architectural historians consider Stick style to be transitional, linking the Gothic Revival and Queen Anne styles. The Stick style's emphasis on using wall surfaces as decoration was an idea embraced by the subsequent Queen Anne style.

Queen Anne

The Queen Anne style was popular in St. Joseph County during the 1880s and 1890s. The style originated in England in the 1860s and was an informal blend of 18th-century English architecture and earlier medieval motifs. As the Queen Anne style spread across the United States, it lost much of its 18th-century character and acquired a vague resemblance to late medieval English architecture. An American contribution to the style was the profusion of readily available wooden ornamentation and the substitution of wooden facade shingles for clay tiles found in the English counterparts.

The style typically featured asymmetrical massing, irregular fenestration, diversity of wall treatments and projecting bays, and a feeling of intentional informality (76016, 80003, 97014). These buildings were statements of individuality

and uniqueness in an increasingly regulated and mass-produced world. Builders used the style chiefly in domestic architecture, though occasionally in commercial architecture, and it is often synonymous with the popular conception of late-Victorian architecture in America.

97045 This c.1900 house in Walkerton is a good example of the Queen Anne style as it transitioned into the Free Classic style. The house has clapboard siding with cornerboards, a hipped roof with cross gables that suggest a pediment and incorporate cornice returns, and a full-width front porch with round columns.

A later variation of the Queen Anne style is referred to here as the **Free Classic** style. This sub-type typically appeared during the first decade of the 20th century as the Queen Anne style's popularity was waning. The Free Classic style has a more formal feel and applies classical features to the asymmetrical massing of the Queen Anne house. Distinctive features may include a Palladian window in the front gable, a porch with classical columns, and a pediment over the entry (07008, 70027, 97046).

Neoclassical/Classical Revival

By the turn of the 20th century, the Neoclassical style emerged as a dominant force in American architecture. In the Neoclassical style, there was concern for historical correctness of detail but not of overall execution or scale. Neoclassical buildings tend to be meticulously detailed and of massive scale, which sets them quite apart from Greek Revival buildings with casually interpreted classical ornamentation and modest scale. Architectural Neoclassicism prevailed into the 1930s, most notably in large public and commercial buildings including skyscrapers. Characteristics of the style include the use of classical elements such as columned porticos, pilasters, keystones, pedimented openings, and dentils along the cornice (11029, 13026, 66015).

13026 LaFortune Student Center at Notre Dame University once housed the Science Hall. Willoughby J. Edbrooke designed the 1883 building in the Classical Revival style.

28

Colonial Revival

Around the turn of the 20th century, the Colonial Revival style gained prominence, and it retained much popularity throughout the 20th century. Several factors accounted for this: the American centennial in 1876, which stimulated an unprecedented interest in American heritage in general and in colonial American architecture in particular; the growing tendency in the late 19th century among America's trend-setting architects to build period houses in a variety of eclectic styles, which often incorporated colonial elements; and the 1893 Chicago Columbian Exposition, which emphasized accuracy and correctness in the use of historical styles and established Neoclassical and Colonial Revival as the dominant styles in American architecture.

Historical accuracy in the Colonial Revival style was confined more to specific elements than to the building as a whole. For instance, a Colonial Revival house is usually of much larger scale than its 17th- or 18th- century prototype, and it may bear the influence of more than one phase of the colonial period. Elements of the style include dentils, heavy cornices, entrances with fanlights and sidelights, pedimented dormer windows, keystones, and quoins (62012, 70009, 75093). A variation on the style that features gambrel roofs is called **Dutch Colonial Revival** (59007, 75019, 76017).

The **Cape Cod** house has its roots in the Massachusetts area from which it takes its name. Originally built by colonists as simple shelter against the unforgiving New England elements, this small house type became popular in the 1930s and endures to this day. A simple house, it was inexpensive to build. Cape Cods are one or one-and-one-half stories, side gabled with an expansive roof and central chimney, with little or no eave overhang. Builders typically clad Cape Cods in clapboard or wood shingle siding (75041, 90004, 92043).

Prairie

Influenced by the Arts and Crafts movement, Chicago architect Frank Lloyd Wright created a completely original American style at the turn of the twentieth century. Dubbed "Prairie" in honor of the Midwest farmlands that served as his inspiration, Wright's style flourished throughout the country, popularized in pattern books. Architects designed all types of buildings in the Prairie style, but it was most common to residential construction (07002, 62021, 92030).

Characterized by low-pitched, hipped roofs having wide, overhanging eaves, Prairie style houses are two-stories in height and have large porches supported by square piers. Ribbon windows and other decorative elements emphasize the horizontal. Intended to blend into the environment, their overall massing is wide and low to the ground. They most often have brick exteriors, but stucco, wood, and stone were also used. Vernacular examples of the Prairie style resemble American foursquares. The two share many similar characteristics; however, true Prairie style structures are architect-designed and asymmetrical in form, while foursquares tend to be symmetrical. The Prairie style faded in popularity after World War I.

Craftsman

In reaction to the ostentatious Queen Anne and Classical Revival styles that were so prevalent at the dawn of the 20th century, the Craftsman style decried ornamentation and pretension. Rooted in the American Arts and Crafts movement as espoused by Gustav Stickley, the Craftsman style utilized natural materials and handmade, rather than mass-produced, goods. It emphasized honesty of design, meaning that whenever possible the designer left construction methods exposed rather than hidden. Low rooflines with exposed rafters and wide eaves supported by knee braces are typical (64017, 80080, 90003). Stone or brick foundations support walls clad in a variety of natural materials. Intended to blend in with the natural landscape, the Craftsman

92001 The 1937 Dell Pearse House in North Liberty has a double-pile plan with central hallway and Colonial Revival ornament.

62021 This house is Olive Township is a notable example of the Prairie style. It exhibits a horizontal emphasis, especially evident in its wide, overhanging eaves.

97037 The Harley & Ida McKesson House in Walkerton is a notable example of a dormer-front bungalow with Craftsman-style details, such as knee braces beneath overhanging eaves and a full-width integral porch with brick piers. The house features a gabled dormer and side chimney.

house exhibits muted earth-tone colors. Bands of multi-pane windows, often asymmetrically placed, lighted the interior. As the style gained popularity before and after World War I, its stylistic elements were applied to various types of houses, such as bungalows and American foursquares. Ironically, by the end of its popularity, the Craftsman style had become little more than surface ornamentation, the very trend that it had been created to protest.

Eclectic Period Revivals

A variety of eclectic styles became popular around the turn of the century and, as in the Neoclassical style, the buildings feature a somewhat free application of carefully studied detail. The diverse styles of these buildings usually bear apt titles such as **Mediterranean Revival**, **Italian Renaissance Revival**, etc. That period houses reached a high point of popularity during the 1920s has been attributed in part to servicemen who, upon returning from World War I, wished to pattern their homes after the picturesque buildings they had seen in Europe.

The **English Cottage** style exhibits very steep gable roofs, picturesque chimneys, and facades of stone veneer or simulated half-timbering (05017, 58014, 63071). The **Pueblo** or **Mission Revival** styles often have stucco facades and tile

63071 This 1920 English cottage in New Carlisle has irregular-cut shingle siding, a jerkin head roof, round-arched door, and a massive front chimney.

13036 Many buildings on the Notre Dame campus were built in the Collegiate Gothic style, including the 1931 Dillon Hall. The Collegiate Gothic style is one of the eclectic period revivals and has both Tudor and Gothic influences; it takes its name from the popularity of the style on college campuses across the nation.

roofs. The **Tudor Revival** style, or **Tudor Gothic**, distinguishable by its Tudor arch, found wide use in early-20th-century religious architecture and was used so regularly in educational buildings that it is sometimes referred to as **Collegiate Gothic** (13036, 66033, 86001). The eclectic styles achieved their highest expression in the often lavish period houses built before the Great Depression but were also applied to a variety of building types other than residential. For instance, many early gas stations were built in the English Cottage style.

Art Moderne

Art Moderne developed during the 1930s and continued in ever-simplified forms through the 1950s. Art Moderne, as opposed to Art Deco, emphasized the horizontal line, often with rounded corners and streamlined decorations. Builders constructed a few residences in the Art Moderne style, but the style was more prevalent in commercial buildings, particularly gas stations (97002).

97002 St. Patrick School in Walkerton was built in 1956 in the sleek Art Moderne style. It contains a stylized, inset relief sculpture of St. Patrick in limestone.

Contemporary

Gaining popularity in the 1950s, contemporary houses ignored the look of the past and were purely modern in inspiration. Often architect-designed, contemporary houses may have flat, gabled or shed roofs. They often incorporate wood, brick, and stone into the facades. Contemporary houses with flat-roofs evolved from the **International** style of architecture and are sometimes classified as International style in this survey (66006, 12013, 95019). The gabled forms often have wide eave overhangs and exposed rafters like Prairie-style homes. Contemporary houses with shed roofs originated in the early 1960s and persist to the present and may exhibit multi-directional sheds, sometimes combined with gables. Contemporary houses are not bound to a particular shape but may have linear, massed, or irregular plans. They have no decorative detailing, instead making use of the textures of materials and landscaping for their ornament.

66006 This c.1950 house in Greene Township is a good example of the International style as it was translated into residences. It boasts a massive chimney of local stone and floor-to-ceiling glass windows.

Agriculture

Traditionally, a close tie exists between agriculture and Indiana's heritage. Since the pioneer days, the raising of crops and livestock has played an important role in the state's economic, social and educational systems. With the passage of the Land Ordinance Act of 1785, the U.S. government established guidelines for the sale of land in the Northwest Territories. The Act provided for the now-familiar rectangular survey system of one-mile squares. This system also provided for a more organized means of land transfers and decreased the possibility of boundary disputes. Settlers could purchase parcels of land in offices established throughout the state. Indiana's earliest agricultural activity centered around southern Indiana. The area's uneven terrain and undeveloped transportation system limited these early farms to subsistence levels, but corn and livestock provided food for the settler and were used as a means of exchange.

As transportation routes developed in northern Indiana, its open prairie and rich soil invited more and more settlers. Agriculture emerged as an important component of the state's economy and farmers diversified their crops. By the 1850s, advances in transportation and technology were producing dramatic changes in agriculture, expanding it beyond the subsistence level. The Morrill Act in 1862, which provided for the establishment of colleges of agriculture and mechanical arts, encouraged this agricultural expansion. Twelve years later, Purdue University opened in West Lafayette. The University offered courses in agriculture and provided extension services for the state's farmers. Local organizations such as the Grange formed to promote social, cultural, and educational programs in rural areas. Grange buildings, farmers' clubs and grain elevators are part of the state's agricultural heritage not associated with individual farms, and many people overlook their importance.

Distant markets became more accessible to farmers via the new railroads, boosting their productivity. Moreover, improved agricultural implements and machinery increased the amount of crops grown and harvested. The resulting agricultural expansion touched other areas of Hoosier life as well. The farmer could now afford to build larger, more elaborate houses and outbuildings. Rural communities and their small businesses prospered, as did the railroads. As agriculture became more sophisticated, it slowly evolved from being a way of life to being a business. More sophisticated farm machinery decreased the amount of labor needed and increased the size of farms. However, a slowly urbanizing society eroded agriculture's dominance of rural life and its economy.

The following are the most common agricultural buildings in St. Joseph County:

Grain Elevators

Integral to the familiar rural landscape is the prairie skyscraper—the grain elevator. Dominating the skyline of many small towns, sometimes even overshadowing the county courthouse, the grain elevator stands in silent testimony to one of the greatest industries in the world—grain farming. Following the axiom "form follows function," grain elevators, with their hodgepodge appearance, do not often appear to the casual observer as notable examples of architectural beauty. However, close examination finds them to be quite stylish in their simplicity of form, honesty in material, and straightforward functionality (62008, 62045, 82002).

As long as farmers have had the ability to produce grain beyond the needs of themselves and their immediate locale, grain elevators have proven a necessity. Typically, there are two classifications of elevators: country or rural elevators that serve a small section of farmland and terminal or urban elevators that serve regions of land. Farmers brought grain to the rural elevator by truck, wagon, or rail. Workers then weighed, sorted, and shipped the grain to the larger terminal elevator, where it could be distributed locally, nationally, or internationally.

Small towns built on feeder tracks of major rail lines often boast elevators constructed of wood or concrete. Whether of crib construction akin to a log cabin or of stud construction similar to a frame house, wood frame elevators are typically sheathed in non-combustible materials such as asbestos shingles or corrugated sheet metal to reduce the danger of fire. Farmers were still building wood frame elevators well into the 20th century, though not as commonly as before 1900. Poured concrete was a safer, sturdier material to use, but it was not until the advent of slipform technology—in which short molds are filled with concrete, then "slipped" up to the next level—that constructing elevators of concrete became cost effective.

By 1915, most farmers built their new elevators of concrete. Concrete elevators were sturdier, had a greater capacity than the framed structures and, most importantly, were fireproof. Sometimes they retained a rectangular footprint like the frame examples, and sometimes they were built with more efficient round bins.

Explosion and fire have been the bane of grain elevators since their inception. Consolidation and abandonment are the current enemies. The

62045 The 1954 St. Joseph County Farm Bureau Co-op Grain Elevator in New Carlisle is the third elevator located at this site.

closing of spur lines and consolidation of shipping signaled the end for many rural elevators. Some may find a niche in the community as retail outlets for agricultural products or storage facilities. Others shut down operations, unable to compete in today's economy. Whether left empty or still used, they acknowledge the historic importance of the farmer, the railroad, and technology in American history.

Indiana's "golden age" of agriculture extended into the 20th century. By 1900, agriculture so dominated the state's economy that the top four industries in Indiana were agriculture related. However, with the rise of other industries, the evolution of an urban society and changes in transportation, agriculture's dominance of the Hoosier lifestyle lessened. Despite this downturn in the agrarian economy, agriculture remains a vital part of Indiana's traditions.

Barns

The barn is the most prominent and recognizable structure within the farm complex. Farmers constructed early barns according to traditional building methods, both in form and craftsmanship. Heavy hand-hewn timbers are characteristic of these traditional barns. Toward the end of the 19th century, traditional barn types gave way to barns whose designs were promoted by agricultural journals, land-grant college programs, and later by the United States Department of Agriculture. Following the Great Depression and World War II, barn building techniques changed drastically, and the construction of pole barns and prefabricated structures almost entirely superseded traditional methods of barn construction.

English Barn

English settlers brought the English barn to the New England and Chesapeake Bay area. It became the dominant barn type there and traveled to the Midwest with few modifications.

English barns are timber-framed and rectangular in plan. They differ from transverse-frame barns in that their major entry is not on the gable end but on the barn's long side. The entry is usually centered and consists of double doors. The English barn is commonly separated into three bays. Farmers used the center space as a threshing area and sections to either side as grain and hay storage. They clad English barns in vertical siding and gave them few windows.

St. Joseph County retains many examples of the English barn (75024, 80046, 80060).

Basement/Bank Barn

The basement, or bank, barn consists of an English barn raised on a stone, concrete, or brick foundation. In addition to the centered door on the barn's long side, small doors on each gable end provide access to the basement. Typically, an earthen wagon ramp provides access to the upper floor. Farmers could also build the barn into a hillside, with the top of the hill providing upper-floor access. They used the lower level of the basement barn to house livestock and the upper level for crop storage and as a threshing floor.

St. Joseph County has several examples of basement/bank barns (10004, 70041, 80071).

Transverse-frame Barn

The transverse-frame barn is the culmination of a barn type that evolved from a basic single-crib log structure. The single-crib barn was simply one square or rectangular crib with a gable roof. It was commonly of log construction and used for grain storage and the stabling of animals. As farmers required additional space, the double-crib and four-crib barns evolved. Both these barn types used the single-crib barn as the basic unit and simply added additional cribs in two distinct configurations.

Similar to the English barn, the double-crib barn consisted of two cribs separated by a breezeway and sharing a gable roof. The four-crib barn had cribs at each corner with a common roof and intersecting aisles that formed a cross.

The transverse-frame barn evolved from the four-crib barn. The cross aisle was closed off and stalls or cribs were built along the wall. Farmers placed entrances to the transverse-frame barn at either end so that they could drive wagons through the structure. Rows of storage cribs or stables lined each side of the barn. Unlike crib

75024 **This English barn in Penn Township is part of the Alfred Curtis Farm and has vertical board siding.**

70041 **This impressive bank/basement barn in Centre Township retains shiplap siding and a large, sliding door. The paired windows have cornices and round-arched openings, a highly-decorative feature for a barn.**

barns, transverse-frame barns were primarily of frame construction (85009, 90042, 95010).

Round/Octagonal Barn

Round and octagonal barns are a unique part of our architectural heritage. Most date from the early 20th century, a time of rising prosperity and innovation in American agriculture. Numerous agricultural and builder's journals disseminated designs for labor- and material-saving round barns.

Both enthusiasm and derision greeted the appearance of round or octagonal barns, which were regarded as something of a fad. The deepening agricultural depression of the 1920s and subsequent changes in agricultural technology and economy curtailed their construction. Today, one octagonal and one round barn remains in St. Joseph County (00026, 85078).

Non-Traditional Barns

Toward the end of the 19th century, forces other than tradition influenced barn building. The use of cut-to-size dimensional lumber rather than heavy timber in barn construction resulted in lighter framing systems that, in turn, allowed for large, unobstructed lofts sheltered by gambrel or round-arched roofs. Research at agricultural experiment stations also had a great impact on barn designs through the promotion of efficiency and sanitation as well as new construction techniques. Many of the dairy and livestock barns built in the early 20th century resulted from these designs. The typical 20th-century livestock barn has a gambrel roof and doors on either the side or the end of the building (75035, 75061, 75076).

Silos

Silos became popular around the turn of the 19th century as a means of storing green crops, or silage, to feed cattle over the winter (05009,

00026 St. Joseph's Farm was established in 1867 by the Brothers of the Holy Cross and the University of Notre Dame to provide food to the University. This octagonal barn dates to 1900.

75033, 80058). Builders constructed the first silos of wood, often in a square shape. At first, the square silos were sometimes built into a corner of the barn, but this reduced the available area for livestock or hay storage. Square silos were also not as practical as round ones because the silage did not pack down into the corners well, which allowed air to get in and rot the mixture.

In the 1920s, concrete and glazed tile silos came into widespread use. Tile was not as popular as concrete because it was fragile, and the curved tiles determined the size of the silo. Concrete

75061 This barn in Penn Township is an excellent example of a gothic-arch barn, sometimes called a rainbow-roof barn. It has vertical weatherboard siding and a large ventilator on the roof's ridge.

was easy to use; builders could pour it in rings or assemble it in vertical staves. Metal was also a popular silo material. After World War II, the familiar blue Harvestore silos began to dot the landscape. Today, wooden silos are very rare in Indiana.

Outbuildings

Historically, several types of outbuildings supported the operations of a farm. Generally smaller than the house and barn, they were usually devoted to one specific function.

The historic farmstead contained a variety of ancillary buildings used in the preparation and storage of food for human consumption. **Smokehouses** (00016, 58031, 66055) for curing meat (often identified by the coating of soot and creosote that has built up on the inside of the door); **milk houses** to keep dairy products cool; **root cellars** for winter storage of apples, potatoes, and onions; and insulated **warm houses** for the storage of canned goods year round exist on numerous farms. These basic structures were usually rectangular in plan and could be of frame, brick, or block construction.

80060 This English barn with attached wood silo in Madison Township is a notable example of an agricultural resource. Surviving wood silos are rare today.

Glazed tile was a popular and sanitary construction material in the 1920s through 1940s.

Many farmsteads retain **summer kitchens**, which removed unwanted heat, odors, and fire risks from the main house. These buildings could either be freestanding or attached to the rear of the house by a covered breezeway.

Another building, the **privy**, was perhaps the humblest of buildings on the farmstead, yet one of the most important. During the 1930s, the Works Progress Administration (WPA) built and distributed plans for "sanitary" privies to replace inadequate structures. Many of the privies remaining on farms today are built to WPA specifications, which are very similar to facilities found in national parks and campgrounds. Ubiquitous until quite recently, privies, like many of the outbuildings associated with the historic farmstead, are increasingly scarce.

Other outbuildings that hold agricultural produce include structures such as **granaries** and **corn cribs**. Corn needs the circulation of air around it, so it is stored in wire mesh or slatted wood cribs. Grain needs to be protected from moisture and vermin, so it is usually stored in more airtight structures that are often raised above the ground on piers (66057, 80015, 95006). At this time, architectural historians do not consider the round metal grain bins seen on many modern farms historic.

00016 **This double-entry smokehouse in Harris Township was once used to cure meat and retains an impressive ashlar foundation.**

80016 **This 1942 granary, part of the Derkson Farm in Madison Township, is a notable example of that outbuilding type.**

Hog pens, hen houses, and brooder houses are a few of the special types of structures that shelter animals. **Hen or chicken houses** are usually long, low, rectangular buildings with many windows. **Brooder houses** are frequently round or octagonal to prevent baby chicks from getting stuck in corners. Farmers often scattered **hog houses** within or around the perimeter of a fenced enclosure, constructing them out of wood or half of a corrugated metal culvert.

Industry

The earliest industries to appear in Indiana relied almost exclusively upon the agricultural economy and accessibility to raw materials. Settlers built water-powered gristmills and sawmills along streams and rivers, encouraging development. These were small, multifunctional operations with only one or two workers. The mills not only served as a place of business but were also used as post offices, polling places, and meeting places. Craftsmen plied their specialized trades in home industries. Coopers, wheelwrights, and blacksmiths were common tradesmen up until the advent of mass-production techniques.

Gristmills were often at the center of early settlements. Corn, the staple of pioneer life, was

milled into flour for food and as a means of exchange. Distilleries, another common early industry, also used corn. Sawmills took advantage of southern Indiana's seemingly inexhaustible supply of timber, so that lumber soon emerged as one of the state's largest industries.

With few overland routes available, the Ohio River developed as the major means of transportation in southern Indiana during the early and mid-19th century. The river provided access to markets for manufactured goods as well as to raw materials. River towns such as Madison and Jeffersonville developed as major manufacturing communities. Madison was at one time the nation's largest pork-packing center. Jeffersonville gained national renown for the hundreds of steamboats built in its shipyards.

With the advent of the railroad during the 1850s, the scope of Indiana's industrial base widened dramatically, although most industry was still found in southern Indiana. While milling and lumbering retained their dominance, the railroad contributed to the emergence of other industries. Workers mined coal from fields in southwestern Indiana to meet the increased demand for energy.

As the railroad network developed, industry slowly became more sophisticated. Increased availability of raw material, access to distant markets, and the demand for manufactured goods as a result of the Civil War spurred Indiana's industrial growth. The state's industrial centers slowly shifted north toward Indianapolis. By the 1880s, many of the state's largest industries made homes in the capital city and in emerging industrial cities such as South Bend and Fort Wayne.

Specialized factories soon appeared, employing sometimes hundreds of workers. Coal, natural gas, and steam replaced water power. Production shifted from the manufacturing of agriculture-based goods to durable goods that were easy to ship to distant markets. The discovery of natural gas in north-central Indiana accelerated the state's industrial growth near the end of the 19th century.

With the advent of the internal combustion engine, industry became more efficient and diversified. The arrival of the automobile introduced a new focus in manufacturing, and the auto industry took on a dominant role in the economy of Indiana.

Around the turn of the century, some buggy manufacturing companies restructured their businesses to begin testing, designing, and producing some of the country's earliest automobiles. By the 1920s, manufacturing had surpassed agriculture as the state's largest industry. Factories were larger, more sophisticated, and operated more efficiently because of the internal combustion engine.

Religion

Religious congregations were often one of the first institutions established in newly settled areas. Initially there were no formal churches in which to worship, so settlers gathered in private homes for services. Itinerant preachers or circuit riders sent from established churches in neighboring areas usually conducted these services. As a region developed, congregations became more organized and formal church buildings were constructed. Typically, early church buildings were crude log structures, replaced gradually by simple frame buildings as the congregations grew. Often these structures were the only public buildings located outside villages, resulting in their use for a variety of functions. Rural communities sometimes used churches as schools and public meeting places. In many cases, several different congregations shared one building. Eventually, as a congregation grew larger and wealthier, it replaced its church building with a more elaborate structure.

French Catholic missionaries in southern Indiana established the state's earliest churches. The

80041 The Mt. Zion Evangelical and Reformed Church in Madison Township dates to 1868 and features a tall steeple and pointed-arch windows with stained glass.

Baptists and Methodists soon followed and developed into Indiana's two dominant religious groups. Both denominations were well established in the South, where many of Indiana's earliest settlers originated. The Methodists and the Baptists provided lay preachers, while other religious groups depended on churches in the East to send trained clergy. Until the 1860s, Presbyterian and Catholic churches, among others, considered Indiana a missionary field. Members of the Friends denomination also heavily settled parts of Indiana.

Sparse population, poor transportation, and lack of clergy severely limited the attendance of religious services. Simple rural churches of log or frame construction dotted the countryside. Often, burial grounds accompanied these rustic buildings. However, as the railroad reached more Indiana communities, larger congregations formed, especially in towns and cities. They built

bigger, more expensive churches to replace the modest frame buildings of only a few years before. The rise of the state's urban areas during the early 20th century hastened the growth of organized religion in Indiana, as congregations supported increasingly larger churches.

However, the gradual migration from a rural to an urban populace, the merging or decline of rural congregations, and the cost of maintaining church buildings have had a negative impact on religious structures in recent years. As the number of abandoned or neglected buildings increases, the challenge of preserving and

97027 Architect LeRoy Bradley designed the late-Gothic Revival Walkerton Methodist Church in 1937. The entry has a limestone surround and is flanked by bronze lanterns. Brick pilasters, reminiscent of buttresses, line the main elevation.

00001 The Salem Church of the Evangelical Association Cemetery in Harris Township has burials dating to c.1850.

reusing these churches becomes more imperative. Despite a decrease in the number of church buildings in recent years, especially in rural areas, religion remains an important part of the state's heritage.

St. Joseph County's religious history is well represented by its collection of rural and urban churches. Typically, the faithful built simple rural churches in the gable-front form of many New England churches (00002, 62024, 80041). As towns boasted larger congregations, they built larger and more impressive churches (13023, 59012, 97028).

An important part of the built environment frequently overlooked is the numerous cemeteries found throughout St. Joseph County (00001, 11018, 95011). Often, cemeteries are historically connected with church buildings. As congregations died out or consolidated, burial grounds were often all that remained. Other rural cemeteries might be family plots, the final resting place of hard-working settlers, their families, and neighbors, such as the Henson Family Cemetery, established c.1849 (70031).

In many cases, cemeteries provide us with the only record of a person's or a family's presence in a time and place. The earliest markers were slabs of sandstone or marble that bore inscriptions and occasionally bas-relief, followed by classically inspired shafts, urns, or obelisks that corresponded to the Greek Revival period in architecture. Later, Gothic markers appeared, using the pointed arch motif. For a few decades in the late 19th century, cast "white bronze" monuments were popular and affordable alternatives to expensive stone monuments. Like the stamped metal cornices common among Italianate buildings, the cast monuments provided many rural areas with a sense of inexpensive opulence.

This survey has attempted to locate cemeteries within St. Joseph County but does not include pre-contact, Native American burial grounds. Laws protect the locations of those burial grounds to prevent looting.

Education

In addition to religious congregations, settlers usually established educational institutions in frontier areas. Familiar one-room schoolhouses dotted the landscape. They were typically subscription schools, in which residents banded together and hired a teacher of suitable training. Like church buildings, schools were multi-functional, serving as meeting places, polling places, and in some instances, churches. As the idea of public education gained support, subscription schools slowly gave way to the opening of tax-supported township schools.

The Land Ordinance Act of 1785 greatly affected Indiana's educational system. Provisions in the Act allowed the leasing of public lands to support local schools and set aside one section of each 36-mile-square township for a school. However, localities did not always adhere to this system and abuses occurred. In many areas, subscription schools and private academies prevailed until the 1850s, when a free public school system began in Indiana. The state authorized the levying of taxes for school construction, established standards for teachers, and provided money for school libraries. It was

during the late 19th century that the familiar brick one- and two-room schoolhouses proliferated. Officials built township schools within several miles of each other so that students could walk to them. The one-room schoolhouse persisted throughout the 19th century into the early 20th century until school consolidation began.

Consolidation of district schools into township schools began in the years before World War I. Better roads and motor transportation led to the creation of centralized, all-grade schools; one by one, the single-room schools were closed, abandoned, or converted into homes, barns, or sheds. The larger township schools, often located in the center of the township or in the closest town, began consolidating in the 1960s. Some of the older township schools then served as elementary schools, but most closed their doors forever.

Consolidation of rural schools presented both positive and negative results. Larger schools allowed for more teachers, better facilities, and more students. With the coming of paved roads and school buses, the school no longer had to be within walking distance. Despite the advantages of consolidation, proponents of the neighborhood school saw its closing as contributing to the exodus of young people from

62004 The Olive Township District No. 1 School has Italianate features such as tall, narrow windows with segmental-arched hoods, and dates to 1867.

86001 The 1931 Lakeville High School is an outstanding example of Collegiate Gothic architecture. It displays limestone insets with shield and scroll medallions and limestone quoins. The raised letters of the school name above the main door are flanked by limestone pilasters. The school is listed in the National Register of Historic Places.

the farm as well as a decline in community spirit. Between the years of 1890 and 1900, more than half of the state's 8,000 one-room schools were abandoned. Officials replaced these schools with larger grade and high schools, usually located in the township's largest community. Like the advent of public schools decades before, school consolidation produced dramatic changes in the educational system. School consolidation continued during the 20th century, resulting in the loss of many historic schools.

St. Joseph County's collection of schools reflects the history of educational trends (00007, 62004, 86001).

Commerce

The areas of commerce and transportation are interrelated; without access to waterways, roads, and railroads, the exchange of goods and services is not possible. That is why an area's earliest commercial activity usually occurred along rivers or Indian trails.

French fur traders established early trading posts at places like Lafayette, Fort Wayne, and Vincennes. Mills were usually the first businesses to appear in a frontier area, providing a variety

of services to the surrounding population. Gristmills produced flour for settlers to use as food and as a medium of exchange before the widespread use of hard currency. Often, the mill was multi-functional, serving as a general store, a post office, and a school.

As settlers poured into the state, the Ohio River took on an important role in Indiana's commercial development. Southern Indiana river ports such as Madison, Jeffersonville, and Evansville became major economic centers. As the state's transportation system developed with the construction of canals and roads, economic growth slowly shifted to central and northern Indiana. The opening of the state's first railroad in 1847 ushered in a period of dramatic changes in the area of commerce. The development of towns along rail lines had a profound impact on commerce, moving it from a subsistence level based on bartering to a more complex activity. Until the advent of the automobile, most business took place in small-town, family-owned specialty stores.

The railroad enabled merchants to offer a wider selection of goods at a cheaper cost. Advances in building technology coupled with product diversification resulted in the development of the familiar late-19th-century commercial building. The introduction of cast iron and advances in the manufacturing of glass enabled the storefront to offer a larger display area. A decorative wood panel on the bottom and a transom with small panes of prism glass on top usually framed the display window. The building's second floor often served as residential space for the business owner and had windows with decorative pressed-metal hoods. An ornate pressed-metal cornice, sometimes with the merchant's name cast into it, might top the building. This type of commercial building dominated the Main Streets of railroad-era towns across Indiana, and its popularity persisted into the early 20th century.

The automobile was responsible for dramatic changes in small-town-based economy and slowly changed the state's commercial focus. By 1930, a large percentage of Indiana's rural

population owned automobiles and were able to drive to larger towns to conduct their business. The Great Depression, which brought a number of bank and business failures and a population shift from rural to urban areas, hit small communities hard. The growth of suburbs after World War II further contributed to a decentralization of the business district and a decline in downtown commercial districts. Clusters of commercial buildings soon appeared along streetcar routes or in suburban areas. Residents no longer conducted business exclusively in downtown areas. As suburbs developed their own commercial areas, people did not need to travel into town to shop. During the mid- to late-20th century, strip shopping centers and the development of the suburban mall further drained business away from downtowns.

Recently, attempts to reverse this trend have met with positive results, and a renewed interest in the small town business district is evident. Since the establishment of the Indiana Main Street Program in 1986, small-town business districts have re-emerged as an important part of a community's commercial activity.

The survey classifies commercial buildings by their styles and/or vernacular types. The most common vernacular types in Indiana follow:

1- or 2-part Commercial Block

The simplest commercial buildings may often be described as 1- or 2-part commercial blocks. These masonry commercial structures have little or no decorative detailing and are usually one or two stories tall, as indicated by the numeral preceding "part." The boxy buildings usually have large glass display windows and flat roofs (82005, 86014, 91006).

Parapet-front

Parapet-front commercial buildings have a principal façade wall that extends vertically

91006 The Pearse Block is a notable example of a 2-part commercial block. It has two storefronts with recessed entries, full display windows, and wood bulkheads.

11016 This commercial building in Portage Township was probably built as an auto repair garage and is an example of a 20th century functional structure.

Fanciful statuary in the Studebaker Fountain. *Courtesy of Historic Preservation Commission of South Bend and Saint Joseph County.*

beyond the roof line. That extension is called a "parapet." Parapets can be simple rectangular extensions, stepped, or elaborately designed in the Spanish Mission style. Often, the building's name or date is placed on the parapet (05008, 58032, 82008).

19th or 20th Century Functional

If a building does not fall into a style or one of the above vernacular-type categories, the survey classifies it as "Functional" according to the century in which it was built. These are generally utilitarian buildings like warehouses, factories, or garages that have little or no decorative features (11016, 13048).

58032 This commercial building in Warren Township exhibits a parapet façade.

A family of young and old are pictured in front of their Harris Township home. *Courtesy of Historic Preservation Commission of South Bend and Saint Joseph County.*

Current Map of St. Joseph County

Right: St. Joseph Hospital, circa 1920. *Courtesy of Historic Preservation Commission of South Bend and St. Joseph County*

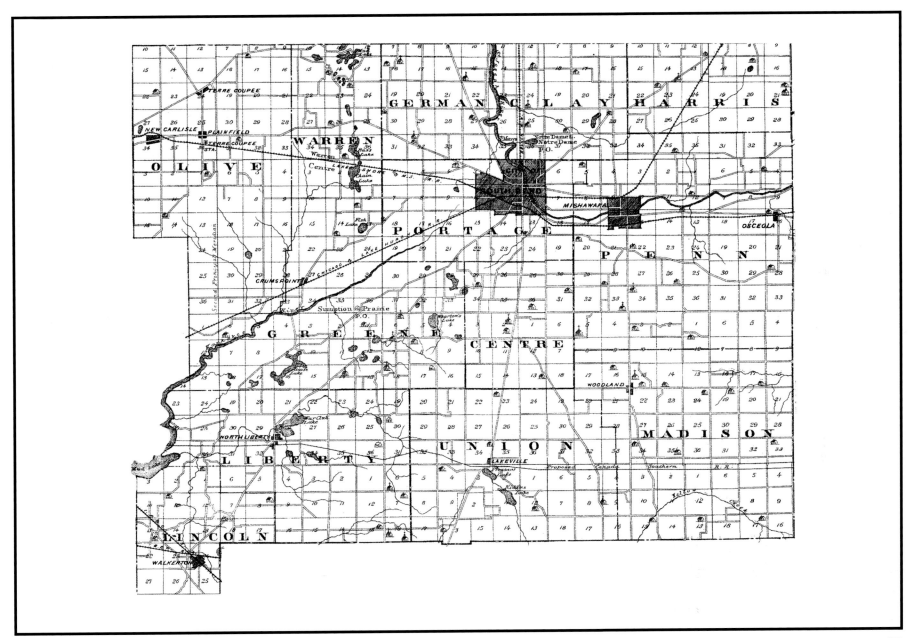

Catalog

How to Read the Catalog

Each section of this catalog begins with the name of the township, community, or historic district, with its range of site numbers printed in parentheses. A map showing the location of the sites follows. For historic districts, towns, and townships, a short descriptive narrative also appears. The actual list of sites included in the inventory follows in numerical order. Each entry provides the following information:

Number

The last three digits of the property's individual site number precede each catalog entry. This three-digit number is also used on the accompanying map to show the site's location.

Rating

The next column of information contains the rating for each inventory entry (O, N, C, or NC). See the section on p. 7, "Criteria and Evaluation," for a full explanation of the rating system.

Description

Name

When original property owners' names were available, the report couples them with the type of resource, e.g. "Smith Farm." It lists institutional properties according to their original names when these are available, such as "Methodist Episcopal Church." If the historic name is unknown, a general name has been used, such as "House," "Commercial Building," or "Farm."

Address

The property's address follows the name. If the street number was not available to the surveyor, the abbreviation "NA" has been used in historic districts.

Form and Style

The report identifies structures by form, style, or a combination of both. A building's form is usually based on folk or vernacular traditions, while its style derives from trends found in architect-designed buildings. In most cases, buildings combine vernacular forms with embellishments derived from architectural styles. For example, when a house is identified as "I-house/Greek Revival," the building's form (I-house) and its style (Greek Revival) are indicated. For sites with more than one structure (farm complexes, for example), both the house and prominent outbuildings are noted. A "1½" preceding the form means that the house is a one-and-one-half-story variant of a normally one- or two-story house type.

Date

An exact date appears when verifiable information exists. Most inventory entries, however, have an approximate date given with the "circa" (c.) notation.

Architect/Builder

The architect or builder, if known, follows the date.

Significance

The report attempts to indicate the category of significance for each entry (except in historic districts). See the section on "Criteria and Evaluation" (p. 7) for a discussion of the categories of significance. A notation indicates if an entry is listed in the National Register of Historic Places (NR), is designated a local landmark by the South Bend and St. Joseph County Preservation Commission (LL), or is recorded by the Historic American Buildings Survey (HABS) or the Historic American Engineering Record (HAER).

USGS Map Number

Except in historic districts, the code number of the USGS quadrangle map on which the entry is located has been noted in parentheses. Figure 3 (p. 10) shows the USGS quad map overlay for Blackford County.

Historic Districts

Historic district entries follow the format given above except for three differences. The report organizes each historic district by street, listing east-west streets first, one side at a time, starting with the northernmost streets in the district and moving south. North-south streets follow, beginning with the westernmost streets and moving east.

The report does not list categories of significance for each entry in a district since the accompanying narrative describes the significance of the district as a whole.

The third difference in historic district listings is that the USGS map number does not appear after each entry but instead is given at the beginning of the narrative description of the district.

Harris Township (00001-027)

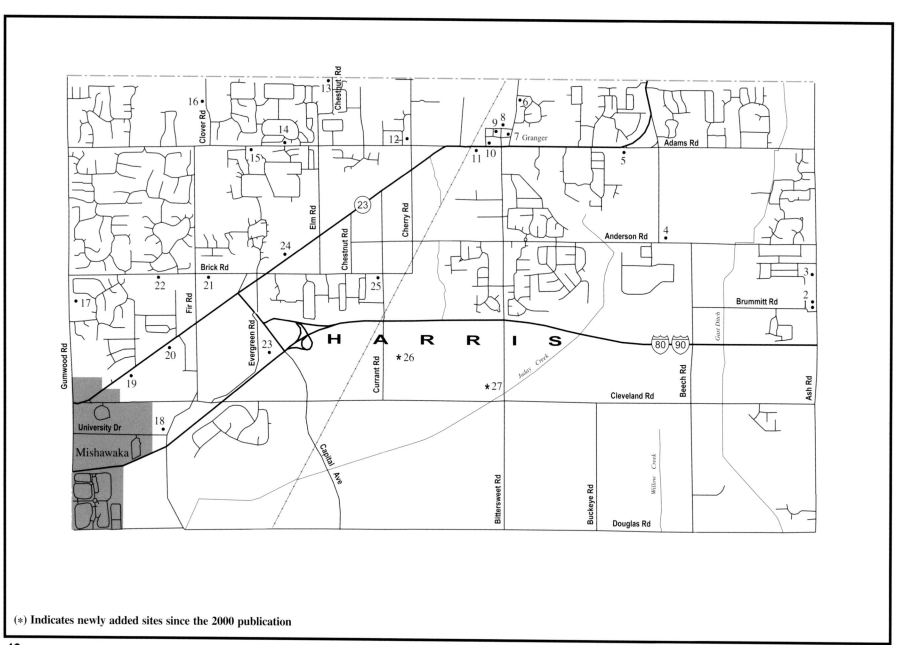

(∗) **Indicates newly added sites since the 2000 publication**

Harris Township was formed in 1836. The new township contained one of the county's finest upland prairies and a large quantity of lowland. Sheffield Creek once traversed the township on its way to the St. Joseph River, but it was converted to a ditch. The township is the second smallest in the county in terms of size, but is home to the small town of Granger.

Some have speculated that Granger's name comes from the Grange, a farmers' social and political organization and agricultural union. Thomas Foster platted Granger in 1883, gobbling up the town of Shaffer, platted a year earlier by Peter Shaffer. Situated along the Grand Trunk Railroad (formerly the Lake Huron & Chicago), Granger is the last Indiana stop before entering Michigan. The town served as a switching point for passengers, freight, and mail, and many rail employees settled there. Granger thrived until the 1930s when rail service ceased. Today it is known as a South Bend suburb, but several resources attest to its past, including a Greek Revival house that served as the meeting place of the first town board (00011).

The township was named in honor of Jacob Harris, an early settler who arrived to the area in 1830 with his son-in-law, Samuel Bell. A Baptist preacher named Adam Miller arrived the same year, as did Adam Ringle. Other early settlers included the Buell, Augustine, Meyer, Hartzell, Kennedy, Aehnle, Irvin, and Lowry families.

Education was important to the people of Harris township and Robert Kennedy served as the first schoolmaster. The earliest schoolhouses were constructed from logs, complete with large fireplaces to provide heat on cold winter days. Later schools were constructed from brick. Harris Township District No. 1 School stands as an example of the brick structures (00021).

Religious congregations, including Presbyterian, Evangelical, and Christian denominations were formed early in the township's history. The 1904 Salem Church stands a significant structure related to Harris Townshp's religious heritage (00002).

HARRIS TOWNSHIP SCATTERED SITES (00001-027)

No. Rtg. Description

001 C **Salem Church of the Evangelical Association Cemetery**; Ash Rd.; c.1850; *Exploration/Settlement, Landscape Architecture, Religion* (483)

002 O **Salem Church of the Evangelical Association**; 52173 Ash Rd.; Queen Anne; 1904; *Architecture, Religion* (483)

003 N **Catherine & John Smith House**; 51991 Ash Rd.; Lazy-T/Italianate; c.1870; *Architecture* (483) **LL**

004 C **Oak Grove School**; 11219 Anderson Rd.; Gabled-ell; 1898; *Architecture, Education* (483)

005 O **Michael Smith House**; 11518 Adams Rd.; Italianate; c.1870; *Architecture* (483) **LL**

00003 This lazy-T house dates to c.1870 and exhibits Italianate-style details.

006 O **William C. Kownover Farm**; 50106 Bittersweet Tr.; L-plan/Italianate; 1877; English barn, summer kitchen; *Agriculture, Architecture* (483) **LL**

007 N **Harris Township Consolidated School**; 12450 Beckley St.; Arts & Crafts; 1929 (Williard M. Elwood, Architect; Vincent Chiabal, Builder); *Architecture, Education* (483)

008 C **House**; 12495 St. Thomas St.; Minimal traditional; c.1935; *Architecture* (483)

009 C **House**; 50311 Alice St.; Queen Anne; c.1890; *Architecture* (483) DEMOLISHED

010 C **House**; 12613 SR 23; Hall-and-parlor; c.1859; *Architecture, Exploration/Settlement* (483)

011 O **John Follmer/Kownover/Milliken House**; 12594 SR 23; Central-passage/Greek Revival; c.1838; Smokehouse; *Architecture, Exploration/Settlement* (483) **LL**

012 O **Joseph & Julie Ann Snyder Farm**; 13271 Adams Rd.; Italianate; 1871 (Joseph Singer, Builder); English barn; *Agriculture, Architecture* (597) **LL**

013 N **John & Mary M. McMichael Farm**; 50017 Chestnut; Greek Revival; c.1833; Barn; *Agriculture, Architecture, Exploration/Settlement* (597)

014 O **Metzger House**; 14309 Adams Rd.; upright-and-wing Greek Revival; 1847; *Architecture, Exploration/Settlement* (597) **LL**

00002 The Salem Church of the Evangelical Association was built in 1904 and features round-arched windows with limestone sills and keystones and stained glass.

00011 The John Follmer/Kownover/Milliken House is an outstanding example of the Greek Revival style. The c.1838 house features clerestory windows and a main entry flanked by sidelights.

015 C Harris Prairie Cemetery; Adams Rd.; c.1840; *Exploration/Settlement, Landscape Architecture, Religion* (597)

016 C Farm; 50157 Clover Rd.; Greek Revival; c.1840; Smokehouse, barn; *Agriculture, Architecture, Exploration/Settlement* (597)

017 N Arbogast Zarhle Farm; 52228 Gumwood Rd.; Upright-and-wing/Federal; 1854; Smokehouse; *Agriculture, Architecture, Exploration/Settlement* (597)

018 O Chearhart House; 1450 University Drive Ct.; Cross-plan/Queen Anne; c.1870; *Architecture* (597)

019 C House; SR 23; Dutch Colonial Revival; c.1930; *Architecture* (597) DEMOLISHED

020 C House; 15258 SR 23; Colonial Revival; c.1930; Garage, privy, well house; *Architecture* (597)

021 O Harris Township District No. 1 School; 14912 Brick Rd.; T-plan/Italianate; 1892 (D. Werst & Sons, Builder); *Architecture, Education* (597) **LL**

022 C House; 15320 Brick Rd.; Greek Revival; c.1850/1875; *Architecture, Exploration/Settlement* (597)

023 C Farm; 52590 Evergreen Rd.; Italianate; c.1875/1915; Barn; *Agriculture, Architecture* (597)

024 O John B. & Henriette F. Metzger House; 14297 SR 23; Cross-plan/Eastlake; c.1880; *Architecture* (597) **LL**

025 O Amos Irwin Farm; 13546 Brick Rd.; Italianate Cube; 1875; Milk house, privy; *Architecture* (597) **LL**

026 N St. Joseph's Farm; 52682 Currant Rd.; Side-gabled; 1870; Apple storage building, bee house, boiler house, creamery, dairy barn, garage, octagonal barn, shed, slaughter house, smokehouse, south residence, stable, workshop; *Agriculture, Architecture, Education* (597)

027 C County Bridge No. S557; Bittersweet Rd. over Judy Creek; Concrete slab; 1953; *Engineering, Transportation* (483)

00021 The T-plan Harris Township District No. 1 School was built by D. Werst & Sons in 1892.

00024 The John B. & Henriette F. Metzger House is a local landmark dating to c.1880. The cross-plan house has Eastlake-style details, most notably, the porch shown here.

00012 The Joseph & Julie Ann Snyder House dates to c.1871 and is an excellent example of the Italianate style applied to a 3-bay I-house.

00014 The Metzger House dates to 1847 and is an outstanding example of the Greek Revival style. It is designated as a local landmark.

Clay Township (05001-056)

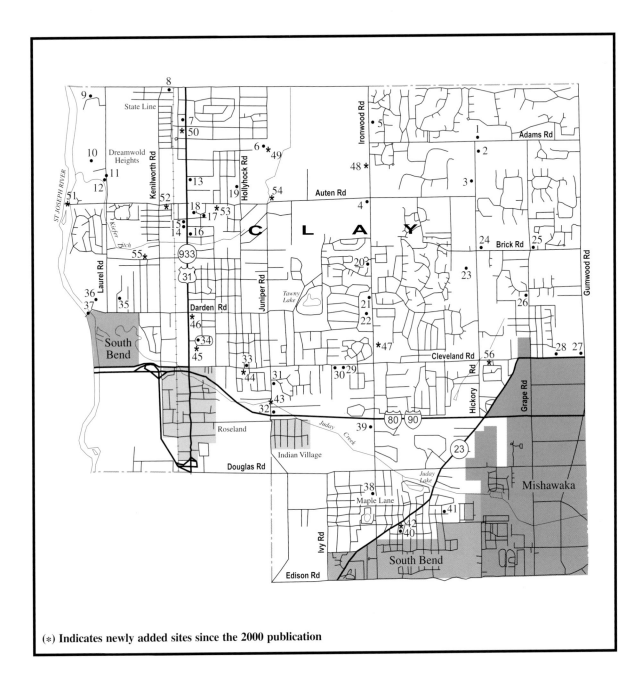

Clay Township was formed in 1840 and was named after the famous American statesman, Henry Clay. Its landscape includes the scenic St. Joseph River and deep blue lakes of Notre Dame. The township's first settlements near the river were among the earliest in the county. At that time, the settlements were located in Portage Township, which later became German Township and finally Clay Township.

Settlers, including Benjamin Potter, John Hague, and William McCombs, arrived to the area as early as 1829. John and Peter Cripe, Thomas Longley, and Peter and Jacob Eaton arrived during the following two years. Other early settlers included the Smith, Drapier, Eyler, McCombs, and Weaver families. Prominent residents included William Drapier, who later moved to Indianapolis and authored the Indiana legislative *Brevier Reports*, and members of the local Bulla family, who were uncompromising opponents of slavery.

Early roads were finely graveled and farms operated throughout the township. Crops did well in the sand and gravel soil, with fruit, corn, and other vegetables the most successfully cultivated. Sheffield Flour Mill stood for many years, generating water power from the steady current of Sheffield Creek. Development was advanced with the coming of the Michigan Central Railroad and the Southern Michigan Railway.

The township's first school was taught in a private home by Charles Murray. When the first schoolhouse was constructed, Daniel Veasey served as its teacher. The Walnut Grove/Eggleston School was originally located in Cass County, Michigan. The building was moved to its current site in 1990 to teach local children about history (05006).

The German Baptist congregation has had a church building in the west-central portion of the township since 1868. For many decades, it was the township's only church other than those found at Notre Dame and St. Mary's. Jacob Cripe, Christian Wenger, and John Wrightsman were among the church's pastors. Today, the Little Flower Catholic Church also serves area residents (05038).

The small communities of Indian Village and Roseland developed in Clay Township. Indian Village has the distinction of being St. Joseph County's youngest and smallest town. Roseland is also one of the county's smallest towns, covering an area of only 348.7 acres. Both of these towns retain structures significant to Clay Township's heritage.

CLAY TOWNSHIP SCATTERED SITES (05001-056)

No. Rtg. Description

001 O Grabowski Barn; 16977 Adams Rd.; Sweitzer barn; c.1880; *Agriculture, Architecture* (597) **LL**

002 C Stable; 51088 Hickory Rd.; c.1880; *Agriculture, Architecture* (597)

003 N Kramer Barn; 51375 Hickory Rd.; Sweitzer/bank barn; 1878; *Agriculture, Architecture* (597)

004 O Farm; 51533 Ironwood Rd.; Gabled-ell; c.1880/1900; Sweitzer barn; *Agriculture, Architecture* (597)

005 O Farm; 50878 Ironwood Rd.; Sweitzer barn; c.1850/1900; Chicken house, English barn, garage, pumphouse, smokehouse, windmill; *Agriculture, Architecture, Exploration/ Settlement* (597)

006 N Walnut Grove/Eggleston School; 19010 Adams Rd.; Gable-front; c.1890; Log house; *Architecture, Education* (597)

007 C House; 50783 SR 33; English cottage; c.1925; *Architecture* (703)

008 C Commercial Building; 19948 State Line Rd; Parapet-front; c.1925; *Architecture, Commerce* (703)

05010 **The Manion Log House is a recreational cabin and has a large, rustic stone fireplace.**

009 O St. Patrick's Farm; 50651 Laurel Rd.; Livestock barn; c.1925; Silos; *Agriculture, Architecture, Education, Landscape Architecture* (703)

010 O Manion Log House; 50651 Laurel Rd.; Rustic; c.1925/c.1947; *Architecture, Landscape Architecture* (703)

011 N County Bridge No. S589; Laurel Rd.; Concrete; c.1940; *Engineering, Transportation* (598)

012 N Barn; 50651 Laurel Rd.; Livestock barn; c.1925; *Agriculture, Architecture* (598)

013 O Charles Hunt House; 51256 SR 933; Gabled-ell/Greek Revival; 1860; Summer kitchen; *Architecture, Exploration/Settlement* (597)

014 C Farm; 51675 SR 933; Hall-and-parlor; c.1900; Transverse-frame barn; *Agriculture, Architecture* (598)

015 C House; 51743 SR 933; American foursquare; c.1915; Garage; *Architecture* (598)

016 N Frederick Cowles House; 19701 Cowles Ave.; T-plan; 1875; Garage; *Architecture* (597) **LL**

017 N House; 51618 E. Myrtle; English cottage; c.1940; Garage; *Architecture, Community Planning* (597)

018 N House; 51561 W. Myrtle; English cottage; c.1940; Garage; *Architecture, Community Planning* (597)

019 N House; 51327 Hollyhock Rd.; Upright-and-wing/Greek Revival; 1874; *Architecture* (597)

020 N Cloverleaf Farm; 52063 Ironwood Rd.; 1837; English/bank barn; *Agriculture, Architecture, Exploration/Settlement* (597) DEMOLISHED

021 N Farm; 52433 Ironwood Rd.; Bank barn; c.1920; Silo; *Agriculture, Architecture* (597) DEMOLISHED

022 N Farm; 52529 Ironwood Rd.; American foursquare; c.1915; Bank/basement barn; *Agriculture, Architecture* (597)

023 N Fickensher Farm; 52163 Hickory Rd.; Italianate; 1878; Bank/basement barn; *Agriculture, Architecture* (597)

024 C Barn; 51986 Hickory Rd.; English barn; c.1930; *Agriculture, Architecture* (597)

025 O Samuel H. & Elizabeth Zaehnle House; 16479 Brick Rd.; Italiante; 1883; *Architecture* (597) **LL**

026 O James and Mary Ann Harris Farm; 52407 Grape Rd.; Upright-and-wing/Greek Revival; 1843; Livestock barn; *Agriculture, Architecture, Ethnic Heritage, Exploration/ Settlement* (597) **LL**

027 O Daniel Ward House; 16021 Cleveland Rd.; Italianate Cube; 1865; *Architecture* (597) **LL, SR**

05025 **The Samuel Zaehnle House is an outstanding example of the Italianate style. Built in 1883, the house features segmental-arched openings and a front porch with decorative square posts and a dentilated frieze.**

028 O **Robert Savidge House**; 16327 Cleveland Rd.; Italianate; 1868; *Architecture* (597) **LL**

029 C **Tutt/Stuckey Cemetery**; 18300 Cleveland Rd.; c.1850; *Exploration/Settlement, Landscape Architecture, Religion* (597) **LL**

030 C **Farm**; 18384 Cleveland Rd.; English cottage; c.1925; Chicken house; *Agriculture, Architecture* (597)

031 O **Alfred Talley House**; 53190 Juniper Rd.; Italianate Cube; 1856; *Architecture, Exploration/Settlement* (597) **LL**

032 C **House**; 53444 Juniper Rd.; Gabled-ell; c.1915; Garage; *Architecture* (597)

033 C **House**; 19237 Cleveland Rd.; Free Classic; c.1900; *Architecture* (597)

034 C **House**; 19657 N. Paxson Dr.; Mission Revival; 1935; *Architecture* (597)

035 N **Ike Lupa House**; 52380 Harvest St.; Art Moderne; 1949-1951 (Lupa Brothers, Builder); *Architecture* (598)

036 O **St. Joseph County Tuberculosis Sanitorium**; 20531 Darden Rd.; Colonial Revival; c.1920/1947 (Schmidt, Garden & Erikson, Architects; Gust. K. Newberg Const. Co., Builder); County Dept. of Corrections, Laurel House; *Architecture, Health/Medicine, Landscape Architecture* (598)

05026 The 1843 James Harris House is an early example of the Greek Revival style. The upright-and-wing plan has a rubble stone foundation, brick walls, and deeply recessed windows.

05028 The Robert Savidge House dates to 1872 and is an outstanding example of the Italianate style. The brick house has a rubble stone foundation, front verandah with turned posts, scrollwork brackets, and a decorated lintel, and arched window openings.

037 O **Darden Road Bridge/St. Joseph County Bridge No. 5**; 21000 Darden Rd.; Pratt through truss; 1885/1906; *Engineering, Transportation* (598) **NR, LL**

038 O **Little Flower Catholic Church**; 45191 Ironwood Rd.; Contemporary; 1957; *Architecture, Religion* (597)

039 O **James Stuckey House**; 53597 Ironwood Rd.; Federal; 1840; *Architecture, Exploration/Settlement* (597) **LL**

040 C **House**; 54560 Northern Ave.; California bungalow/Craftsman; c.1920; Garage; *Architecture* (597)

041 N **Robert Kollar House**; 54382 32nd St.; Minimal ranch/Modern; 1952-53 (Robert Kollar, Architect and Builder); Garage; *Architecture* (597)

042 C **Henry F. Smith House**; 54540 Northern Ave.; English cottage; 1928; Sears, Roebuck & Co. catalog house; *Architecture* (597)

043 C **St. Joseph County Bridge No. S564**; Juniper Rd. over Judy Creek; Concrete slab; 1925; *Engineering, Transportation* (597)

044 C **House**; 19252 Cleveland Rd.; Dormer-front bungalow/Craftsman; c.1920; Garage; *Architecture* (597)

045 C **House**; 19640 S Paxon Dr.; Spanish Colonial Revival; c.1935; *Architecture* (597)

046 C **La Salle's Camp Historical Marker**; SR 933; *Exploration/Settlement* (598)

05036 The St. Joseph County Tuberculosis Sanitorium encompasses three buildings on the campus. The main building, pictured here, was designed in 1947 by architects Schmidt, Garden & Erikson.

047 C **Farm**; 52866 Ironwood Rd.; T-plan; c.1880; Chicken house; *Agriculture, Architecture* (597) DEMOLISHED 2006

048 C **Farm**; 51185 Ironwood Rd.; L-plan; c.1900; Garage, machine shed, pumphouse; *Agriculture, Architecture* (597)

049 C **Log House**; 19010 Adams Rd.; Single-pen; c.1850; *Architecture, Exploration/Settlement* (597)

050 C **House**; 50817 SR 933; English cottage; c.1930; Garage; *Architecture* (703)

051 C **County Bridge No. 214**; Auten Rd. over St. Joseph River; Steel plate girder; 1953; *Engineering, Transportation* (598)

052 C **House**; 19956 Auten Rd.; California bungalow; c.1930; Garage; *Architecture* (598)

053 C **House**; 19464 Auten Rd.; Upright-and-wing; c.1870; *Architecture* (597)

054 C **Vandel Horvath Farm**; 18939 Auten Rd.; Western bungalow; 1927; Brooder house, garage, workshop; *Agriculture, Architecture* (597)

055 C **Farm**; 20159 Brick Rd.; Side-gabled/Craftsman; c.1920; Chicken house, garage; *Agriculture, Architecture* (598)

056 C **House**; 17510 Cleveland Rd.; Italianate; 1876; *Architecture* (597)

Indian Village Scattered Sites (06001-003)

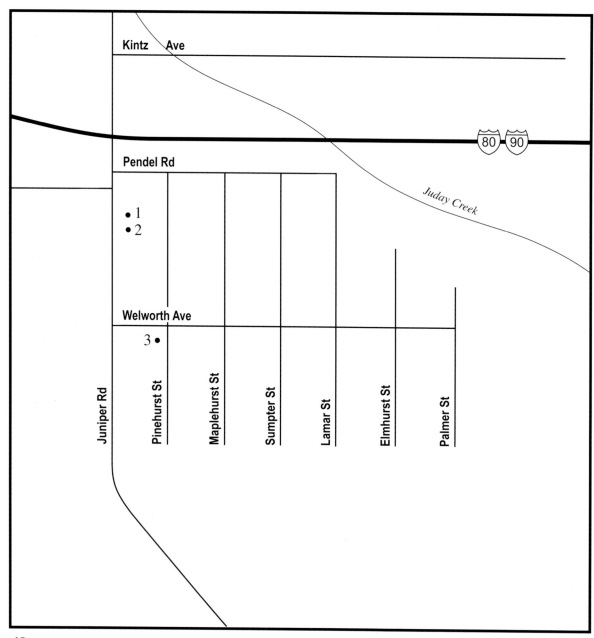

Indian Village consists of twelve city blocks southeast of Juniper Road and the toll road. It is entirely residential and is St. Joseph County's youngest and smallest town.

James Stuckey was the first settler in the area during the 1830s, followed by Jacob Chearhart in 1845. In 1925, the Reliance Development Company platted the area; engineer Charles Cole divided the plat into 300 lots and named it Indian Village. The town of thirty-two was finally incorporated in 1940 and the newly elected officials set about establishing building codes. Extant historic resources all date to the period before Indian Village was incorporated.

INDIAN VILLAGE SCATTERED SITES (06001-003)

No.	Rtg.	Description
001	C	**House**; 53530 Juniper Rd.; Central-passage; c.1889/1925; Garage; *Architecture* (597)
002	C	**House**; 53548 Juniper Rd.; Greek Revival; 1889; Garage; *Architecture* (597)
003	C	**Joseph Blanh House**; 18964 Welworth Ave.; California bungalow; 1923; *Architecture* (597)

Roseland Scattered Sites (07001-008)

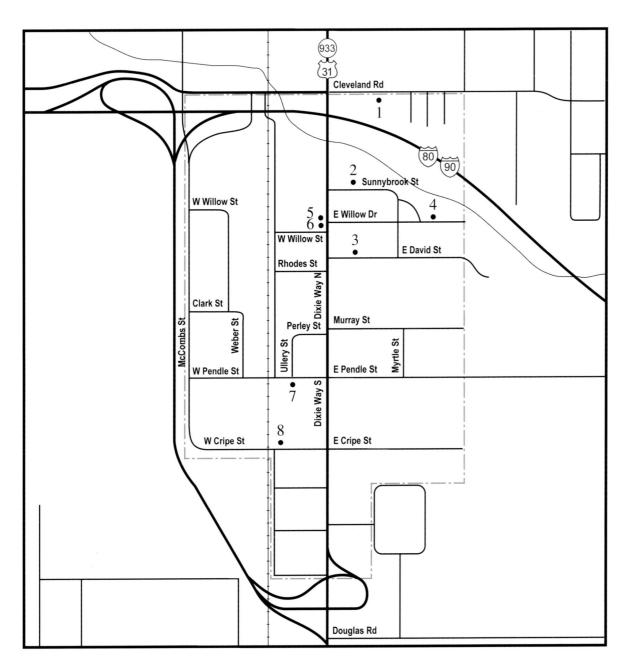

Roseland was first located in German Township until Clay was formed from it in 1840. Roseland is one of St. Joseph County's smallest towns, covering only 348.7 acres. Joseph and Stephen Ullery were the earliest settlers to the area. Stephen operated a carding mill near the creek and south of Cleveland Road. The Ullery Cemetery is significant for its association with the early settlement of the county (07001), having stones dating to the 1850s.

During the second half of the nineteenth century, the Michigan Central Railroad passed through Roseland connecting South Bend with Niles, Michigan. The stretch of rail was very profitable and added to Roseland's development. Much of the area was platted as the turn of the century, after the interurban railway arrived. The South Michigan Interurban ran north and south, parallel to the Michigan Central, and connected South Bend with St. Mary's College, Bertrand, Niles, Berrien Springs, and St. Joseph, Michigan. Roseland was first called Rose Lawn and in 1915, some residents feared that it would be annexed to South Bend. Consequently, the town incorporated in 1916 and changed its name to Roseland. It experienced rapid growth until 1929.

Roseland's earliest structures were situated along Niles Road (US 33) and have been lost to developmental pressures. However, a handful of historic structures remain, including the Alden Hack House (07008), which is a nice example of the Free Classic style. David Guilfoyle platted the Roseland Woods Addition in 1927 and his home is an example of a California bungalow having Craftsman-style details (07003).

Industry in Roseland was limited due to its small acreage. Nineteenth-century residents were predominantly farmers and since the early 1900s, most residents found employment in South Bend. However, during the 1930s and 40s several businesses existed along the Dixie Highway, including a lumber company, grocery store, dry cleaner, and gas station. Today, the area along US 33 is home to commercial business strips and much automobile traffic. Due to its small boundaries, Roseland faces many developmental pressures that often result in the destruction of historic structures (07002).

07002 The Noel Ducomb House was a notable example of an American foursquare with Prairie-style influences. Unfortunately, the house has been demolished since it was originally surveyed in 1999.

07008 The Aiden Hack House dates to 1909 and is an example of the Free Classic style, a transitional style from the Queen Anne at the turn of the 20th century.

ROSELAND SCATTERED SITES (07001-008)

001   C   **Ullery Cemetery**; 19671 Cleveland Rd.; 1868; *Exploration/Settlement, Landscape Architecture, Religion* (597)

002   N   **Noel Ducomb House**; 135 Sunnybrook Ct.; American foursquare/Prairie; c.1915; *Architecture* (597) DEMOLISHED

003   C   **David Guilfoyle House**; 125 E David St.; California bungalow/Craftsman; 1927; Garage; *Architecture* (597)

004   N   **Stevens House**; 231 E Willow St.; Minimal traditional; c.1952; Garage; *Architecture* (597)

005   C   **Garland Building**; 409-417 Dixie Way North/SR 933; Two-part commercial block; c.1950; *Architecture, Commerce* (598)

006   C   **Stevens Building**; 401-407 Dixie Way North; Two-part commercial block; c.1950; *Architecture, Commerce* (598)

007   C   **House**; 128 W Pendel St.; Dormer-front bungalow/Craftsman; c.1925; *Architecture* (598)

008   N   **Alden Hack House**; 137 W Cripe St.; Free Classic; 1909; *Architecture* (598)

07003 The 1927 David Guilfoyle House is a good example of a California bungalow with Craftsman style details. The house retains original, narrow clapboard siding, an integral porch with battered piers, and original double-hung windows.

Blake Gardens in Roseland. *Courtesy of Historic Preservation Commission of South Bend and St. Joseph County.*

German Township (10001-020)

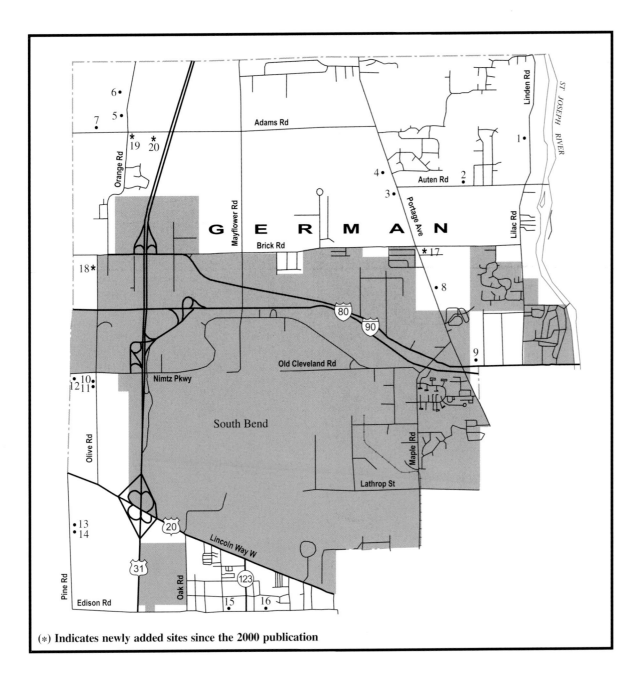

(∗) **Indicates newly added sites since the 2000 publication**

German Township was formed in 1884, the first township to be carved from the original three townships in St. Joseph County. Portage Prairie covers the greater part of the township, constituting one of the finest farming districts in the world. Because of this, the township was favored and said to be the wealthiest per capita in Indiana. The famous portage between the St. Joseph and Kankakee Rivers crosses German and Portage Townships. The portage was used to transport traders and merchants between the Great Lakes and the Mississippi River for centuries, including Marquette, La Salle, and Charlevoix.

Near the area known as Mount Pleasant, a great Miami village once thrived. It was there in 1681 that La Salle made his celebrated treaty with the Miamis. The county's original seat, also called St. Joseph, was located at the junction of the portage with the St. Joseph River. Further upriver was the small and important town of Portage, where a ferry crossed the river. Today there are no structures associated with the towns of Mount Pleasant, St. Joseph, and Portage that speak of their urban pasts.

Due to its advantageous location, settlers were attracted to German Township early. William Brokfield arrived in 1827 and became its first surveyor, laying out the first and second county seats. Church congregations formed as early as 1831 when the township's first pastor, Elder David Miller, organized one. However, it wasn't until 1851 that the first church building was constructed (10019). It was followed by a Methodist Church in 1854, which later became a Baptist church. A Universalist church organized in 1858. The township's first schoolhouse was built at Mount Pleasant; from the simple log structures of early settlers to the comfortable edifices of modern schools, education had remained an important aspect of the township's heritage (10003, 10011).

51

GERMAN TOWNSHIP SCATTERED SITES (10001-020)

No.	Rtg.	Description

001 O **George V. Fisher House**; 51177 Lilac; Gabled-ell/Greek Revival; c.1875; Garage, shed; *Architecture* (703); LL

002 C **Farm**; 21563 Auten Rd.; American foursquae; c.1910; Barn; *Agriculature, Architecture* (598) DEMOLISHED

003 N **Wagner/German Township District No. 1 School**; 51755 Portage Ave.; Craftsman; c.1920; *Architecture, Education* (598)

004 O **Wetz/Bestle Farm**; 51387 Portage Ave.; T-plan/Italianate; 1883; Bank/basement barn; *Agriculture, Architecture, Landscape Architecture* (598) **LL, NR**

005 N **Farm**; 50929 Orange Rd.; T-plan/Italianate; c.1880; Dairy barns, garage, milk house, silos, spring house; *Agriculture, Architecture* (703)

006 O **Jacob Whitmer/Miller Farm**; 50759 Orange Rd.; Italianate; c.1872; Silos, transverse-frame barn; *Agriculture, Architecture* (703) **LL**

007 C **Portage Prairie Cemetery**; 25201 Adams Rd.; c.1830; *Exploration/Settlement, Landscape Architecture, Religion* (703)

10004 The Italianate Wetz/Bestle House dates to 1883. It has segmental-arched window openings and a porch with scrolled brackets.

008 N **Molnar House**; 52400 Portage Ave.; Free Classic; 1910; *Architecture* (598)

009 C **Cripe-Witter Cemetery**; 20501 Cleveland Rd.; c.1850; *Exploration/Settlement, Religion* (598) **LL**

010 C **House**; 53081 Olive Rd.; Hall-and-parlor; c.1890; Garage; *Architecture* (598)

011 C **German Township School**; 53117 Olive Rd.; c.1890; *Education* (598); LL

012 O **Aaron N. Miller Farm**; 24888 Cleveland Rd.; Upright-and-wing/Greek Revival; c.1855; Barn, corn crib, sheds, Sweitzer barn; *Agriculture, Architecture, Exploration/Settlement* (598) **LL**

013 N **House**; 54166 Pine Rd.; Colonial Revival; 1912; *Architecture* (598)

014 N **Barn**; 54270 Pine Rd.; English barn; c.1880; Silos; *Agriculture, Architecture* (598)

015 C **House**; 23691 Edison Rd.; California bungalow/Craftsman; c.1925; Garage; *Architecture* (598) DEMOLISHED

016 C **Mount Pleasant Cemetery**; Edison Rd.; c.1880; *Education, Exploration/Settlement, Landscape Architecture, Religion* (598)

017 C **House**; 52086 Portage Ave.; Gable-front/Greek Revival; c.1870; Garage, privy; *Architecture* (598)

018 C **Farm**; 52097 Olive Rd.; L-plan; c.1880; Garage, grain bin, livestock barn, summer kitchen; *Agriculture, Architecture* (598)

019 C **Brethren Church**; 24460 Adams Rd.; Gable-front; 1851; *Architecture, Exploration/Settlement, Religion* (703)

020 N **Farm**; 24222 Adams Rd.; American foursquare/Free Classic; 1913; Drive-thru corncrib, grain bin, pumphouse, shed, silo; *Agriculture, Architecture* (703)

10012 The Miller House is an outstanding early example of the Greek Revival style. It exhibits a heavy cornice with returns and a full-width dentilated front porch.

10001 This gabled-ell house dates to c.1875 and boasts a wide cornice and carved window surrounds.

10006 The Italianate Jacob Witmer/Miller House retains original clapboard siding, windows with carved surrounds, and an elaborate porch with double fluted square posts and decorative brakets.

Portage Township (11001-032)

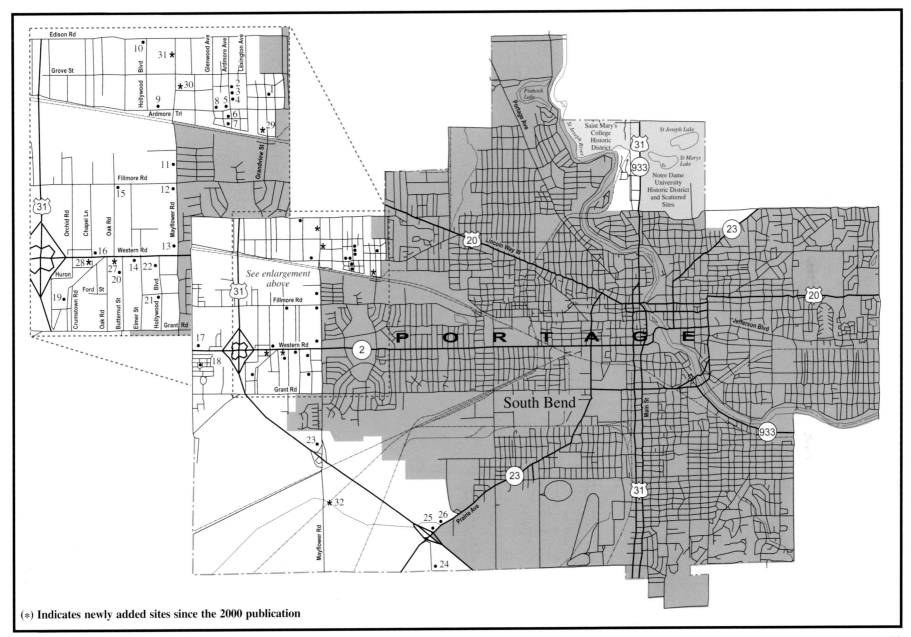

(∗) **Indicates newly added sites since the 2000 publication**

Portage Township was formed in 1882, encompassing an area of high and slightly rolling lands. The St. Joseph River traverses Portage Township and the city of South Bend developed, as its name suggests, at a bend in the river where it turns north. The famous portage between the St. Joseph and Kankakee Rivers crosses Portage and German Townships. The portage was used to transport traders and merchants between the Great Lakes and the Mississippi River for centuries, including Marquette, La Salle, and Charlevoix.

Much of the township's history centers on the development of South Bend, St. Joseph County's largest city. The first permanent settler to the area was Pierre Navarre, an agent of the American Fur Company, who arrived in 1820. He was followed by Alexis Coquillard, appointed by the same company, in 1823. Coquillard is generally considered to be the founder of South Bend. Colonel Lanthrop M. Taylor joined Navarre and Coquillard in 1827 and served as Southold's first postmaster. Residents of South Bend are familiar with these names, as many places in the city were named after these men. Settlement increased after 1830 when the government lands recently acquired from the Potawatomi were placed on the open market. Taylor and Coquillard purchased land in 1831 and subdivided it as the town of South Bend, changing its name from Southold. In 1865, South Bend was incorporated as a city.

In 1828, the Indiana General Assembly passed an act to survey and mark a road from Lake Michigan to Indianapolis. The Michigan Road made the frontier lands of Portage Township more readily accessible. South Bend's Michigan Street and Lincolnway West mark the course of Michigan Road through the city. Most early settlers were involved in agricultural pursuits, as the light, sandy soil of the St. Joseph valley was well suited to farming. Wheat, oats, and corn were among the crops produced.

The township's first churches and schools were located in what is today the city of South Bend. The First Methodist Church opened its doors on North Main Street in 1835, followed by an 1836 Presbyterian Church at the corner of Water and Lafayette Streets. By 1879, South Bend was home to Baptist, Episcopal, Lutheran, Evangelical, Adventist, Roman Catholic, Brethren, and Jewish places of worship. In 1842, Father Edward Sorin founded the University of Notre Dame, an institution that made South Bend internationally known. Its sister institution, St. Mary's College, was established in 1855 by Mother Mary Angela. Quality education was an important goal of St. Joseph County residents as early as the 1830s and 40s when district schoolhouses were constructed.

William McCartney erected the township's first flour mill along McCartney's Creek in 1831, followed by the first tannery. By the 1850s, the harnessing of water power from the river, first used to power grist and saw mills, spurred manufacturing. Makers of farm implements and wagons became South Bend's first successful industrialists. The Studebaker Brothers Manufacturing Company eventually grew to be the world's largest manufacturer of wagons. In the twentieth century, the Studebaker Corporation produced automobiles, dominating South Bend's industrial economy through the 1950s. South Bend's second-largest employer, Oliver Chilled Plow Works, also capitalized on agricultural needs, perfecting an efficient plow. Other industries made use of the locally plentiful timber. Companies included the South Bend Furniture Manufacturing Company, the paper mill Beach and Keedy, and the flour and feed mill Knoblock, Ginz and Company.

In 1851, the Michigan Southern and Northern Indiana Railway reached South Bend and later became the Lakeshore and Michigan Southern. The Michigan Central arrived at South Bend by 1870. The city continued to grow with a large quantity of homes and commercial building being constructed until the onset of the Great Depression. After World War II, a small housing boom occurred throughout the city, but it was short-lived. During the 1950s and 60s many industries moved or closed down and much of the city's historic resources were lost to demolition or neglect.

While it is impossible to separate the histories of Portage Township and South Bend, the city of South Bend has its own survey of historical resources, *The City of South Bend Summary Report*. Therefore the following documented sites are located outside the city boundaries.

PORTAGE TOWNSHIP SCATTERED SITES (11001-032)

No.	Rtg.	Description
001	C	**House**; 22835 Hartzer Rd.; Gable-front; 1927; *Architecture* (598)
002	N	**House**; 55348 Moss Rd.; American four-square; c.1920; Garage; *Architecture* (598)
003	N	**House**; 55372 Moss Rd.; Castellated; c.1925; Garage; *Architecture* (598)
004	C	**House**; 55400 Moss Rd.; Western bunga-low/Craftsman; c.1925; Garage; *Architecture* (598)
005	N	**Ardmore School**; 23181 Ardmore Tr.; Classical Revival; 1914; *Architecture, Education* (598)
006	C	**House**; 55555 Moss Rd.; American four-square; c.1920; Garage; *Architecture* (598)
007	C	**House**; 55589 Moss Rd.; California bunga-low/Craftsman; c.1925; Garage; *Architecture* (598)
008	C	**House**; 23265 Ardmore Tr.; Colonial Revival; c.1940; *Architecture* (598)

11003 This house is an unusual castellated residence with a crenellated parapet.

11005 Ardmore School boasts two projecting octagonal bays that have segmental-arched openings.

009 N **House**; 23651 Ardmore Tr.; American foursquare; c.1925; *Architecture* (598)

010 N **House**; 23712 Edison Rd.; English cottage; c.1927 ("The Barrington" catalog house); *Architecture* (598)

011 C **House**; Mayflower Rd.; Gable-front/Italianate; *Architecture* (598)

012 C **House**; 56021 Mayflower Rd.; California bungalow/Craftsman; c.1925; *Architecture* (598)

013 O **Holy Family School**; 56407 Mayflower Rd.; Modern; 1953; *Architecture, Education* (598)

014 O **House**; 23784 Western Ave./SR 2; Italianate; 1872; *Architecture* (598)

015 C **House**; 23990 Fillmore Rd.; California bungalow/Craftsman; c.1925; *Architecture* (598)

11006 This American foursquare retains original clapboard siding, five-over-one double-hung windows, and a full-width front porch with large, square posts.

016 C **Commercial Building**; 24133 Western Ave./SR 2; 20th century functional; c.1930; *Architecture, Commerce, Transportation* (598)

017 C **Sacred Heart Cemetery**; Western Ave./SR 2 & Pine St.; c.1900; Chapel, shed, statue; *Art, Architecture, Ethnic Heritage, Landscape Architecture, Religion* (598)

018 N **St. Joseph's Cemetery**; Pine St. & Western Ave./SR 2; c.1905; Chapel, memorial marker, statues; *Art, Architecture, Ethnic heritage, Landscape Architecture, Religion* (598)

019 N **House**; 56927 Crumstown Rd.; Gable-front; c.1860; *Architecture, Exploration/Settlement* (598)

020 N **House**; 56589 Butternut Rd.; English cottage; c.1925; *Architecture* (598)

11013 Holy Family School is an outstanding example of a modern building, having this impressive entryway that recalls some elements of the Art Deco style.

11014 This 1872 house is an outstanding example of the Italianate style. It features a low, hipped roof, segmental-arched window openings, and an open porch with decorated capitals and a dentilated lintel.

021 N **House**; 56771 Hollywood Blvd.; Tudor Revival; c.1925; *Architecture* (598)

022 C **House**; 56547 Hollywood Blvd.; Western bungalow/Craftsman; c.1920; *Architecture* (598)

023 N **George & Anna Dodd House**; 57537 Mayflower Rd.; Colonial Revival; 1936; *Architecture* (598)

024 N **House**; 58920 Magnolia Rd.; Gable-front; c.1870; Garage, shed; *Architecture, Exploration/Settlement* (598)

025 C **House**; 22195 Prairie Ave./SR 23; American foursquare; c.1910; Garage; *Architecture* (598)

026 N **Dr. Petrosi Farm**; 22027 Prairie Ave./SR 23; Chateauesque; c.1880/c.1940; *Agriculture, Architecture* (598)

027 C **Commercial Building**; 23946 SR 2; Parapet-front; 1943; *Architecture, Commerce* (598)

028 C **Monson Chapel Methodist Episcopal Church**; 24172 SR 2; Gothic Revival; 1885; *Architecture, Religion* (598)

029 C **Chicago, South Shore & South Bend Railroad Grandview Substation**; 55674 Grandview Ave.; Neoclassical; c.1925 (Northern Indiana Public Service Company, Builder); *Architecture, Transportation* (598)

11018 The huge St. Joseph's Cemetery includes this monument to the men of Polish descent who fought in World War I, and a limestone chapel.

030 N **House**; 55362 Mayflower Rd.; American foursquare; c.1920; Garage; *Architecture* (598)

031 C **Mainer House**; 55167 Mayflower Rd.; English cottage; c.1928 ("The Dover" Sears, Roebuck & Co. catalog house); *Architecture* (598)

032 C **Indiana, Illinois and Iowa Railroad Bridge**; Concrete slab; c.1900; *Engineering, Transportation* (598)

11029 The Northern Indiana Public Service Company built the c.1925 Chicago, South Shore & South Bend Railroad Grandview Substation in the Neoclassical style. It is one of two in the county that provide electricity to the Railroad, which is considered the last interurban in the country.

11023 The George & Anna Dodd House is a notable example of the Colonial Revival style. It exhibits a symmetrical plan, a side porch with classical columns, and an entry with a fan and side lights.

St. Mary's College Historic District (141-598-12001-050)

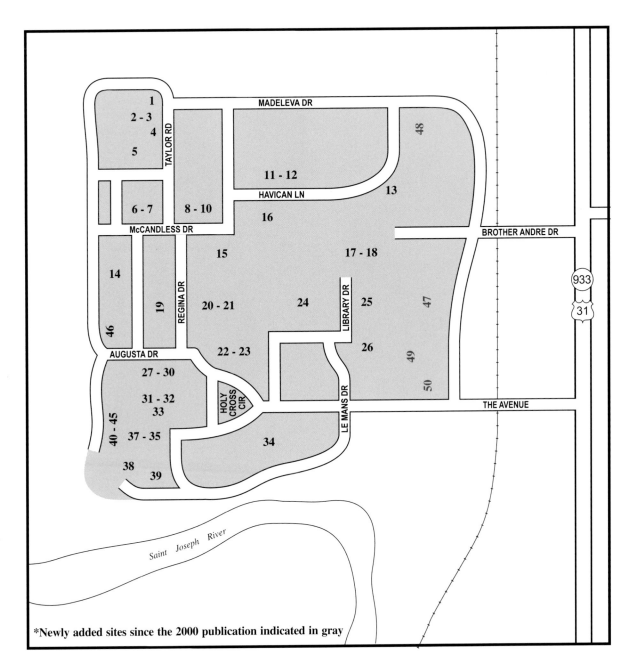

*Newly added sites since the 2000 publication indicated in gray

The St. Mary's College Historic District encompasses the campus of St. Mary's College, whose history began in 1844 by the Sisters of the Holy Cross. The Sisters, a religious order started in Le Mans, France, initially chose Bertrand, Michigan, as the site of their school. The Sister's School as it was originally known educated and cared for orphaned, deaf, and lower class children. By 1854 Bertrand had not developed into a thriving metropolis and Father Edwin Sorin, founder of Notre Dame University, purchased the school for $300 and moved it to its present location just north of South Bend. Father Sorin and Sister Mary Angela dedicated the new school and convent called, in tribute to the Blessed Mother, St. Mary's of the Immaculate Conception in 1855. Sister Mary Angela, regarded as the founder of St. Mary's College, was the first of three dynamic sisters who led the college for more than a century.

The State of Indiana empowered St. Mary's at its founding to grant degrees and it became one of the earliest Catholic women's colleges in the country. In 1860 St. Mary's awarded its first graduation medals to six women. The niece of Sister Mary Angela earned the first degree in 1898.

Bertrand Hall (12035) built in 1861 housed the entire school. Father Sorin and William Thomas of Chicago designed the building in the Classical Revival style. Constructed of yellow "Notre Dame" brick, Bertrand Hall was funded by monies the Sisters made from caring for wounded Civil War soldiers. The oldest building on campus, the Chapel of Loretto dates to 1856 (12040). Sister Mary Angela's brother, Father Neal Gillespie, C.S.C., brought its plans from Rome. The Chapel, only thirty-one feet by thirteen feet, was moved in 1886 to make room for the main church.

The 1956 Church of our Lady of Loretto (12038) is the second church located at that site. The new church, designed by Paul Jacques Grillow with

South Bend architect Otto Seeler, was built on the first church's foundation and contains windows and statues from the older building.

In 1889 the Administration Building or Tower Building was constructed and provided office space, a convent, and a noviate (12029). Between 1892-93 the Novitiate was constructed to house the novices and postulants who had been staying in the Administration Builiding. After being opened to students, it was renamed Augusta Hall in honor of Mother Mary Augusta, the first Superior General Mother (12029).

The Students' Infirmary was completed in 1901 and served as an administration building and residence hall for the sisters, known as Immaculata Hall. Architects Egan and Prindeville designed a new all-purpose facility named Collegiate Hall in 1903. It housed the entire student body and contained a library, dining hall, bookstore, post office, classrooms, guest rooms, health center, and chapel. It was later known as the Freshman Hall for College Students and Holy Cross Hall (12032).

The college focused on more than just constructing buildings at the turn of the twentieth century; between 1897 and 1911, the entrance gate and wall, Lake Marian and its island (12026), and St. Michaels' Shrine (12030) were built, along with a horse barn, numerous sheds, and chicken and orchard houses. Those agricultural structures were lost to a 1934 fire and replaced by a steel and concrete barn. In 1918, the Sisters of the Holy Cross gifted the Sacred Heart Shrine to Mother Perpetua, the Superior General.

During the 1910s a great deal of construction tool place under Mother Mary Pauline's administration. Rosary Hall was constructed in 1911 as a residence hall and kitchen for the sisters (12028). In 1914, St. Joseph's (12043), St. John's (12044), and St. Michael's (12045) Halls were built, providing quarters for the Brothers of the Holy Cross and other men working on campus. Loretto Convent was built that same year (12041).

Le Mans Hall began in 1925, adopted from the thesis of Maurice Carroll, a fifth-year Notre Dame

architecture student. Initially called New College, the building housed the upper classes and provided classroom and office space for the administration (12024).

During the distinguished tenure of Sister Mary Magdaleva, South Bend architects Austin and Shambleau designed Reidinger Alumnae House. A home economics lab, students lived there managing its operation on a supervised budget (12021). Three years later, the Alumnae Centennial Library completion marked the centennial of the founding of the Sisters of the Holy Cross (12025).

In the 1950s and 60s the Campus School (12013), Science Hall (12018), and Moreau Hall and O'Laughlin Auditorium (12023) were constructed. Buildings under forty years old include the 1977 Angela Athletic Facitly (12012), the 1982 Cushwa-Leighton Library (12017), and the recent Noble Family Dining Hall and Student Center (12015). These more recent buildings will gain historical significance in the coming years.

ST. MARY'S COLLEGE HISTORIC DISTRICT (141-598-12001-050)

No.	Rtg.	Add.	Description
001	NC	NA	**Maintenance Building**; Pole barn; 1960
002	C	NA	**Maintenance Shed**; Quonset hut; c.1950
003	C	NA	**Maintenance Shed**; Quonset hut; c.1950
004	C	NA	**Outbuildings**; 20th century functional; c.1934; Barns, silos
005	NC	NA	**Central Utilities Plant**; 20th century functional; c.1970
006	C	NA	**St. Bridget's Convent**; Massed ranch; c.1950
007	NC	NA	**Andre House**; Massed ranch; c.1970
008	C	NA	**Bethany House**; Western bungalow; c.1920

12014 **The Our Lady of Peace Cemetery has been used by the Sister's of the Holy Cross as a final resting place for its members for over 150 years.**

009	C	NA	**House of Shalem**; Western bungalow; c.1925
010	NC	NA	**Facilities Building**; Parapet-front; c.1965
011	NC	NA	**Tennis Courts**; c.1980
012	NC	NA	**Angela Athletic Facility**; 20th century functional; 1977 (C.F. Murphy and Associates, John Helmet, James Goettsch, Architects; Hickey Construction Company, Builder)
013	N	NA	**Havican Hall/Campus School**; International; 1950
014	N	NA	**Our Lady of Peace Cemetery**; 1868
015	NC	NA	**Noble Family Dining Hall & Student Center**; Neo-Gothic; 2002/ 2005
016	C	NA	**McCandless Hall**; International; 1963
017	NC	NA	**Cushwa-Leighton Library**; Neo-eclectic; 1982 (Evans Woollen, Architect)
018	C	NA	**Science Hall**; Late-Gothic Revival; 1955

12024 The outstanding-rated New College/Le Mans Building built in 1925 in the Collegiate Gothic style features a center tower with arched entryway.

019	C	NA	**Regina Hall**; Modern; 1963
020	O	NA	**Sacred Heart Shrine**; Late-Gothic Revival; 1918
021	N	NA	**Riedinger Alumnae/Adaline Crowley Residence House**; Tudor Revival; 1939 (N. Roy Shambleau, Architect)
022	C	NA	**Security Building**; Craftsman; 1903
023	C	NA	**Moreau Center for the Performing Arts**; Modern; 1964
024	O	NA	**New College/Le Mans Hall**; Collegiate Gothic; 1925 (Maurice Carroll, Architect; H.G. Christman Company, Builder)
025	N	NA	**Alumnae Centennial Library/ Haggar Student Center**; Colonial Revival; 1942 (Jens Frederick Larson, Architect; Thomas L. Hickey, Builder)
026	C	NA	**Lake Marian & Bridge**; 1907
027	NC	NA	**Lillie O'Grady Center**; Modern; c.1970
028	N	NA	**Rosary Hall**; Colonial Revival; 1911 (Brothers of the Holy Cross, Architects and Builders)
029	O	NA	**Novitiate/Augusta Hall**; Classical Revival; 1893 (Brothers of the Holy Cross, Architects and Builders)
030	C	NA	**St. Michael's Shrine**; 1906
031	O	NA	**Administration/Tower Building**; Classical Revival; 1888 (Brothers of the Holy Cross, Architects and Builders)
032	O	NA	**Collegiate/Holy Cross Hall**; Second Empire; 1903 (Eganard Prindeville, Architect)
033	N	NA	**Lourdes Hall**; Second Empire; 1872 (Brothers of the Holy Cross, Architects and Builders)
034	C	NA	**Clubhouse**; Craftsman; 1922 DEMOLISHED
035	N	NA	**Old Academy/Bertrand Hall**; Classical Revival; 1862 (William Thomas, Architect; Fathers Patrick Dillon and Edward Sorin, Builders)
036	N	NA	**Music Hall**; Second Empire; 1866 (Brothers of the Holy Cross, Architects and Builders)
037	C	NA	**St. Mary's Convent**; Modern; 1954 (Ray Gavger, Architect; Walter Butler, Builder)
038	N	NA	**Church of Our Lady of Loretto**; Late-Romanesque Revival; 1956 (Paul Jacque Grillo, Architect; Lotto Seeler, Engineer)

12020 The Gothic Revival Sacred Heart Shrine features ornate cornices and Corinthian columns.

12031 Built in 1888 the Classical Revival Administration/Tower Building exhibits Ionic columns, an ornate gable-front, and simple stone masonry window frames.

039	N	NA	**Students' Infirmary/Immaculata Hall/Guest House**; Classical Revival; 1901
040	O	NA	**Chapel of Loretto**; Greek Revival; 1856
041	N	NA	**Rectory/Loretto Convent**; Classical Revival; 1914
042	C	NA	**Plant and Maintenance Building**; 20th century functional; 1932
043	C	NA	**St. Joseph's Hall**; 20th century functional; 1914 (Brothers of the Holy Cross, Architects and Builders)
044	C	NA	**St. John's Hall**; 20th century functional; 1914 (Brothers of the Holy Cross, Architects and Builders)
045	N	NA	**St. Michael's Hall**; Classical Revival; 1914 (Brothers of the Holy Cross, Architects and Builders)
046	NC	NA	**Garage**; 20th century functional; c.1965
047	C	NA	**Madeleva Hall**; International; 1966
048	NC	NA	**Opus Hall**; Neo-Colonial; 2004
049	NC	NA	**Dalloway's Coffee House**; Neo-Craftsman; 2000
050	NC	NA	**Welcome Center**; Neo-Tudor; 2000

Notre Dame Historic District (141-597-13001-065)

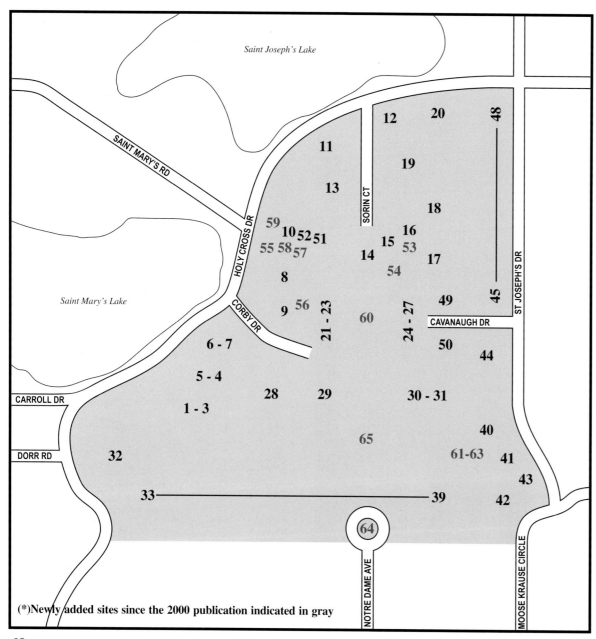

Saint Joseph's Lake

SAINT MARY'S RD

HOLY CROSS DR

Saint Mary's Lake

CORBY DR

SORIN CT

ST JOSEPH'S DR

CAVANAUGH DR

CARROLL DR

DORR RD

MOOSE KRAUSE CIRCLE

NOTRE DAME AVE

12 20 48

11

19

13

18

59 10 52 51
55 58 57

16
15 53
14

17

54

8

9 56

21 - 23

60

24 - 27

49

45

50

6 - 7

44

5 - 4

28 29

30 - 31

1 - 3

40

65

32

61-63 41

43

33 39 42

64

(*)Newly added sites since the 2000 publication indicated in gray

60

The Notre Dame Historic District encompasses most of the campus of the University of Notre Dame, a nationally prominent Roman Catholic university. Its history dates back to c.1830, when Father Stephen Badin, a French missionary, purchased 524 acres and built a small chapel. Architect William Arnett constructed a reproduction of that chapel at its approximate original location in 1906 (13005). Badin sold his land at a nominal fee to the Vincennes diocese with the hope that it would be used for a school and orphanage. In 1842, Father Edward Sorin and six French religious brothers arrived as the site. In less than two years, Father Sorin realized Badin's dream, having built a Catholic men's college, an apprentice's vocational school, a preparatory high school, and a religious novitiate. In 1844, the University received its charter from the Indiana General Assembly.

During its early years, Notre Dame was a self-sustaining community. The Holy Cross brothers farmed the University's land and eventually the college had its own bakery, sugar house, wheat granary, slaughterhouse, and icehouse. In 1842, brick production began and until the early 1880s, university kilns produced distinctive tan "Notre Dame brick" to be used in all campus construction. Father Sorin and Brother Francis Patois built the first classroom structure in 1843. Known today as the Old College, it is the only extant building from the University's first decade (13006). In 1855, Father Sorin and Brother Patois designed several new buildings to serve the needs of the Sisters of the Holy Cross, including Brownson Hall (13013) and the Earth Sciences Building (13053). That area was known as the French Quarter because the buildings' designs were influenced by French architecture.

During the Civil War, eight Notre Dame priests acted as chaplains of the Union Army. Holy Cross nuns from Notre Dame also served in the war, caring for the wounded on the battlefields and at military hospitals. The nuns who lived and worked at Notre Dame first came from France in 1843. They staffed kitchens, laundries, infirmaries, and the Minim School for Young Boys. When Father Sorin established St. Mary's College in 1855, the nuns became the teachers and administrators of that school.

In 1868, Father Sorin was elected Superior General of the Congregation of the Holy Cross and transferred its international headquarters from Le Mans, France to Notre Dame. The following year, William Thomas designed the Presbytery in the Second Empire style (13051). Likewise, the French Gothic Revival design of Sacred Heart Basilica, which was begun in 1871 and took more than fifteen years to complete, recalls the homeland of the priests and brothers (13023). Contained within the basilica are two fine pieces of sculpture by Ivan Mestrovic, the celebrated Croatian artist.

The basilica was still under construction when a disastrous fire swept the Notre Dame campus on April 23, 1879. It destroyed the Second Main Building, the St. Francis Elderly Men's Home, the infirmary, and the music hall. Less than a month later, the University broke ground for a new main building. Designed by Willoughby Edbrooke, the new Administration Building would become Notre Dame's most famous landmark with its golden dome (13014).

Given its French cultural background, the university valued dramatic, musical, and fine arts. The 1881 Washington Hall was built to replace the music hall that had burned down in 1879. Also designed by Willoughby Edbrooke, it was the center for Notre Dame's musical and dramatic arts (13027). The 1882 St. Edward's Hall originally functioned as the Minim School for Boys until 1929 when the school was discontinued. The dormitory, noted for its stained glass windows, suffered extensive fire damage in the summer of 1980, but has been restored (13015). The 1883 Science Hall housed significant scientific research conducted by university scholars including John A. Zahm, and Fathers Julius Nieuwland, Francis Wenninger, and Alexander Kirsh (13026).

Between 1919 and 1932, the University experienced tremendous growth, with its student body and faculty nearly tripling in size. Fifteen major building projects were completed during this period. Howard (13003), Lyons (13001), and Morrissey (13002) Halls were constructed in the Collegiate Gothic style to provide housing for the expanding university community. The 1927 South Dining Hall was constructed to resemble a medieval guild hall (13035). Academic changes were also taking place, as the elementary and preparatory programs were phased out and increased emphasis was given to college-level instruction and graduate studies. In 1930, the University constructed the Law School (13038), followed by the Hurley College of Business Administration in 1932 (13030) to meet those academic needs.

Also during those years, the fame of Notre Dame's "Fighting Irish" football team won national renown. Knute Rockne, a Notre Dame graduate and faculty member, became head coach in 1918. During his thirteen-year tenure, the University's football record was 105 wins, twelve losses, and five ties. The Osborn Engineering Company constructed Notre Dame Stadium of Belden brick in 1930 (14004). Known as "the house that Rockne built," the coach was killed in a plane crash just one year after its construction. In 1938, the University built the Rockne Memorial Building athletic facility in his honor (13032).

During the Second World War, Notre Dame served as a training facility for young men preparing to serve in the armed forces. The Navy established a Naval Reserve Officers Training Corps at the University in 1941 and the naval V-7 and V-12 officer training programs in 1942-43. Almost 12,000 men completed their training at Notre Dame between 1942 and 1946.

Father Theodore Hesburgh was ordained in 1943 and became president of the University in 1952. He held his presidential post longer than any of his predecessors and during that time brought extensive growth and change to Notre Dame, which included the admission of women in 1972.

Twenty-four new structures were completed between 1952 and 1976. These include the O'Shaughnessy Hall of Liberal and Fine Arts (13041); the Radiation Research Building (14003); the Notre Dame Memorial Library, which contains more than 600,000 volumes and valuable special collections (14002); and the Hayes-Healy Center, which houses the graduate division of the college of business administration (13024).

Recent construction includes the 1980 Snite Museum of Art (13042) and the 1982 Stepan Chemistry Building (13044). In 1978, the Main and South Quadrangles of the University were listed in the National Register of Historic Places. This survey includes structures located within that district, along with additions along St. Joseph's Drive.

NOTRE DAME HISTORIC DISTRICT (141-597-13001-066) NR

No.	Rtg.	Add.	Description
001	N	NA	**Lyons Hall**; Collegiate Gothic; 1927 (Francis Kervick and Vincent Fagan, Architects)
002	N	NA	**Morrissey Hall**; Collegiate Gothic; 1925
003	N	NA	**Howard Hall**; Collegiate Gothic; 1924
004	N	NA	**Bond Hall**; Italian Renaissance Revival; 1917 (Edward Titton, Architect)
005	N	NA	**Log Chapel**; Gable-front; 1906 (William Arnett, Architect) (597)
006	O	NA	**Old College**; Pyramidal-roof; 1843 (Father Edward Sorin and Brother Francis Patois, Architects)
007	N	NA	**Founders Monument**; 1906
008	N	NA	**Corby Hall**; Italianate; 1893 (Brother Charles Hardin, Builder)
009	C	NA	**Rev. William C. Corby Statue**; 1906
010	O	NA	**Our Lady of Lourdes Grotto**; Rustic; 1896 (Father Edward Sorin, Architect)

011 C NA **Lewis Hall**; Modern; 1965

012 NC NA **St. Michael's Laundry**; Modern; c.1980

013 N NA **Convent of the Sisters of the Holy Cross/Brownson Hall**; Second Empire; 1855 (Father Edward Sorin and Brother Francis Patois, Architects)

014 O NA **Administration Building**; Second Empire; 1879 (Willougby J. Edbrooke, Architect; Brother Charles Harding, Builder)

015 N NA **St. Edward's Hall**; Second Empire; 1882 (Father Edward Sorin and Brother Charles Harding, Architects)

016 N NA **Zahm Hall**; Collegiate Gothic; 1937

017 N NA **Cavanaugh Hall**; Collegiate Gothic; 1936 (Magihnis and Walsh, Architects)

018 N NA **Keenan/Stanford Hall**; Modern; 1957

019 N NA **Student Infirmary**; Collegiate Gothic; 1934 (Maginnis and Walsh, Architects)

020 C NA **Wenniger-Kirsch/Haggar Hall**; Art Moderne; 1937

13014 The Administration Building, known as the Main Building, dates to 1879 and carries a massive tower topped by a gold dome. Inside, murals by Luigi Gregori are located along the walls of the second floor entry hall and the inner dome.

62

13019 Many buildings on the Notre Dame campus were built in the Collegiate Gothic style, including the 1934 Student Infirmary. The Collegiate Gothic style is one of the eclectic period revivals and has both Tudor and Gothic influences; it takes its name from the popularity of the style on college campuses across the nation.

021 N NA **Walsh Hall**; Italian Renaissance Revival; 1909 (William J. Brinkman, Architect)

022 N NA **Sorin Hall**; Italian Renaissance Revival; 1889 (Willougby J. Edbrooke, Architect)

023 O NA **Sacred Heart Basilica**; Gothic Revival; 1871-88 (Father Alexis Granger, Father Edward Sorin, and Brother Charles Harding, Architects)

024 C NA **Hayes-Healey Center/Hurley Hall**; Modern; 1968 (Graham, Anderson, Probst and White, Architects)

025 N NA **Institute of Technology/Haynes College of Law/Crowley Hall of Music**; Classical Revival; 1893 (Brother Charles Hardin and Father John Zahm, C.S.C., Architects)

026 N NA **Science Hall/LaFortune Student Center**; Classical Revival; 1883 (Willoughby J. Edbrooke, Architect)

027 N NA **Washington Hall**; Second Empire; 1881

028 N NA **Badin Hall**; Second Empire; 1897 (Brother Columkille Fitzgerald, Architect and Builder)

029 N NA **Knights of Columbus Council Hall**; Collegiate Gothic; 1931

030 N NA **Hurley Hall**; Collegiate Gothic; 1932 (Graham, Anderson, Probst and White, Architects)

031 C NA **Riley Hall**; Art Deco; 1920 (Edward Titton, Architect)

13023 Sacred Heart Basilica has served as a place of worship for the Notre Dame community since its construction between 1871-88. The Gothic Revival style church has a cruciform plan and features a massive central tower and spire.

13025 The Crowley Hall of Music dates to 1893 and began as the Institute of Technology; it also housed the Haynes College of Law between 1918 and 1976.

032 N   NA   **Knute Rockne Memorial Building**; Art Deco; 1938 (Maurice Carroll and Chester E. Dean, Architects)

033 C   NA   **Pangborn Hall**; Art Deco; 1955

034 C   NA   **Fisher Hall**; Modern; 1953

035 N   NA   **South Dining Hall**; Collegiate Gothic; 1927 (Ralph Adams Cram, Architect; Francis Kernick and Vincent Fagan, Assoc. Architect)

036 N   NA   **Dillon Hall**; Collegiate Gothic; 1931

037 N   NA   **Alumni Hall**; Collegiate Gothic; 1931 (Maginnis and Walsh, Architects)

038 N   NA   **Law School**; Collegiate Gothic; 1930

039 N   NA   **Cushing Hall of Engineering/ Fitzpatrick Hall**; Collegiate Gothic; 1933 (Francis Kernick and Vincent Fagan, Architects)

040 C   NA   **Shaheen-Mestrovic Memorial Park**; c.1963

041 N   NA   **O'Shaughnessy Hall of Liberal and Fine Arts**; Collegiate Gothic; 1953 (Ellerbe Associates, Architects)

042 NC NA   **Snite Museum of Art**; International; 1980 (Ambrose Richardson, Architect)

043 C   NA   **Sculpture Studio**; Collegiate Gothic; 1955 (Ellerbe Associates, Architects)

044 NC NA   **Stepan Chemistry Hall**; International; 1982

045 N   NA   **Breen-Phillips Hall**; Collegiate Gothic; 1939 (Maginnis and Walsh, Architects)

046 N   NA   **Farley Hall**; Collegiate Gothic; 1947 (Maginnis and Walsh, Architects)

047 C   NA   **North Dining Hall**; Collegiate Gothic; 1957

048 N   NA   **Fire Station**; 20th century functional; 1946 (Wendell Phillips, Architect)

049 NC NA   **Field House Mall Memorial**; 1986

13027 The 1881 Washington Hall has a mansard roof covered by slate shingles to form horizontal stripes; the central tower features a steep pyramidal roof.

13051 The 1869 Presbytery was designed by architect William Thomas in the Second Empire style.

050 C   NA   **Nieuwland Science Hall**; Modern; c.1950

051 N   NA   **Presbytery**; Second Empire; 1869 (William Thomas, Architect)

052 N   NA   **Earth Sciences Building**; Second Empire, Gothic Revival; 1855 (Father Edward Sorin and Brother Francis Patois, Architect)

053 C   NA   **Our Lady Statue**; c.1920

054 C   NA   **St. Edward Statue**; c.1920; Froc-Robert, Sculptor

055 NC NA   **Thomas Dooley Statue**; 1986; Rudolph E. Torrini, Sculptor

056 C   NA   **St. Jude Statue**; c.1920

057 C   NA   **Blessed Brother Andre, C.S.C. Statue**; c.1939; Rev. Anthony Lauch, C.S.C., Sculptor

058 C   NA   **St. Francis of Assisi Statue**; c.1910

059 C   NA   **Christ Statue**; c.1910

060 C   NA   **Sacred Heart Statue**; c.19??; Robert Casiani, Sculptor

061 C   NA   **St. John the Evangelist Sculpture**; c.1955; Ivan Mestrovic, Sculptor

062 C   NA   **Christ and the Samaritan at Jacob's Well Sculpture**; 1957; Ivan Mestrovic, Sculptor

13052 The 1855 Earth Sciences Building was designed by Father Edward Sorin and Brother Francis Patois and features tall, narrow windows with segmental-arched tops.

Father Edward Sorin built Our Lady of Lourdes Grotto (13010) in 1896 in the Rustic style. *Courtesy of Historic Preservation Commission of South Bend and St. Joseph County.*

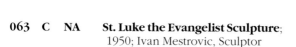

063 C NA **St. Luke the Evangelist Sculpture**; 1950; Ivan Mestrovic, Sculptor

064 C NA **Our Lady of the University Statue**; 1954; Anthony Lauck, C.S.C., Sculptor

065 C NA **Father Sorin Statue**; 1905; Ernesto Blondi, Sculptor

13055 This statue depicts St. Edward in bronze and copper holding a replica of the Sacred Heart Basilica in his left hand and a staff in his right hand.

This Art Deco-style stadium features vertical columns with limestone coping. *Courtesy of Historic Preservation Commission of South Bend and St. Joseph County.*

Notre Dame Scattered Sites (14001-008)

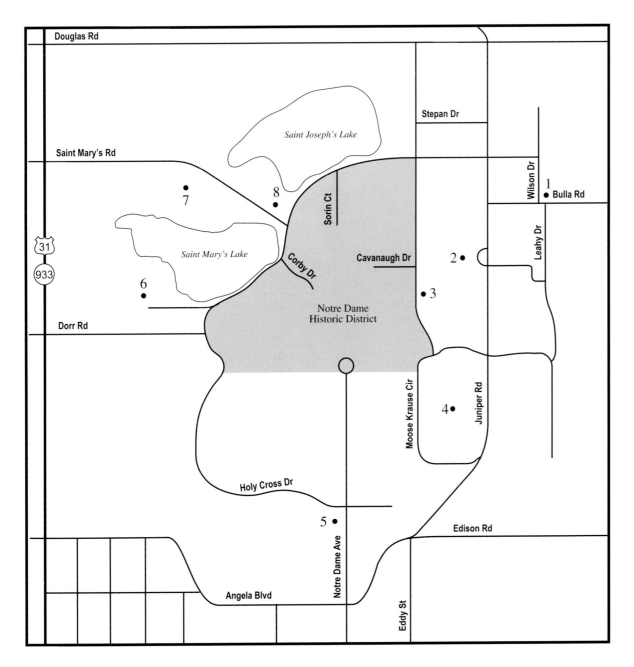

NOTRE DAME SCATTERED SITES (14001-008)

No. Rtg. Description

001 C Wilson Commons; Bulla Rd.; Greek Revival; 1850; *Architecture, Education* (597)

002 N Notre Dame Memorial/Hesburgh Library; Juniper Rd.; Modern; 1963 (Ellerbe Associates, Architects); *Architecture, Education* (597)

003 N Radiation Research Building; St. Joseph's Dr.; Modern; 1963 (Skidmore, Owings & Merrill, Architects); *Architecture, Education* (597)

004 N Notre Dame Stadium; Juniper Rd.; 20th century functional; 1930/c.1996 (Osborn Engineering, Architect); *Architecture, Education, Entertainment/Recreation* (597)

005 N Cedar Grove Cemetery and Chapel; Notre Dame Ave.; c.1840-Present; *Architecture, Art, Landscape Architecture, Religion* (597)

006 O Dujarle/Carroll Hall; Carroll Dr.; Italian Renaissance Revival; 1906 (Brother Charles Harding, Architect); *Architecture, Education* (597)

007 N Holy Cross Federation/Community Cemetery; St. Mary's Rd.; c.1868-Present; *Religion* (597)

008 N Holy Cross Community House/Columbia Hall; St. Mary's Rd.; Italian Renaissance Revival; 1895 (A.O. Hebulis, Architect); *Architecture, Education* (597)

14002 Ellerbe Associates designed the Notre Dame Memorial Library, also known as Hesburgh Library, in 1963. The Modern style building features this mosaic of "Touchdown Jesus" on the south face of the central tower.

14005 The Cedar Grove Cemetery is located on the campus of Notre Dame. Originally open to the public for burial, it has been reserved for Notre Dame faculty and staff since the 1970s. Its chapel is the oldest continually used chapel at the university.

14007 The Holy Cross/Community Cemetery has been in use by the Brothers of the Holy Cross since 1868 as a final resting place for its members. Prior to that, brothers, priests, and nuns were buried at the current site of Columbia Hall. In 1868, the bodies of the brothers and priests were moved here, while the nuns were moved to Our Lady of Peace Cemetery at Saint Mary's College.

14004 Notre Dame football fans have been cheering on the Fighting Irish at the stadium since 1930.

14006 Brother Charles Harding designed Dujarie/ Carroll Hall in 1906.

14008 Architect A.O. Hebulis designed Columbia Hall in 1895 in the Italian Renaissance Revival style.

Warren Township (58001-044)

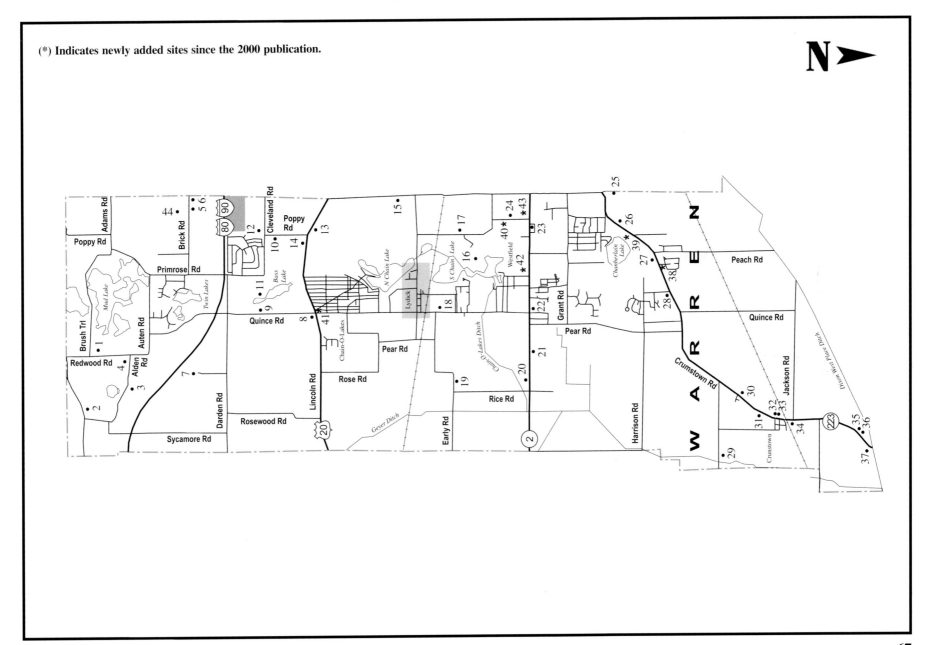

(*) Indicates newly added sites since the 2000 publication.

N

Warren Township was formed in 1838 and was named after Warren County, Ohio, from where many of the township's first inhabitants came. The township is distinguished by its many lakes, which extend throughout the length of the township from the Michigan border to the Kankakee River. Among the lakes are Clear Lake, which partially lies in Michigan, Mud, Deer, Twin, Augustine, Woolverton, Bass, Chain, and Fish/Chamberlain lakes. The Chain Lakes are drained by a branch of the Grapevine, through which waters find their way to the Kankakee River. Though many of the smaller lakes had become shallow and marshy by 1907, Bass, Chain, and Clear lakes were popular picnic and boating sites.

The prairie, lakes, and woodlands of the township made it favorable to inhabitants. Reynolds Dun, the first white settler, arrived in 1831. He farmed land to the northwest of Chain Lakes. Other early settlers included the Brick, Wikoff, Witter, Kingery, Field, Frame, Wilson, Phillips, Buckles, Dunbar, Jones, Price, Jackson, Myler, Skiles, Case, Mikesell, Dunnahoo, Brown, Platts, and Crum families.

The first log school building is believed to have been constructed as early as 1839. Hardy pioneers combined labors to voluntarily build these early structures. An 1882 school illustrates the expansion of the district school system (58033), and a 1935 school stands as a reminder of school consolidation (58030). German Baptists were among the first denominations to organize and they eventually built a church in 1879.

Three railroads crossed the township: the Lake Shore, the Grand Trunk, and the St. Joseph & Southern. In addition, two interurban lines were constructed to bring visitors to Chain Lakes: the Chicago, South Bend & Northern Indiana (the Indiana Railway) and the Chicago, Lake Shore, and South Bend. Two towns developed along the railroads; Lydick, formerly called Warren Center, Sweet Home, and Lindley, was a station along the Lake Shore. The other town, Crum's Point, was located along the Grand Trunk. The township's significance as a recreational destination is reflected in its historic resources, including the

Cresswell Tourist Camp (58008) and the South Bend Country Club (58016).

WARREN TOWNSHIP SCATTERED SITES (58001-044)

No. Rtg. Description

001 O **Barn**; 50726 Redwood Rd.; Bank/basement barn; c.1890; *Agriculture, Architecture* (700)

002 C **Joseph B. and Sarah Wells Inn/Farm**; 27680 Chicago Tr.; Gabled-ell; 1866; Livestock barn, transverse-frame/bank barn; *Agriculture, Architecture, Exploration/ Settlement, Transportation* (700)

003 C **Maple Lawn Farm**; 27386 Alden Rd.; Gabled-ell/Greek Revival; c.1858; Livestock barn; *Agriculture, Architecture, Exploration/Settlement* (372)

004 C **Garret Morris House**; 51235 Redwood Rd.; Central-passage/Greek Revival; c.1859; *Architecture, Exploration/Settlement* (372)

005 C **Farm**; 25218 Brick Rd.; Upright-and-wing; 1875/c.1900; Barns, garage, sheds; *Agriculture, Architecture* (598)

006 O **Henry & Mary Jane Sellers House**; 25026 Brick Rd.; T-plan/Eastlake; c.1875; Privy, sheds; *Architecture* (598)

007 C **John Rush Farm**; 52133 Rose Rd.; I-house/Italianate; c.1850/c.1875; Barn, chicken house, garages, granary, log crib barn; *Agriculture, Architecture* (372)

008 N **Cresswell Tourist Camp**; 26571 US 20; Rustic; 1925; Tourist cabins; *Architecture, Entertainment/Recreation* (372)

009 C **Barn**; 52986 Quince Rd.; English barn; c.1910; *Agiculture, Architecture* (372)

010 N **William Jackson House**; 53135 Poppy Rd.; Lazy-T; c.1880; *Architecture* (598)

011 N **House**; 52931 Primrose Rd.; Upright-and-wing; c.1840; *Architecture, Exploration/ Settlement* (372)

012 C **Barn**; 25471 Cleveland Rd.; Bank/basement barn; c.1920; *Agriculture, Architecture* (598)

013 C **Alex Cocsis House**; 25468 US 20; Western bungalow/Craftsman; 1915; Garage, privy, shed; *Architecture* (598) DEMOLISHED

014 N **Ralph Kizer House**; 25641 US 20; English cottage; 1932; *Architecture* (598)

015 N **Barn**; 54745 Pine Rd.; Bank/basement barn; c.1890; Pumphouse; *Agriculture, Architecture* (598)

016 O **South Bend Country Club**; 25800 Country Club Rd.; Dutch Colonial Revival; 1916; *Architecture, Entertainment/Recreation, Social History* (598) DEMOLISHED

017 O **House**; 55624 Country Club Rd.; Tudor Revival; c.1920; *Architecture* (598)

Historic view of the Sellers Farm with two outbuildings in the background. *Courtesy of Historic Preservation Commission of South Bend and St. Joseph County.*

58008 The Cresswell Tourist Camp is said to be the earliest in the area and it retains five cabins built at various times during the camp's history.

018 N **George Dunahoo Farm**; 55334 Quince Rd.; Upright-and-wing/Greek Revival; 1864; English barn; *Agriculture, Architecture* (372)

019 C **Irvin J. Tobalski Farm**; Early Rd.; California bungalow/Craftsman; c.1930 (Irvin Tobalski, Builder); Livestock barn, transverse-frame barn; *Agriculture, Architecture* (372)

020 C **House**; 27387 SR 2; American foursquare; c.1915; *Architecture* (372)

021 C **House**; 26868 SR 2; Western bungalow/Craftsman; c.1925; Garage; *Architecture* (372)

022 N **Varslager House**; 26368 SR 2; English cottage; 1940; Garage; *Architecture* (372)

023 C **House**; 25406 SR 2; California bungalow/Craftsman; c.1920; *Architecture* (598)

024 N **House**; 56262 Peppermint Rd.; Colonial Revival; 1923; *Architecture* (598)

025 C **Mathys/Shady Lane Farm**; 57706 Crumstown Hwy.; Colonial Revival; c.1929/1947; Dairy barn, pumphouse; *Agriculture, Architecture* (598)

026 N **House**; 57810 Crumstown Hwy.; Gabled-ell; c.1880; *Architecture, Ethnic Heritage* (598)

027 C **House**; 58075 Crumstown Hwy.; Spanish Colonial Revival; c.1930; Garage; *Architecture* (598)

028 NC **House**; 58339 Crumstown Hwy.; T-plan; c.1890; Garage; *Architecture* (372)

029 C **Farm**; 28298 Inwood Rd.; English barn; c.1950; Garage; *Agriculture, Architecture* (372)

030 O **Crumstown School**; 59340 Crumstown Hwy.; Mission Revival; 1931; *Architecture, Education* (372)

031 O **Riddle Farm**; 59675 Crumstown Hwy.; English barn; c.1878; Carriage house, smokehouse; *Agriculture, Architecture* (372)

58016 Unfortunately, the outstanding-rated South Bend Country Club was demolished since being surveyed in 1999.

032 C **Commercial Building**; 59675 Crumstown Hwy.; Parapet-front; c.1910; *Architecture, Commerce* (468)

033 N **Warren Township District No. 5 School**; 59703 Crumstown Hwy.; Gable-front; 1882; *Architecture, Education* (468)

034 N **Farm**; 59991 Crumstown Hwy.; California bungalow/Craftsman; c.1920; Dairy barn, garage, shed; *Agriculture, Architecture* (468)

58010 The William Jackson House has a lazy-T plan and features a front porch with square posts and scrolled brackets.

58014 The Ralph Kizer House is a notable example of an English cottage. The brick walls contain a belt course of soldiers at the water table line, the entry has a round-arched top, and the windows are six-over-one double-hung sashes.

58017 This house is an outstanding example of the Tudor Revival style. The house boasts a massive chimney, a steeply pitched roof with gray and purple slate shingles, and a variety of window openings, including segmental-arched and square windows with casement sashes.

58027 This house is a unique resource, having stucco walls, a clay tile roof, openings with geometric-patterned surrounds, and distinctive casement windows.

035 C   Emiel Maenhout House; 60900 Crumstown Hwy.; Cape Cod; c.1945; *Architecture, Ethnic Heritage* (468)

036 N   Remie Maenhout House; 60920 Crumstown Hwy.; English cottage; 1947; Garage; *Architecture, Ethnic Heritage* (468)

037 C   Crumstown Cemetery; Crumstown Hwy.; 1843; *Ethnic Heritage, Exploration/Settlement, Landscape Architecture, Religion* (468)

038 C   House; 58110 Crumstown Hwy.; Upright-and-wing; c.1880; Garage; *Architecture* (598)

039 C   Paul and Sophia Hetman Farm; 57845 Crumstown Hwy.; Western bungalow; c.1930 (Paul Hetman and Stanley Dylewski, Builders); Chicken house, garage, smokehouse; *Agriculture, Architecture* (598)

58034 This California bungalow has walls of cobblestone, a tall chimney stack, and concrete window sills and lintels.

040 N   House; 56191 Peppermint Rd.; American foursquare; c.1910; Grain bin, garage; *Architecture* (598)

041 C   Commercial Building; 26548 US 20; Gable-front; c.1900; *Architecture, Commerce* (700)

042 O   House; 25967 SR 2; Tudor Revival; c.1930; *Architecture* (598)

043 C   Farm; 25245 SR 2; Western bungalow; c.1900; Chicken house, workshop; *Agriculture, Architecture* (598)

044 C   Farm; 25509 Brick Rd.; Double-pile; c. 1870; Dairy Barn, Corn Crib Barn, Nontraditional Barn, Silo; *Agriculture, Architecture* (598)

58006 The historic Sellers House (above) has not been altered much throughout the years, as evidenced by the historical image below. *Courtesy of Historic Preservation Commission of South Bend and St. Joseph County.*

58030 The Mission Revival style is rarely seen applied to Indiana school building, making this resource significant, despite alterations to the window openings.

58042 This c.1930 Tudor Revival house is an outstanding example of the style. It bears stone walls with stucco beneath the gable ends, gabled dormers in the rear, a massive chimney, a slate roof, and original six-over-six windows.

Lydick Scattered Sites (59001-013)

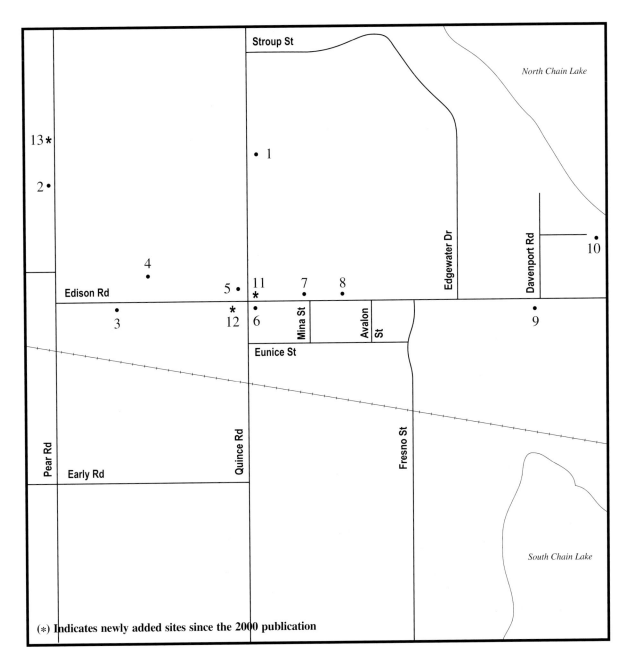

Stroup St

North Chain Lake

13 *

2 •

• 1

Edgewater Dr

Davenport Rd

• 10

4
•

Edison Rd

5 • 11
      •
      *

7
•

8
•

Mina St

Avalon St

• 9

3
•

12
*

• 6

Eunice St

Pear Rd

Quince Rd

Fresno St

Early Rd

South Chain Lake

(∗) Indicates newly added sites since the 2000 publication

Lydick is located at the center of Warren Township. Like many small towns, Lydick developed around the railroad and depended upon it for its livelihood. In 1851, the first train of the Michigan Southern and Northern Indiana Railway Company reached South Bend. Shortly thereafter, the company merged and became the Lake Shore and Michigan Southern. By 1875, there was a depot and telegraph office in the town that was then called Warren Center. Warren Center's post office, however, was called Sweet Home.

In 1901, Ashbury and Mina Lindley recorded the original town plat and changed the town and post office's name to Lindley. The same year, a railway delivery mix-up involving a man named Irvin Lydick resulted in the railroad depot being renamed Lydick. Both names, Lindley and Lydick, were used for about a decade, until the town came to be known as Lydick.

In 1903, the Chicago, South Bend and Northern Indiana Railway purchased land and began service from South Bend to Chicago a few years later. This interurban company survived until 1935 and its power house remains today (59004). A second interurban, the Chicago, South Shore and South Bend, arrived in 1908. The builders of these lines hoped they would bring pleasure-seekers to area lakes. A fourth rail line operated between 1900 and 1924. The branch of the Michigan Central extended from South Bend to St. Joseph, Michigan and was popularly called the Pumpkin Vine because it carried fruit.

By 1925, Lydick was booming. A new school was constructed, new businesses opened, including the Lumber and Coal Company, and new houses were built. The boom was short-lived, however, and during the 1930s and 40s the railroads declined and so did Lydick. The town has struggled to exist since that time, but remnants of its past glory remain.

LYDICK SCATTERED SITES (59001-013)

No. Rtg. Description

001 C **House**; 54744 Quince Rd.; American four-square; 1926; *Architecture* (372)

002 C **House**; 54835 Pear Rd.; English cottage; c.1950; Garage; *Architecture* (372)

003 C **House**; 26720 Edison Rd.; American four-square; c.1925; Garage; *Architecture* (372)

004 N **Northern Indiana Railway Power Station**; 26667 Edison Rd.; Romanesque Revival; c.1908; *Architecture, Transportation* (372)

005 N **House**; 26513 Edison Rd.; Western bungalow/Craftsman; 1920; *Architecture* (372)

006 NC **House**; 26498 Edison Rd.; American four-square; c.1920; *Architecture* (372)

007 C **Albert Wedel House**; 26419 Edison Rd.; Dutch Colonial Revival; 1929; *Architecture* (372)

008 C **House**; 26377 Edison Rd.; Dormer-front bungalow/Craftsman; c.1920; *Architecture* (372)

009 C **House**; 26080 Edison Rd.; Cross-plan; 1900; *Architecture* (598)

010 C **House**; Indiana St.; Side-gabled/Craftsman; c.1925; *Architecture* (598)

011 C **House**; 26497 Edison Rd.; Colonial Revival; c.1925; *Architecture* (372)

012 C **Lydick United Methodist Church**; 26510 Edison Rd.; Late-Gothic Revival; 1954; *Architecture, Religion* (372)

013 C **House**; 54768 Pear Rd.; Dormer-front bungalow; c.1920; *Architecture* (372)

59012 The Lydick United Methodist Church was built in 1954 on the foundation of an earlier church and has a 1961 addition of a recreation hall, classrooms, and offices.

59004 The Northern Indiana Railway Power Station dates to c.1908. Although converted to a residence, it still retains brick corbeling and windows with radiating voussoirs and limestone keystones.

59007 The 1929 Albert Wedel House has a gambrel roof, which helps identify it as Dutch Colonial Revival in style. The house retains original weatherboard siding, ten-over-one double-hung sash windows, and a contributing garage.

Olive Township (62001-047)

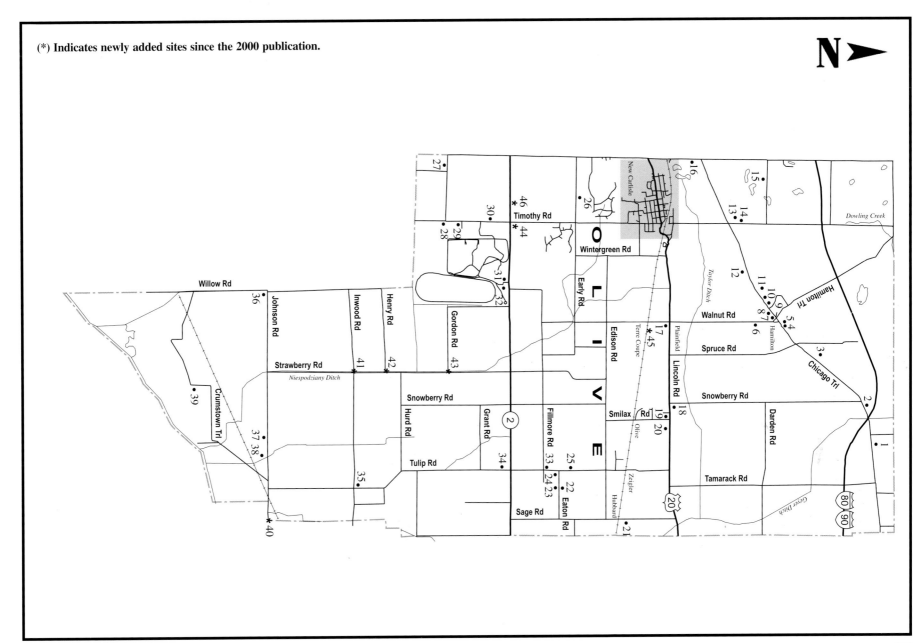

(*) Indicates newly added sites since the 2000 publication.

N

Olive Township was formed in 1832 and is the county's second largest township in area, exceeded only by Penn Township. The township's most significant geographical feature is the vast Terre Coupee Prairie, which extends roughly seven miles by five miles. The prairie land produced fine crops, which encouraged inhabitants to settle there. Eventually, the towns of Hamilton and New Carlisle developed, further increasing the population of the township.

The first settlements were made in 1830 when Charles Vail and his wife Olive arrived; the township was named in Olive's honor. Other early settlers included the Haines, Adams, Rush, Druliner, Garwood, Hubbard, Nickerson, White, Carskaddon, Egbert, Boyd, Garoutte, Redding, Smith, Ranstead, and Reynolds families. Many came from Warren County, Ohio by way of Niles, Michigan or Crawfordsville, Indiana, where the land office was located. Israel Rush served as the first justice of the peace and John Banker was an associate judge of the St. Joseph Court. Judge Banker, who lived on Terre Coupee Prairie, walked to South Bend to perform his judicial duties. John Druliner hosted the township's first election in his log house.

In about 1836, Samuel Garwood sold a tract of prairie land to Jonathan Hubbard, who platted the town of Terre Coupee. A man named Hamilton built a hotel in the new town and the town eventually became known as Hamilton. Reverend James Armstrong was the Methodist Church's first missionary to St. Joseph County and he helped found a Methodist society near Hamilton at the house of Paul Egbert in 1830. In 1852, a school was built that was used for church services until the new Methodist Episcopal church was constructed in 1858-59.

A man named Bourissau first owned the land upon which New Carlisle was built. After his death, his children sold the land to Richard Carlisle, who platted the town and gave it his name. Richard Cranner built a hotel in New Carlisle in 1836. After being sold to Joseph Ivens, it gained a reputation as one of the best establishments along the stage line.

OLIVE TOWNSHIP SCATTERED SITES (62001-047)

No. Rtg. Description

001 C Farm; 29655 Chicago Tr.; Cross-plan; c.1865; Dairy barn; *Agriculture, Architecture* (700)

002 C Proud Oaks Farm; 30133 Chicago Tr.; Colonial Revival; c.1894/1939; Dairy barn, English barn; *Agriculture, Architecture* (700)

003 C John Reynolds House; 30905 Chicago Tr.; Italianate Cube; c.1875; Milk house; *Architecture* (700)

004 N Olive Township District No. 1 School; 31479 Chicago Tr.; Italianate; 1867 (T.J. Garoutte, Builder); Garage; *Architecture, Education* (700)

005 N Hamilton Church & Cemetery; 31555 Chicago Tr.; Greek Revival; 1838 (Oliver Emery, Architect and Builder); *Architecture, Exploration/Settlement, Landscape Architecture, Religion* (372)

006 O James & Nancy H. Reynolds Farm; 52720 Walnut Rd.; Italianate; 1861; English barn; *Agriculture, Architecture* (372)

62006 The 1861 James Reynolds Farm is an outstanding example of the Italianate style. It has tall, narrow window openings with carved hoods, a paneled wood cornice with decorative scrolled brackets beneath overhanging eaves, and three bay windows.

62008 This grain elevator was originally part of the Haven Hubbard Farm. The c.1900 structure was still in use at the time of the survey in 1999.

007 NC House; 31544 Chicago Tr.; Greek Revival; c.1840; *Architecture, Exploration/Settlement* (372)

008 N Grain Elevator; 31675 Chicago Tr.; 20th century functional; c.1900; *Agriculture, Architecture* (372)

009 N Hubbard Farm Carriage House; 31895 Chicago Tr.; Second Empire; c.1880; *Agriculture, Architecture* (372)

010 O Haven and Armine Hubbard Farm; 31895 Chicago Tr.; Queen Anne; 1910; Carriage house, barn; *Agriculture, Architecture* (372)

011 O Haven Hubbard Memorial Home; 31895 Chicago Tr.; Tudor Revival; 1922; *Architecture, Health/Medicine* (372)

012 N House; 32272 Chicago Tr.; Colonial Revival; c.1940; Garage; *Architecture* (372)

013 C Power Substation; 52939 Timothy Rd.; Art Deco; c.1950; Brick structures, steel derrick; *Architecture, Engineering* (450)

014 C House; 52959 Timothy Rd.; Colonial Revival; c.1940; Garage; *Architecture* (450)

015 C Farm; 33620 Darden Rd.; Upright-and-wing; c.1900; Barns, privies, sheds; *Agriculture, Architecture* (450)

016 C Farm; 53650 County Line Rd.; Gable-front/T-plan; c.1852/1906; English barn; *Agriculture, Architecture* (450)

017 N Jacob Rush House; 31486 US 20 East; Upright-and-wing/Greek Revival; c.1850/c.1875; *Architecture, Exploration/Settlement, Transportation* (372)

018 C House; 30233 US 20 East; I-house; c.1885; *Architecture* (372)

019 N School; 30008 US 20 East; Gable-front/Italianate; c.1890; *Architecture, Education* (372)

020 C House; 29917 US 20 East; T-plan; c.1890; *Architecture* (372)

021 N House; 54620 Sage Rd.; Prairie; c.1920; *Architecture* (372)

022 N Farm; 28969 Eaton Rd.; American four-square; c.1910; Barns, privy; *Agriculture, Architecture* (372)

62010 The Haven and Armine Hubbard House dates to 1910 and is an outstanding example of the Queen Anne style. The roof carries several dormers with Palladian windows, a dentilated frieze and decorative projecting cornices, and a large classical porch with second story solarium.

62012 This Colonial Revival house displays a symmetrical plan with a central entry flanked by side lights and topped by a fan light. Window openings feature limestone sills, while the door opening has a limestone quoin surround.

023 N House; 28978 Eaton Rd.; T-plan; 1897; *Agriculture, Architecture* (372) LOG BARN DESTROYED

024 N St. Stanislaus Kostka Church; 55756 Tulip Rd.; Late-Gothic Revival; 1905/1927; Rectory; *Architecture, Ethnic Heritage, Religion* (372)

025 C Miller House; 55485 Tulip Rd.; Colonial Revival; c.1940; Garage; *Architecture* (372)

026 C Miller House; 33440 Early Rd.; Gable-front; c.1863; *Architecture* (450)

027 N Farm; 33854 Gordon Rd.; Bank/basement barn; 1898; Silo; *Agriculture, Architecture* (450)

028 C William Hooten House; 57250 Timothy Rd.; Colonial Revival; c.1915; *Architecture* (450)

029 C Olive Chapel Cemetery; Timothy Rd.; c.1837; *Exploration/Settlement, Landscape Architecture, Religion* (450)

030 N Jobe Smith House; 56875 Timothy Rd.; Hall-and-parlor; c.1850/c.1875; Shed, windmill; *Architecture, Exploration/Settlement* (450)

031 O Studebaker Clubhouse & Tree Sign; 32132 SR 2; Colonial Revival; 1926/1938 (Ernest W. Young, Architect); *Architecture, Entertainment/Recreation, Landscape History, Transportation* (372) **LL, NR**

032 O Studebaker Proving Grounds; 32104 SR 2; Parapet-front; 1926; *Architecture, Commerce, Engineering, Landscape Architecture, Transportation* (372)

033 C Olive Township District No. 9 School; 55969 Tulip Rd.; Art Deco; c.1915; *Architecture, Education* (372)

034 C Farm; 56659 Tulip Rd.; California bungalow; c.1920; Garage, livestock barn; *Agriculture, Architecture* (372)

035 N Jasinski Farm; 58995 Tamarack Rd.; Transverse-frame barn; 1926; Milk house; *Agriculture, Architecture* (372)

036 C Farm; 31990 Johnson Rd.; American four-square; c.1915; Livestock barn; *Agriculture, Architecture* (468)

037 N Barn; 29690 Johnson Rd.; English barn; 1906; *Agriculture, Architecture* (468)

038 C Barn; 29550 Johnson Rd.; English barn; c.1900; Windmill; *Agriculture, Architecture* (468) HOUSE DEMOLISHED

039 C House; 61701 Crumstown Tr.; T-plan; c.1900; Barns, garage; *Agriculture, Architecture* (468)

040 N County Bridge No. 12; Johnson Rd. over Geyer Ditch; Concrete; 1925; *Engineering, Transportation* (468)

041 C County Bridge No. S580; Inwood Rd. over Niespodziany Ditch; Concrete; 1929; *Engineering, Transportation* (372)

62011 The Haven Hubbard Memorial Home was given to the Evangelical church in 1920 by Mrs. Hubbard. The main part of the building was constructed in 1921-22; a center wing dates to 1967.

75

62017 This house in Olive Township exhibits an Upright-and-wing plan with Greek Revival elements added to it, such as cornice returns. The house was the home of Jacob Rush, who contracted to clear the path for the Michigan Road from Plymouth to LaPorte.

62031 The Studebaker Clubhouse has a slate roof, a large front porch with six round columns, and six-over-four double-hung sash windows.

Studebaker is integral to the history of Olive Township as it is home to the Studebaker Proving Grounds, Clubhouse, and Tree Sign. *Courtesy of Historic Preservation Commission of South Bend and St. Joseph County.*

042 C **County Bridge No. S581**; Henry Rd. over Niespodziany Ditch; Concrete; 1935; *Engineering, Transportation* (372)

043 C **County Bridge No. S583**; Gordon Rd. over Niespodziany Ditch; Concrete; 1935; *Engineering, Transportation* (372)

044 C **Olive Chapel**; 32987 SR 2; Gable-front; 1869; *Architecture, Religion* (450)

045 C **St. Joseph County Farm Bureau Co-op Grain Elevator**; 54300 Walnut Rd.; 20th century functional; 1954; Fertilizer warehouse, scalehouse, workshop; *Agriculture, Architecture* (700)

046 C **House**; 32867 SR 2; Upright-and-wing; c.1870; Chicken houses, shed, silo; *Agriculture, Architecture* (450)

047 C **Olive Township District No. 12 School**; 30750 Inwood Rd.; Greek Revival; 1925; *Architecture, Education, Social History*.

62024 The St. Stanislaus Kostka Church was built in 1905 as a mission church from St. Hedwig's Polish Church in South Bend after the original building burned.

An 1875 drawing of the former Jon Smith Farm in Olive Township. *Courtesy of Historic Preservation Commission of South Bend and St. Joseph County.*

New Carlisle Historic District (141-450-63001-091)

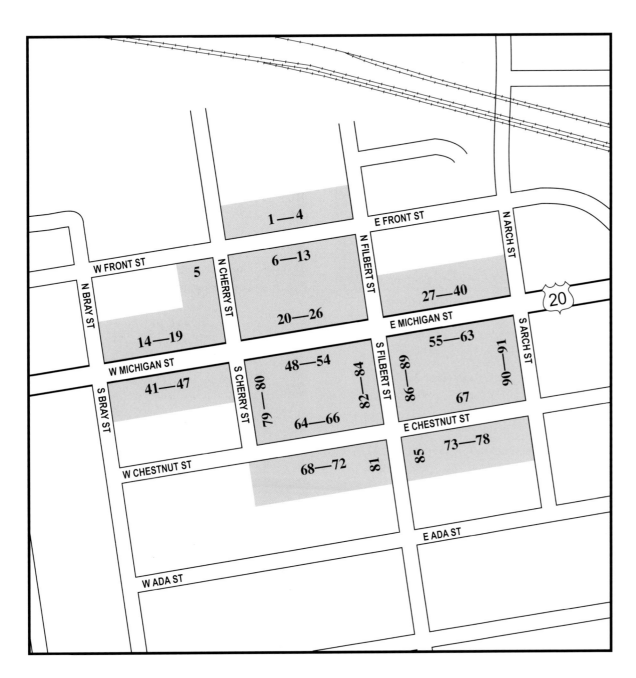

The New Carlisle Historic District encompasses a large portion of the city of New Carlisle. The town served a thriving agricultural community and its commercial district is remarkably intact. Local merchants, professionals, and farmers built homes that reflected the popular architectural styles of the time.

Richard Carlisle purchased the land and platted the village of New Carlisle in 1835, naming it after himself. The village's main street, Michigan, was part of the newly constructed Michigan Road. The George Matthews House (63041) dates to this period and also housed a general store. Matthews served as New Carlisle's first postmaster and was the stepfather of Schuyler Colfax, the United States Vice President under Grant. Colfax is believed to have lived in the house between 1836 and 1841. The Abraham Pyle House (63053) is also believed to date to the pre-railroad period, built in the Greek Revival style.

The 100 block of East Michigan Street became a commercial center and its earliest buildings were of frame construction. More substantial brick structures soon followed, especially in the decades after the Civil War. Many of these buildings survive, including the Italianate Warner Drug Store Building (63040) and the Queen Anne E. H. Harris Building (63039).

The town's advantageous location on one of the few improved roads in the state was further enhanced in 1851 when the Lake Shore Railroad, later called the Lake Shore and Michigan Southern, arrived, roughly paralleling Michigan Road a few blocks away. After the turn of the twentieth century two interurban companies, the Chicago Lake Shore and the South Bend Railway, served New Carlisle. The South Bend Railway failed during the Great Depression and its tracks were removed, but the South Shore continues operation today.

Unlike other towns that faltered as the railroads declined, New Carlisle's location along an improved road ensured its survival as the automobile rose in popularity. In 1915, the Lincoln Highway was routed through New Carlisle along the old Michigan Road. The highway was the first of the privately administered transcontinental roads routed in response to a public demand for better roads. Tourists and travelers were ushered right into New Carlisle's downtown and businesses thrived. The downtown offered banks, groceries, drug stores, dry goods shops, a hardware store, and a library. The Farmers State Bank closed during the Great Depression, but its 1919 building still stands (63063).

Some of the notable residential structures in the district include the Ransom Hubbard House (63005), an outstanding example of an Italian Villa, and the Italianate George Service House (63048). Numerous vernacular dwellings in the district exhibit a strong Queen Anne influence (63045, 63049, 63083). Twentieth-century styles are well represented in the district, reflecting the prosperity of the town through the 1920s. These include several houses influenced by the Prairie style, including the E. L. Maudlin House (63086).

The New Carlisle Historic District was listed in the National Register of Historic Places in 1992.

NEW CARLISLE HISTORIC DISTRICT (141-450-63001-091) NR

No. Rtg. Add. Description

WEST FRONT STREET (*north side*)

001	O	127-29	New Carlisle Methodist Church and Parsonage; Gothic Revival (church)/Hall-and-parlor (parsonage); 1858/c.1860/c.1930
002	C	117	House; I-house; 1890
003	C	109	House; L-plan; 1880
004	C	101	James Hooten House; Italianate; 1870

63001 Originally the New Carlisle Methodist Church, this Gothic Revival building has a central tower and window openings with both pointed-arch and flat tops.

WEST FRONT STREET (*south side*)

005	O	202	Ransom Hubbard House; Italianate; 1881 **LL**
006	C	130	William T. Flanigan House; Gabled-ell; 1885
007	C	126	House; Gabled-ell; 1895
008	C	122	Henry Reinhart House; Lazy-T; 1880/c.1930
009	C	118	House; Gabled-ell; 1890
010	C	114	House; Gabled-ell; c.1890
011	C	110	House; Hall-and-parlor; 1890
012	C	106	House; Hall-and-parlor; 1890
013	N	102	Anthony N. & Mary R. Van Ryper House; Italianate; 1880

WEST MICHIGAN STREET (*north side*)

014	C	229	Samuel Lancaster House; Italianate; 1875 (450)
015	N	221	Francis & Andell Warner House; T-plan; c.1880
016	O	217	Charles L. & Sarah C. Taylor House; Gabled-ell; c.1880
017	C	213	George F. Miller House; Prairie; c.1920
018	NC	209	House; Gabled-ell; c.1890/c.1950
019	O	201	New Carlisle Christian Church; Romanesque Revival; 1927
020	O	129	James & Loretta Reid House; Shingle Style/Free Classic; 1900
021	C	125	Mark Brummitt House; T-plan; c.1880
022	C	121	House; Craftsman; 1910
023	C	113	House; Craftsman; 1915
024	C	109	House; Prairie; 1910

63005 The Ransom Hubbard House is an example of the Italianate style; its corner tower is reminiscent of Italian villas. The 1881 house displays an irregular plan and ornate window hoods. It is a local, single-site historic district.

025 C 105 **House**; Queen Anne; 1905

026 C 101 **House**; American foursquare; 1915

EAST MICHIGAN STREET (*north side*)

027 NC 101 **Garage**; 20th century functional; 1950/c.1980

028 NC 101-07 **Telephone Company Building**; 20th century functional; 1965

029 NC 109-11 **Commercial Building**; 1-part commercial block; 1960

030 C 113 **Commercial Building**; Italianate; c.1880

031 N 115 **Commercial Building**; Italianate; c.1880

032 C 117 **Grocery & Butcher Shop**; Italianate; c.1885

033 NC 119 **Commercial Building**; 1-part commercial block; c.1980

034 C 123 **William Brummitt & Son Building**; Italianate; 1889

035 N 125 **E. H. Harris Grocery**; Italianate; 1895

036 NC 127 **Commercial Building**; 2-part commercial block; 1878/c.1980

037 C 129 **E. C. Taylor Building**; Italianate; 1886

63019 Originally the New Carlisle Christian Church, this late-Romanesque Revival structure displays a portico with three large, round-arched openings that mirror the window and door.

63020 The James & Loretta Reid House is an outstanding example of the Shingle Style. The c.1900 house possesses a full-width integral front porch with paired columns.

038 C 131 **Fair Building**; Italianate; 1890

039 C 133 **E. H. Harris Building**; Queen Anne; 1882 **LL**

040 O 135 **Warner & Garoutte Building**; Italianate; 1874 **LL**

WEST MICHIGAN STREET (*south side*)

041 C 230 **George W. Matthews House**; Gable-front; 1835

042 C 226 **Edward & Carrie S. Harris House**; American foursquare; 1916

043 C 222 **House**; Dutch Colonial Revival; 1930

044 C 218 **House**; Craftsman; 1930

045 N 214 **Francis & Andell Warner House**; Queen Anne; 1893

046 C 210 **Emma H. Stevens House**; Craftsman; 1928

047 C 202 **House**; Ranch; 1955

048 O 130 **George H. Service House**; Italianate; 1875 **LL**

049 O 122 **Mary Davis Peters House**; Queen Anne; 1891

050 C 120 **House**; Queen Anne; 1900

051 C 116 **House**; Upright-and-wing/Greek Revival; 1850

052 C 110 **House**; Gabled-ell; 1880

053 C 106 **Abraham Pyle House**; Hall-and-parlor; c.1910

054 C 102 **House**; Upright-and-wing/Greek Revival; 1850/c.1900

EAST MICHIGAN STREET (*south side*)

055 NC 102 **Gas Station**; 20th century functional; c.1950

056 NC 108 **Elda Rapp General Store**; Italianate; 1905

057 NC 110 **Commercial Building**; Italianate; c.1890

058 C 112 **Charles C. Carney Harness Shop**; Italianate; c.1890

059 N 114-18 **First National Bank of New Carlisle**; Italianate; 1900

060 O 124-26 **New Carlisle-Olive Township Library**; Craftsman; 1921 **LL**

061 C 128 **Commercial Building**; Parapet-front; c.1930

63040 The Warner & Garoutte Building is a local, single-site historic district. The Italianate commercial building dates to 1874 and features a bracketed cornice, narrow windows with decorative hoods, and cast-iron columns in the storefront.

63048 The 1875 George H. Service House is an outstanding example of the Italianate style. It has an ornate cornice and windows with decorative hoods.

| 062 | NC | 132 | **Commercial Building**; 1-part commercial block; c.1980 |
| 063 | N | 136 | **Commercial Building**; Craftsman; c.1915 |

WEST CHESTNUT STREET (*north side*)

064	C	121	**Anthony & Rose Herzog House**; Upright-and-wing; 1879
065	C	117	**House**; Gable-front; c.1900
066	NC	109	**House**; Ranch; c.1980

EAST CHESTNUT STREET (*north side*)

| 067 | C | 121 | **United States Post Office**; Contemporary; 1964 |

WEST CHESTNUT STREET (*south side*)

068	C	126	**Ernie Myers House**; Dutch Colonial Revival; 1931
069	C	118	**Milton Thompson House**; Cross-plan; 1885 **LL**
070	C	114	**House**; Gabled-ell; 1880
071	N	110	**Charles & Emily Larson House**; English cottage; 1921

63049 The 1891 Mary Davis Peters House is an outstanding example of the Queen Anne style. The house is covered in decorative shingles and features an open porch with patterned spindlework.

| 072 | C | 106 | **House**; Colonial Revival; 1920 |

EAST CHESTNUT STREET (*south side*)

073	C	110	**Double House**; T-plan; c.1900
074	C	114	**House**; Gable-front; c.1920
075	C	118	**William & Mary Brummitt House**; T-plan; 1886
076	C	122	**Moffitt House**; Gabled-ell; 1890
077	C	126	**House**; T-plan; 1890
078	O	130	**Jacob Augustine/Brown House**; Stick Style; 1887

SOUTH CHERRY STREET (*east side*)

| 079 | C | 107 | **House**; Gabled-ell; c.1900 |
| 080 | C | 114 | **House**; Ranch; c.1960 |

SOUTH FILBERT STREET (*west side*)

| 081 | C | 201 | **House**; Gabled-ell; c.1900 |

63085 The Smith/Trowbridge House in New Carlisle is an outstanding example of the Italianate style. The "L" plan house has segmental-arched windows with decorative hoods, and ornate spindlework in the gable ends.

082	C	121	**House**; California bungalow/Craftsman; 1921
083	C	117	**House**; Queen Anne; c.1880
084	C	113	**Mary A. Smith House**; Queen Anne; 1893

SOUTH FILBERT STREET (*east side*)

085	O	202	**Morgan & Mary A. Smith/William Trowbridge House**; Italianate; 1887 **LL**
086	C	120	**Edward L. Maudlin House**; American Foursquare/Prairie; 1912
087	C	116	**House**; Western bungalow/Craftsman; c.1920
088	NC	106	**Commercial Building**; 20th century functional; c.1970
089	NC	104	**Commercial Building**; 1-part commercial block; c.1960

SOUTH ARCH STREET (*west side*)

| 090 | C | 117 | **House**; Cross-plan; c.1900 |
| 091 | N | 113 | **City Hall**; Craftsman; 1950 |

New Carlisle Scattered Sites (64001-029)

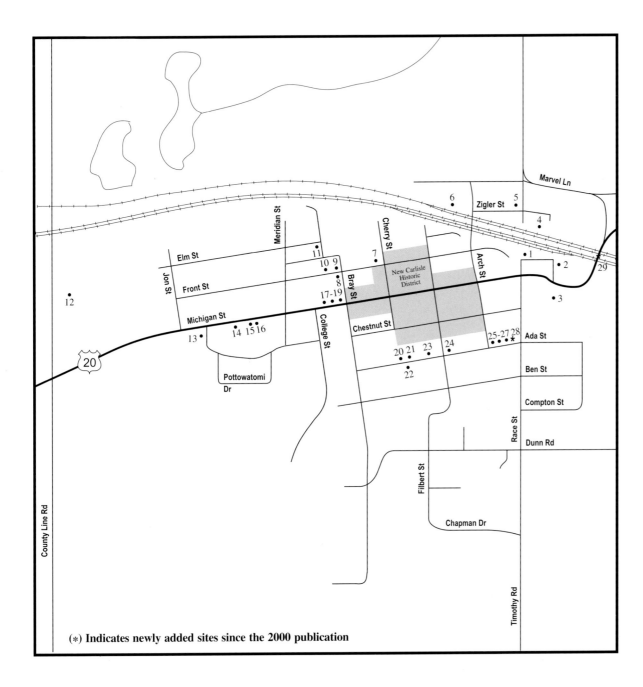

(✻) **Indicates newly added sites since the 2000 publication**

Richard Carlisle platted and named New Carlisle after himeslf in 1835. The village's main street, Michigan, was part of the new Michigan Road. The town's advantageous location on one of the few improved roads in the state resulted in successful businesses that could transport goods to other locations easily and offer services to visitors traveling the Michigan Road.

The town's accessibility was further enhanced in 1851 when the Lake Shore Railroad, later called the Lake Shore and Michigan Southern, arrived. After the turn of the twentieth century, two interurban companies, the Chicago Lake Shore and the South Bend Railway, served New Carlisle. The South Bend Railway failed during the Great Depression and its tracks were removed, but the South Shore continues operation today. A Classical Revival substation is a strong reminder of New Carlisle's rail heritage (64004).

Unlike other towns that faltered as the railroads declined, New Carlisle's location along an improved road ensured its survival as the automobile rose in popularity. In 1915, the Lincoln Highway ran through New Carlisle along the old Michigan Road. The highway, the first of the privately administered transcontinental roads, responded to a public demand for better roads.

A number of New Carlisle's significant historic structures lie outside the boundaries of the historic district. The National-Register listed and local landmark Jeremiah Service House was home to one of New Carlisle's most prominent citizens (64003); Service served one term in the Indiana State Legislature. Also built in the Italianate style, the Theodore L. Borden House is an outstanding-rated resource (64013). In addition, twentieth-century types and styles represented include American foursquares (64009, 64015), period revivals (64014, 64022), and Craftsman (24017) houses.

81

NEW CARLISLE SCATTERED SITES (64001-029)

No. Rtg. Description

001 N   Zahl's Elevator & Feed Mill; Timothy Rd.; 20th century functional; c.1947/1951; *Agriculture, Architecture* (450)

002 C   Fred Huffman Cooper Shop; 311 E Michigan St.; Italianate; 1925; Silos; *Architecture, Commerce* (450)

003 O   Jeremiah Service House/Old Republic; 304 E Michigan St.; Italianate Cube; 1861; *Architecture* (450) **NR, LL**

004 N   Chicago, South Shore & South Bend Railroad New Carlisle Substation; E Zigler St.; Classical Revival; c.1925 (Northern Indiana Public Service Company, Builder); *Architecture, Commerce, Engineering, Transportation* (450)

64003 This impressive Italianate Cube house, shown here prior to rehabilitation, was built for Jeremiah Service, one of New Carlisle's most prominent citizens who served one term in the Indiana State Legislature in 1852. His wife Sarah lived in the house until 1901. In 1998, Historic New Carlisle purchased the house, commonly known as the Old Republic, and rehabbed it as an inn and offices. The house is listed in the National Register of Historic Places.

64017 This c.1925 Craftsman-style house has wood shingle siding, a front porch with large, square posts, and multi-light windows and front door.

005 C   House; 237 Zigler St.; Italianate; 1875; Shed; *Architecture* (450)

006 C   House; 121 Zigler St.; Gabled-ell; 1890; *Architecture* (450)

007 C   Harvey Runnels House; 201-03 W Front St.; Italianate; c.1870; *Architecture* (450)

008 C   Andreas Maurer House; 302 W Front St.; T-plan; c.1880; *Architecture* (450)

009 C   House; 301 W Front St.; American foursquare; c.1915; *Architecture* (450)

010 C   House; 309 W Front St.; Hall-and-parlor; c.1880; *Architecture* (450)

011 C   David Hay House; 306 Elm St.; Italianate; 1870; *Architecture* (450)

012 N   New Carlisle Cemetery; 799 W Michigan St.; 1863; War memorial; *Exploration/Settlement, Landscape Architecture, Religion* (450)

013 O   Theodore L. Borden House; 732 W Michigan St.; Italianate; 1868; *Architecture* (450)

014 N   House; 538 W Michigan St.; English cottage; c.1925; *Architecture* (450)

015 C   House; 526 W Michigan St.; American foursquare; 1929; *Architecture* (450)

016 C   House; 518 W Michigan St.; Dutch Colonial Revival; c.1930; *Architecture* (450)

017 C   House; 321 W Michigan St.; Craftsman; c.1925; *Architecture* (450)

018 C   James S. Parnell House; 309 W Michigan St.; T-plan; 1880; *Architecture* (450) **LL**

019 C   House; 301 W Michigan St.; Upright-and-wing/Italianate; 1885; *Architecture* (450)

020 C   House; 125 W Ada St.; Minimal traditional; c.1930; Garage; *Architecture* (450)

021 C   Wilber VanDusen House; 117 W Ada St.; Gabled-ell; 1896; *Architecture* (450)

022 C   House; 118 W Ada St.; Colonial Revival; c.1930; *Architecture* (450)

023 N   Richard C. Teeters House; 109 W Ada St.; T-plan; 1893; *Architecture* (450)

024 C   Oren Tippy House; 220 S Filbert St.; Gabled-ell; 1880; *Architecture* (450)

025 C   Pilgrim Holiness Church; 201 E Ada St.; Gable-front; 1902; *Architecture, Religion* (450)

026 C   House; 205 E Ada St.; Hall-and-parlor/Greek Revival; c.1880; *Architecture* (450) DEMOLISHED

027 C   House; 209 E Ada St.; Gable-front; c.1900; *Architecture* (450)

028 C   House; 213 E Ada St.; Hall-and-parlor; c.1880; Garage; *Architecture* (450)

029 C   New York Central Railroad New Carlisle Bridge; Over US 20; Concrete; 1925; *Engineering, Transportation* (450)

64018 The James S. Parnell House exhibits a T-plan, retains original clapboard siding and double-hung windows, and decorative fretwork in the gable end.

Greene Township (66001-060)

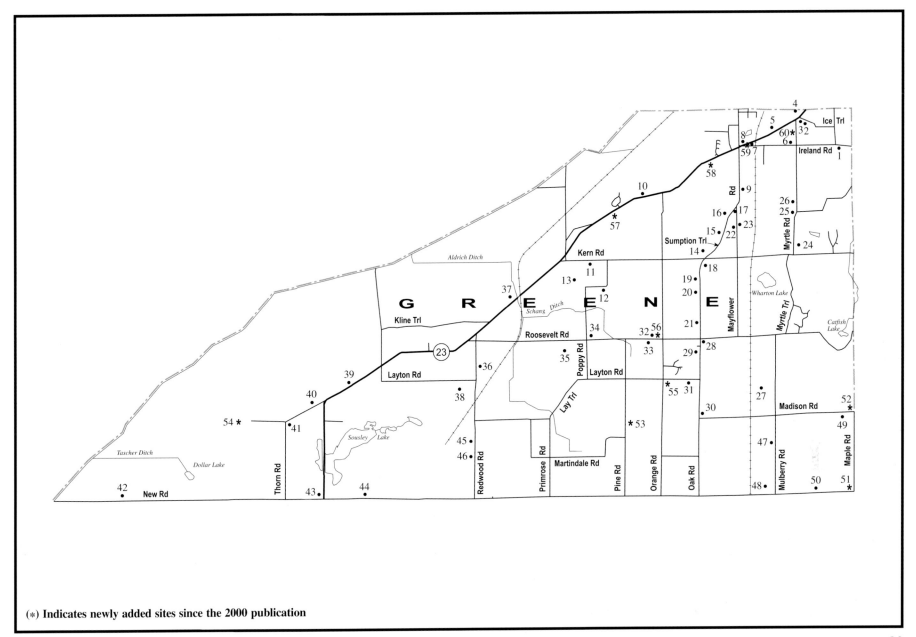

(∗) **Indicates newly added sites since the 2000 publication**

Greene Township was formed in 1836. Within its boundaries was Sumption Prairie, one of St. Joseph County's richest prairies. The fertility of the land made it well-suited to agriculture and agriculture remains the primary occupation of the township. Like Warren Township, Greene contains numerous lakes, including Goose, Duck, Wharton, and Bolin Lakes.

Settlers came early, attracted by the beauty and fertility of the land. The prairie was named after George Sumption, who settled upon it in 1830. The township was named after John Greene, who first visited the area on horseback in April of 1830. After further exploring northern Indiana and southern Michigan, he returned in 1832 and permanently settled. He brought with him friends and family from Greene County, Ohio. Samuel Leeper first came to the St. Joseph Valley in August of 1829. In March of the following year, he returned with his family from Ohio, eventually settling upon Sumption Prairie.

The Methodist church was the first established in the township in 1832 under Reverend Nehemiah B. Griffith. Services were initially held in private homes and log school houses until a building was constructed in 1841. Reverend Alfred Bryant of South Bend organized the first Presbyterian church in 1836. The church was constructed in 1838 on the farm of church member John McCullough. Elders Samuel Miller and Peter Hummer organized a Baptist society in 1846. They constructed a church building between 1852 and 1855. The German Baptists, also called Dunkards, built the Oak Grove Church at an early date.

The township's residents came together to fund and build the first school building in 1832. It was a simple log structure. The township's educational heritage is reflected in its surviving historic schools, including the 1873 Hoosier School (66028), a Greek Revival schoolhouse (66040), and the consolidated 1929 Greene Township School (66033).

Resources from the settlement period remain and include the Sumption Prairie Cemetery (66014)

and the George Sumption House (66016). The township's historic buildings also reflect its agricultural heritage. Situated on area farms are simple wood-framed and brick houses (66002, 66008, 66047), more elaborate Greek Revival (66028, 66049) and Italianate (66010, 66044) houses, and fine barns (66009, 66012).

GREENE TOWNSHIP SCATTERED SITES (66001-060)

No. Rtg. Description

001 C Farm; 22280 Ireland Rd.; Colonial Revival; c.1939; Livestock barn; *Agriculture, Architecture* (598)

002 C House; 22670 Ice Tr.; Side-gabled; c.1900; *Architecture* (598)

003 N House; 22708 SR 23; Dormer-front bungalow/Craftsman; c.1920; Garage; *Architecture* (598)

004 C Jacob J. & Marm M. Kirby House; 22727 SR 23; Queen Anne; 1911 (Catalog house); *Architecture* (598)

005 N Farm; 23007 SR 23; Gabled-ell; c.1900; English barn, workshop; *Agriculture, Architecture* (598)

006 N House; 22875 Ireland Rd.; International; c.1950; *Architecture* (598)

66010 The John & Lydia Rupel House is a fine example of the Italianate style. It displays paired, scrolled brackets beneath overhanging eaves, paired windows with round-arched tops on the second story, and ten-over-ten double-hung sash windows with carved surrounds on the first story.

66019 The Thomas & Drucilla Holloway House possesses a mansard-like roof with decorative, circular vents, and an oversized entry suround.

007 C House; 23356 SR 23; American foursquare; c.1915; *Architecture* (598)

008 C House; 23487 SR 23; Gabled-ell; c.1900; *Architecture* (598)

009 N Barn; 60100 Mayflower Rd.; Bank/basement barn; c.1900; *Agriculture, Architecture* (339)

010 O John J. and Lydia C. Rupel House; 24845 SR 23; Italianate; 1859; *Architecture* (339), **LL**

011 C Barn; 25450 Kern Rd.; Bank/basement barn; 1915; *Agriculture, Architecture* (339)

012 N Barn; 25200 Kelly Rd.; Bank/basement barn; c.1890; *Agriculture, Architecture* (339)

013 O Camp Millhouse; 25600 Kelly Rd.; T-plan/ Rustic; c.1940; Basketball court, cabins, garage, infirmary, nature center, pool, poolhouse, recreation hall, sheds; *Architecture, Entertainment/Recreation, Health/ Medicine, Social History* (339)

014 N Sumption Prairie Cemetery; 23999 Kern Rd.; c.1830; *Exploration/Settlement, Landscape Architecture, Religion* (339)

015 N Andrew Longhley House; 60559 Sumption Tr.; Gable-front/Italianate; c.1854/1875; *Architecture, Exploration/Settlement* (339)

016 O George & Elizabeth Sumption House; 60413 Sumption Tr.; Federal; 1832; *Architecture, Exploration/Settlement* (339) **LL**

017 C House; 60177 Mayflower Rd.; English cottage; c.1940; *Architecture* (339)

018 N House; 61074 Oak Rd.; Gabled-ell; c.1890; Garage; *Architecture* (339)

019 O Thomas L. & Drucilla M. Holloway Farm; 61229 Oak Rd.; Late-Georgian Revival; c.1860/1941; Barns, garage, house, sheds, summer kitchen, Sweitzer barn; *Agriculture, Architecture* (339)

020 O John Greene House; 61383 Oak Rd.; Greek Revival; c.1850; Grange hall, transverse-frame barn; *Agriculture, Architecture, Exploration/Settlement* (339)

021 O Seth Hammond Farm; 61723 Oak Rd.; Stick Style; 1885; Barns, garage, sheds; *Agriculture, Architecture* (339), **LL**

022 N House; 60535 Mayflower Rd.; American foursquare; c.1920; *Architecture* (339)

023 C House; 60502 Mayflower Rd.; Gabled-ell; c.1890; *Architecture* (339)

024 C House; 60800 Myrtle Rd.; Upright-and-wing; c.1895; *Architecture* (339)

025 C House; 60415 Myrtle Rd.; Greek Revival; c.1845; *Architecture, Exploration/Settlement* (339)

026 C House; 60255 Myrtle Rd.; California bungalow/Craftsman; c.1925; *Architecture* (339)

66015 **The Andrew Longhley House has evolved over time. Its rear tower was added sometime after it was featured in the 1875 atlas, when the house was updated to the popular Italianate style. The Classical Revival porch was added sometime before 1930.**

66021 **The Seth Hammond House has a T-plan, clapboard siding, and decorative vertical and diagonal siding with spindlework in the gable ends.**

027 C Farm; 62503 Mulberry Rd.; Italianate; 1872; Livestock barn; *Architecture* (339)

028 N Hoosier School; 62012 Oak Rd.; Greek Revival; 1873; Concrete block barns; *Agriculture, Architecture, Education* (339)

029 C House; 62129 Oak Rd.; Italianate; c.1875; Summer kitchen; *Architecture* (339)

030 C Barn; 62950 Oak Rd.; Bank/basement barn; c.1880; *Agriculture, Architecture* (339)

031 C House; 24136 Layton Rd.; Dormer-front bungalow/Craftsman; 1915; *Architecture* (339)

032 C House; 24621 Roosevelt Rd.; Cross-gable square; c.1905; *Architecture* (339)

033 O Greene Township School; 24702 Roosevelt Rd.; Collegiate Gothic; 1929; *Architecture, Education* (339)

034 C House; 25459 Roosevelt Rd.; California bungalow/Craftsman; c.1915; *Architecture* (339)

035 C Farm; 25836 Roosevelt Rd.; Gabled-ell; 1900; Sweitzer barn; *Agriculture, Architecture* (339)

036 N House; 62254 Redwood Rd.; Gable-front; c.1900; *Architecture* (468)

037 N Ephraim Rupel Farm; 26573 SR 23; Italianate; c.1863; Dairy barn, silo; *Agriculture, Architecture* (468)

038 C Farm; 27348 Layton Rd.; Upright-and-wing; c.1840; Bank/basement barn; *Agriculture, Architecture* (468)

66025 **This early Greek Revival house in Greene Township dates to c.1845 and features original siding, small window openings, and a molded cornice with returns.**

66033 The Greene Township school is an outstanding example of the Collegiate Gothic style, having some Art Deco influences, such as the diamond stonework.

039 C **Barn**; 28629 SR 23; Bank/basement barn; c.1900; *Agriculture, Architecture* (468)

040 C **Kankakee District No. 7 School**; 29149 Lath Tr.; Greek Revival; 1880; *Architecture, Education* (468)

041 N **Farm**; 29400 Lath Tr.; c.1860; Milk house, privy, summer kitchen, transeverse-frame barn, trough house; *Agriculture, Architecture* (468)

042 C **Farm**; 31605 New Rd.; Gabled-ell; c.1900; Corn crib, transverse-frame barn; *Agriculture, Architecture* (468)

043 C **House**; 63981 SR 23; Side-gabled; c.1925; Garage, gas station; *Architecture, Commerce, Transportation* (468)

044 O **Christopher & Catherine N. Eisenmenger Farm**; 28525 New Rd.; Italianate; 1873; Bank/basement barn, silo, summer kitchen; *Agriculture, Architecture* (468)

045 C **House**; 63185 Redwood Rd.; American foursquare; c.1915; *Architecture* (468)

046 C **House**; 63541 Redwood Rd.; Gable-front; c.1920; *Architecture* (468)

047 N **C. Myers Farm**; 63251 Mulberry Rd.; Gabled-ell; c.1898; Bank/basement barn; *Agriculture, Architecture* (339)

048 N **Barn**; 63877 Mulberry Rd.; Sweitzer barn; c.1900; *Agriculture, Architecture* (339)

049 N **John Smith House**; 22100 Madison Rd.; Gable-front/Greek Revival; c.1858; *Architecture, Exploration/Settlement* (339)

050 N **Barn**; 22553 New Rd.; Bank/basement barn; c.1910; *Agriculture, Architecture* (339)

051 C **Maple grove Methodist Episcopal Church**; 22019 New Rd.; Gable-front; 1878; *Architecture, Religion* (339)

052 C **House**; 22055 Madison Rd.; T-plan; c.1895; Sheds; *Architecture* (339)

053 C **Reeves Cemetery**; 63068 Pine Rd.; 1849-1902; *Religion* (339)

054 N **House**; 30008 Madison Rd.; Double-pile; c.1880; Stable; *Architecture* (468)

055 C **Farm**; 62516 Orange Rd.; Free Classic; c.1905; Smokehouse, stables, summer kitchen; *Agriculture, Architecture* (339)

056 C **Sumption Prairie Methodist Church**; 24535 Roosevelt Rd.; Gable-front/Contemporary; 1960 (Kyle and Associates, Architects; Harry Veller Contractor, Inc., Builder); Parsonage; *Architecture, Religion* (339)

057 C **Charles O. & Clara S. Rupel Farm**; 25248 SR 23; Free Classic; c.1902; Bank/basement barn, brooder house, corn crib, garage, granary; *Agriculture, Architecture* (339)

058 C **House**; 23824 SR 23; Western bungalow/Craftsman; c.1920; Chicken house, garage; *Architecture* (598)

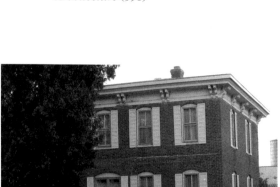

66044 The 1873 Christopher & Catherine Eisenmenger House has overhanging eaves supported by scrolled brackets, segmental-arched window openings, and a side porch with decorative sawtooth and scrollwork.

66056 A good example of a recent-past resource is the Sumption Prairie Methodist Church, built in 1960 by architects Kyle and Associates from LaPorte, Indiana.

059 C **Commercial Building**; 23420 SR 23; Contemporary; c.1950; *Architecture, Commerce* (598)

060 N **Jacob and Elizabeth H. Russell Farm**; 59375 Myrtle Rd.; Uright-and-wing; 1840 (Jacob Russell, Builder); Chicken houses, cold cellar, corn crib, English barn, garage, granary, hog house, privy, shed, smokehouse, tool shed, wood shed; *Agriculture, Architecture* (598) **LL**

Centre Township (70001-056)

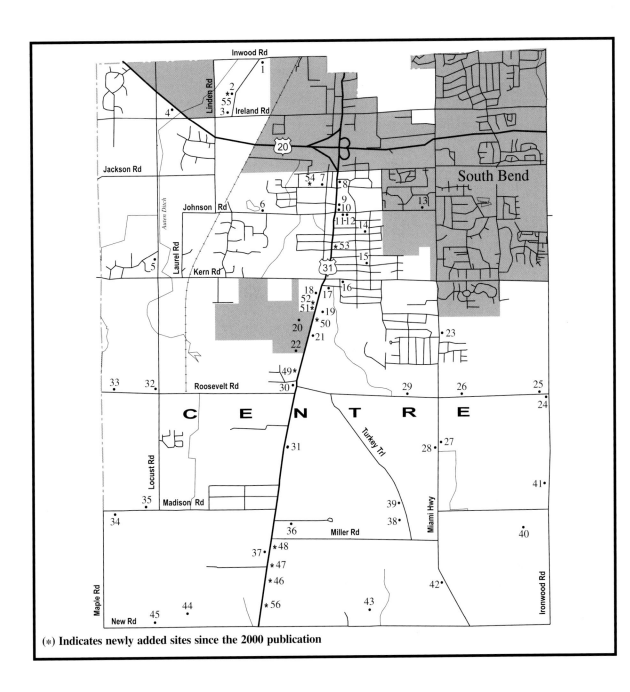

Inwood Rd

Linden Rd

1

2
*
55
3. Ireland Rd

4.

US 20

Jackson Rd

Auten Ditch

Johnson Rd

6

Laurel Rd

Kern Rd

5.

54 7
*

8

9
10

11 12
14

*53

US 31

15

18.
52 *
51 *
17
*19

20
*50

22
*21

23

49*

33   32.
Roosevelt Rd
30

29
26
25
24

C   E   N   T   R   E

Locust Rd

31

Turkey Trl

28.   .27

41.

35
Madison Rd

39.
38.

34

36
Miller Rd

40

37.   *48
*47
*46
42.
*56
43

Maple Rd

45
44

New Rd

Ironwood Rd

Miami Hwy

South Bend

13

(*) Indicates newly added sites since the 2000 publication

Centre Township was formed in 1840 and, along with Lincoln Township, is one of only two St. Joseph County townships whose limits have remained unchanged since their formation. It is the county's smallest township and the old Michigan Road traverses the township from north to south. The township's soil could be characterized as a strong clay and in the northwest portion there was a lot of lowland that has largely been reclaimed by drainage, making it the most valuable land in the township. Rupel Lake lies in that vicinity and the land is drained by Wenger's Creek, which flows through Portage Township, reaching the St. Joseph River almost at the exact south bend of the river.

The first settlements were made in the early 1830s, although some believe that Nathan Rose purchased his land from the Potawatomi in 1829. Other early settlers included the Milling, Stull, Rupel, Smith, Lamb, Hungerford, Bray, Inwood, Phillips, and Robertson families. Palmer Prairie was named after early settlers James and Ashur Palmer. Mathias Stover served as the first justice of the peace.

A log school house was built on Nathan Rose's Farm along the Michigan Road in 1835. A short time later, a frame building was built on Colonel John Smith's farm, also along the Michigan Road. Unfortunately, no historic schools survive today to attest to the township's educational heritage. The German Baptists built Palmer Prairie Church in 1859, with David Miller and Christian Wenger serving as early pastors. St. Joseph County's first infirmary was located in Centre Township between 1846 and 1855.

The Vandalia Railroad ran north and south through the township. Nutwood Station was located on the railroad, but other than this station, the township remained purely agricultural. The prosperity of area farmers is reflected in existing historic resources, including the huge bank barn that is part of the 1870s Vanden Bosch Farm (70032). Other outstanding farms include the Franklin Rupel Farm (70002), the George Schafer Farm (70027), and the Francis Donahue Farm (70038).

CENTRE TOWNSHIP SCATTERED SITES (70001-056)

No. Rtg. Description

001 C Elias Rupel House; 20550 W Chippewa; Italianate; c.1875; *Architecture* (598)

002 O Franklin & Martha R. Rupel Farm; 59449 Keria Tr.; Italianate; 1873; Cemetery, Chicken house, English barn, power house; *Agriculture, Architecture* (598) **NR**

003 N Cover House; 20909 Ireland Rd.; Prairie; c.1920; *Architecture* (598)

004 N Janasch House; 21371 Ireland Rd.; Gabled-ell; c.1880; *Architecture* (598)

005 O Emil & Anna J. Johnson Farm; 60717 Locust Rd.; Tudor Revival; 1914 (Indiana Lumber Company, Builder); *Architecture* (339) **LL**

006 N House; 20545 Johnson Rd.; American foursquare; c.1915; *Architecture* (339)

007 C House; 20041 Jewell Ave.; Minimal traditional; c.1920; *Architecture* (339)

008 N House; 19848 Ruth Ave.; English cottage; c.1940 (Sears, Roebuck & Co. catalog house); *Architecture* (339)

009 N Forest H. Hay House; 60284 US 31; Colonial Revival; 1946; *Architecture* (339)

010 C Indiana Territorial Line Historical Marker; US 31 & Johnson St.; 1966; *Exploration/ Settlement* (339)

011 C House; 19866 Johnson Rd.; Craftsman; c.1925; *Architecture* (339)

012 C House; 19842 Johnson Rd.; Gable-front; c.1925; Garage; *Architecture* (339)

70005 The Emil and Anna Johnson House is a good example of the Tudor Revival style. It has steeply-pitched, gabled dormers with half-timbering and a porte-cochere.

013 O Topper/Hay Farm; 19109 Johnson Rd.; Queen Anne; c.1900; English barn; *Agriculture, Architecture* (694) IN SOUTH BEND **LL**

014 O House; 19645 Dice St.; Western bungalow; 1924; Garage; *Architecture* (694)

015 C House; 19615 Detroit Ave.; American foursquare; c.1915; *Architecture* (694)

016 C House; 19880 Kern Rd.; Bungalow/Craftsman; c.1925; *Architecture* (339)

017 C House; 19946 Southland Ave.; Bungalow/Craftsman; c.1925; Garage; *Architecture* (339)

018 N Ullery/Joseph Farneman House; 61191 US 31; Italianate Cube; 1866; Garage; *Architecture* (339) **LL**

019 C Southlawn Cemetery; 61300 US 31; c.1850/c.1920 (office); *Exploration/Settlement, Landscape Architecture, Religion* (694)

020 C House; 61401 US 31; Gabled-ell/Craftsman; c.1880/1920; Chicken house, barn, sheds; *Agriculture, Architecture* (339) IN SOUTH BEND

021 N Shafer Farm; 61550 US 31; Italianate; 1895; Bank/basement barn, corn crib, garage; *Agriculture, Architecture* (339)

022 C Houses; 61601 US 31; California bungalow/Craftsman; c.1925; English barn; *Agriculture, Architecture* (339) IN SOUTH BEND

023 N Farm; 61396 Miami Rd.; Sweitzer barn; c.1900; Silo; *Agriculture, Architecture* (694)

024 C Van Buskirk Cemetery; 61156 Ironwood Rd.; c.1850; *Exploration/Settlement, Religion* (694) **LL**

025 N James Leach House; 18075 Roosevelt Rd.; Gabled-ell; c.1860; *Architecture* (694) **LL**

026 O Peter Schafer Farm; 18799 Roosevelt Rd.; Queen Anne; 1901; Bank/basement barn, barn, corn crib, garages, machine shed, shed, summer kitchen; *Agriculture, Architecture* (694)

027 O George & Elizabeth Schafer Farm; 62290 Miami Rd.; Free Classic; 1908; Bank/basement barn, English barn, milk house, pump-house, silo; *Agriculture, Architecture* (694) **LL**

028 N Farm; 62485 Miami Rd.; Gabled-ell; c.1910; Bank/basement barn, grain bin, silo, shed; *Agriculture, Architecture* (694)

029 C George F. Shafer Farm; 19251 Roosevelt Rd.; Free Classic; 1908; Bank/basement barn, milk house; *Agriculture, Architecture* (694) **LL**

70013 This c.1900 house has a pyramidal roof with multiple gables and dormer windows. It retains original clapboard siding and a full-width front porch with round columns.

70014 This 1924 western bungalow has a hipped dormer and boasts a clay tile roof. The property retains a matching garage.

030 C **Weller House**; 61953 US 31; Queen Anne; 1910; *Architecture* (339)

031 C **House & Henson Family Cemetery**; 62472 US 31; American foursquare; c.1849/c.1915 (house); *Architecture, Exploration/Settlement, Religion* (339)

032 O **James Q. C. & Mary Jane Vandenbosch Farm**; 61955 Locust Rd.; Second Empire; 1876; English barn, milk house; *Agriculture, Architecture* (339) **LL**

033 C **Barn**; 21855 Roosevelt Rd.; English barn; c.1890; *Agriculture, Architecture* (339)

034 C **Farm**; 21914 Madison Rd.; Dormer-front bungalow/Craftsman; c.1925; Bank/basement barn, Chicken houses, silo; *Agriculture, Architecture* (339)

035 N **George Fox House**; 21595 Madison Rd.; Free Classic; c.1900; *Architecture* (339)

036 C **House**; 20328 Baughman Ct.; Dutch Colonial Revival; c.1920; *Architecture* (339)

037 C **House**; 63419 US 31; T-plan; 1890; *Architecture* (339)

038 O **Francis & Rosanne H. Donaghue Farm**; 63049 Turkey Tr.; Italianate; 1861; Chicken house, garage, pumphouse, Sweitzer barn; *Agriculture, Architecture* (694) **LL**

039 C **House**; 62919 Turkey Tr.; Gable-front; c.1900; Garage, sheds; *Architecture* (694)

040 C **Farm**; 18250 Madison Rd.; Gabled-ell; c.1890; Barn, corn crib, milk house, privy, pump house, silo, summer kitchen, Sweitzer barn; *Agriculture, Architecture* (694)

70027 The 1908 George and Elizabeth Schafer House is an outstanding example of the Free Classic style. It has a pyramidal roof and a wrap-around porch with cast block piers and round columns.

041 N **Farm**; 62697 Ironwood Rd.; Upright-and-wing; c.1850; Bank/basement barn, garage; *Agriculture, Architecture* (694)

042 C **Schrader House**; 63599 Miami Rd.; English cottage; 1940; *Architecture* (694)

043 C **House**; 19591 New Rd.; L-plan; c.1886; *Architecture* (694)

044 NC **House**; 21045 New Rd.; Dormer-front bungalow/Craftsman; c.1920; *Architecture* (339)

045 N **House**; 21405 New Rd.; Queen Anne; 1895; *Architecture* (339)

70032 James Vandenbosch built this Second Empire house in 1876. Vandenbosch had emigrated to America from Holland in 1840 with his wife Mary Jane.

70038 The 1861 Francis & Rosanne Donaghue House is Italianate in style, boasting overhanging eaves supported by paired, scrolled brackets, paired round-arched windows, and an elaborate front porch with square, fluted columns.

046 C **Sacred Heart of Jesus Church**; 63568 US 31; Gambrel-front/Colonial Revival; 1933; Rectory; *Architecture, Religion* (339)

047 C **Mount Calvary Cemetery**; US 31; 1953-Present; *Religion* (339)

048 C **House**; 63344 US 31; French Eclectic; c.1940; Workshop; *Architecture* (339)

049 C **House**; 61851 US 31; Minimal traditional; c.1940; Garage, shed; *Architecture* (339)

050 C **House**; 61430 US 31; Gable-front; c.1920; Garage; *Architecture* (339)

051 C **House**; 61313 US 31; California bungalow; c.1920; *Architecture* (339)

052 C **House**; 61259 US 31; Western bungalow; c.1920; Garage; *Architecture* (339)

053 C **House**; 60756 US 31; Gable-front/Neoclassical; 1939; Shed; *Architecture, Religion* (339)

054 C **House**; 2021 Jewell Ave.; Gable-front; c.1920; Garage; *Architecture* (339)

055 C **Rupel Family Cemetery**; 59449 Keria Tr.; c.1839-c.1861; *Exploration/Settlement, Religion* (598)

056 C **Farm**; 63760 US 31; Craftsman; c.1920; Chicken houses; *Agriculture, Architecture* (339)

Penn Township (75001-108)

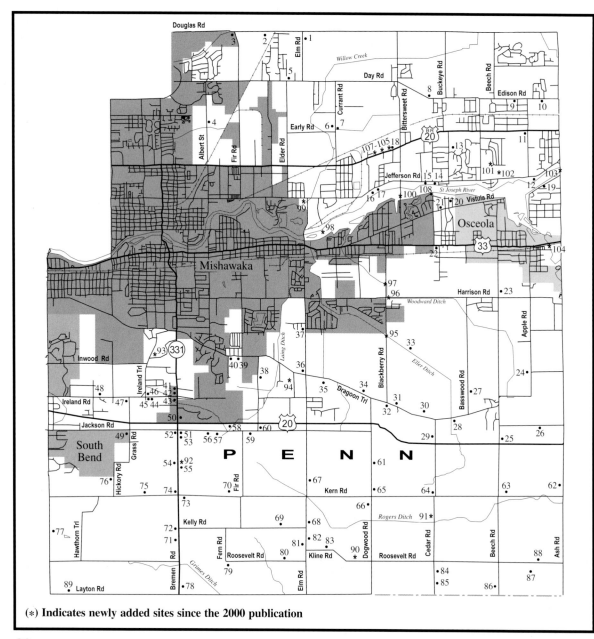

Penn Township was formed when the St. Joseph County Board divided the county into three townships in 1832. Subsequent subdivisions of Penn Township resulted in the creation of Harris and Madison Townships and parts of Clay, Centre, and Union Townships. Despite the large amount of land removed from Penn Township, it remained the largest township in the county. Its rich lands are among the most fertile in the county, with the St. Joseph River and the Twin Branch and Baugo streams flowing through its boundaries. Through drainage in the late-nineteenth century, the lowlands became tillable.

A unique industry grew from the cultivation of Penn Township's fertile swamp lands, particularly from the La Salle Swamp. It was found that these reclaimed lowlands were perfectly adapted to the cultivation of peppermint. The world's supply of high-grade peppermint oils and flavors eventually came from northern Indiana, southern Michigan, and Wayne County, New York, while the low-grade supply came from Japan. Outstanding farms in the township include the Alfred Curtis Farm (75024) and the Henry Crofoot Farm (75071).

Penn Township settlers came from New England and German communities in Pennsylvania and area farms reflect these different building traditions. The first settlements occurred early, when William and Timothy Moat arrived in 1828. Other early settlers include the Holt, Skinner, Cottrell, Bell, Huntsinger, Macy, Byrkit, Curtis, Ireland, West, Eutzler, Coe, Hollingshead, Edwards, McKnight, Chandler, Webster, and Parks families. The early settlers' public life was to a great extent concentrated near the towns of Mishawaka and Osceola. The city of Mishawaka has its own survey of historic sites and structures, *The City of Mishawaka Summary Report*, not included in this publication.

As in other townships, schools and churches were organized early and early religious congregations held services in school houses. The first school building was built in 1832, while the first church building was built in Mishawaka. The c.1880 Cook School (75032) and the 1926 Fulmer and Boner Schools (75054, 75064) attest to the township's educational heritage. A saw mill was built near Osceola in 1832, powered by the little stream of Baugo Creek. The Zelotes Bancroft family was intimately connected to the township's milling business until the early-1900s.

The Lake Shore Railroad and the Grand Trunk Railroad passed through Penn Township, as did the interurban line formerly known as the Indiana Railway.

PENN TOWNSHIP SCATTERED SITES (75001-108)

No. Rtg. Description

001 C **House**; 54230 Elm Rd.; Double-pen/Greek Revival; c.1880; Privy, shed; *Architecture* (597)

002 C **Farm**; 14504 Douglas Rd.; Hall-and-parlor; c.1880/1900; English barn; *Agriculture, Architecture* (597)

003 C **House**; 54125 Fir Rd.; Craftsman; c.1925; Livestock barn; *Agriculture, Architecture* (597) IN MISHAWAKA

004 C **House**; 55310 Filbert Rd.; American four-square; 1917; Grotto; *Architecture* (597)

005 C **House**; 14251 Day Rd.; Italianate Cube; c.1874/1900; *Architecture* (597)

006 C **House**; 55527 Currant Rd.; American four-square; c.1915; *Architecture* (597)

007 C **Farm**; 55570 Currant Rd.; Dormer-front bungalow/Craftsman; c.1925; Chicken house, transverse-frame barn; *Agriculture, Architecture* (597)

008 C **House**; 12046 Day Rd.; Gable-front; c.1860; Garage; *Architecture* (483)

009 O **Samuel Heiss/William Thornton House**; 10708 Edison Rd.; Italianate; 1875; *Architecture* (483) **LL**

010 C **Adam Smith House**; 10234 Edison Rd.; Greek Revival; 1856; *Architecture* (483)

011 C **House**; 55527 Apple Rd.; Colonial Revival; c.1915; *Architecture* (483)

012 N **Eugene Holycross House**; 10430 Jefferson Rd.; Tudor Revival; 1932/1938 (Eugene Holycross, Builder); Terraces; *Architecture, Landscape Architecture* (483)

013 C **Farm**; 55700 Birch Rd.; Greek Revival; c.1860/c.1900; English barn; *Agriculture, Architecture* (483) DEMOLISHED

014 N **Stone Piers**; 11980 E Jefferson Rd.; Rustic; c.1935; *Art* (483)

015 N **House**; 12104 E Jefferson Rd.; Italianate; c.1880; *Architecture* (483)

016 C **House**; 12810 E Jefferson Rd.; California bungalow/Craftsman; c.1920; Garage; *Architecture* (483)

017 C **House**; Jefferson Rd.; English cottage; c.1940; Garage; *Architecture* (483)

018 C **Gas Station**; 12661 McKinley Hwy.; House-with-canopy; c.1930; *Architecture, Transportation* (483) DEMOLISHED

019 C **House**; 10326 Vistula St.; Dutch Colonial Revival; c.1920; Shed; *Architecture* (483)

020 C **House**; 56555 Island Ave.; Colonial Revival; c.1925; *Architecture* (483)

021 N **Hannifal House**; 11891 Vistula Rd.; Italianate; 1860; *Architecture* (483)

022 C **House**; 11910 SR 933; Upright-and-wing; c.1890; Garage; *Architecture* (483)

023 C **John Wesley Leonard House**; 57900 Beech Rd.; Upright-and-wing; c.1868; *Architecture* (483)

75009 The Samuel Heiss/William Thornton House is a designated local landmark. The 1875 Italianate features a stone foundation, brick walls, round-arched windows with decorative heads, and an ornate brick frieze with cross-shaped openings.

75012 The Eugene Holycross House incorporates local cobblestone as a building material. Eugene Holycross built the main part of the house in 1932 and added the west wing in 1938. The property includes a designed landscape with terraces of cobbled retaining walls leading to the St. Joseph River.

024 O **Alfred Curtis Farm**; 59101 Apple Rd.; Lazy-T/Italianate; c.1875; English barn, shed; *Agriculture, Architecture* (483) **LL**

025 N **Eby Farm**; 60290 Beech Rd.; Dormer-front bungalow/Craftsman; 1928; Bank/basement barn, chicken house, transverse-frame barn, sheds; *Agriculture, Architecture* (656)

026 C **Barn**; 10390 Jackson Rd.; English barn; c.1890; *Agriculture, Architecture* (656)

027 C **Barn**; 59500 Basswood Rd.; English barn; c.1875/1910; Chicken house, chimney ruin, sheds; *Agriculture, Architecture* (483)

028 N **Farm**; 11652 Dragoon Tr.; American four-square; c.1920; *Architecture* (483)

029 N **Beers Farm**; 60049 Cedar Rd.; Italianate Cube; c.1870; Chicken house, granary; *Agriculture, Architecture* (656)

030 C **Barn**; 12097 Dragoon Tr.; Transverse-frame barn; c.1900/1915; Shed; *Agriculture, Architecture* (483)

031 N **Barn**; 12675 Dragoon Tr.; Sweitzer barn; c.1880; *Agriculture, Architecture* (483)

032 N **Cook School**; 12768 Dragoon Tr.; T-plan/Italianate; 1880; *Architecture, Education* (383)

033 N **Farm**; 58650 Blackberry Rd.; c. 1880/1900; Chicken house, granary, milk house, pumphouse, transverse-frame barn, shed, silos, windmill, workshop; *Agriculture, Architecture* (483)

034 C Barn; 13092 Dragoon Tr.; Sweitzer barn; c.1900; *Agriculture, Architecture* (483)

035 N Barn; 13826 Dragoon Tr.; Dairy barn; c.1920; *Agriculture, Architecture* (597)

036 O George Eutzler Farm; 14016 Dragoon Tr.; Italianate; c.1865; *Architecture* (597)

037 C House; 58513 Elm Rd.; Craftsman; c.1920; *Architecture* (597)

038 C House; 59150 Clover Rd.; Colonial Revival; c.1930; *Architecture* (597)

039 C House; 15038 Dragoon Tr.; California bungalow/Craftsman; c.1925; *Architecture* (597)

75021 This 1860 house exhibits characteristics of the Italianate style and is an example of the transition from the Greek Revival to the Italianate. Its broad, unbracketed cornice is typical of the Greek Revival style, but the tall, narrow windows with segmental-arched openings are hallmarks of the Italianate.

75024 This Italianate House dates to c.1875 and is part of the Alfred Curtis Farm. The house retains its original porch with scrolled brackets and scalloped applique lintel, and segmental-arched openings with keystones.

040 C House; 15174 Dragoon Tr.; American foursquare; c.1925; *Architecture* (597)

041 C House; 59247 SR 331; Cape Cod; c.1939; Garages; *Architecture* (597)

042 C House; SR 331; Colonial Revival; c.1935; *Architecture* (597) DEMOLISHED

043 C House; 59375 SR 331; American foursquare; c.1915; *Architecture* (597) IN MISHAWAKA

044 C House; 16448 Ireland Rd.; Minimal tranditional; c.1950; Garage; *Architecture* (597)

045 C House; 16472 Ireland Rd.; English cottage; c.1950; *Architecture* (597)

046 C Eck House; 16471 Ireland Rd.; Minimal traditional; 1949; Garage; *Architecture* (597)

047 N Keil Farm; 59589 Grass Rd.; American foursquare; 1922; Chicken house, garage, granary, livestock barn, shed; *Agriculture, Architecture* (597)

048 C Frank Fries House; 17213 Ireland Rd.; Free Classic; 1908; Corncrib, sheds; *Architecture* (597)

049 N Barn; 59979 Grass Rd.; Bank/basement barn; c.1900; Spring house; *Agriculture, Architecture* (694) IN SOUTH BEND

050 C Farm; 59700 SR 331/Bremen Hwy.; Queen Anne; c.1904; Barn; *Agriculture, Architecture* (597) IN SOUTH BEND; Moved Apr. 2006

051 N Coalbush United Methodist Church; 15977 Jackson Rd.; Late-Gothic Revival; 1958; *Architecture, Religion* (694)

052 C House; SR 331; Gabled-ell; c.1890; Milkhouse, shed; *Architecture* (694)

053 N G.W. Minnick Farm; 60020 SR 331/Bremen Hwy.; Cross-plan; 1881; Bank/basement barn, garage, privy, shed; *Agriculture, Architecture* (694)

054 N Fulmer School; 60415 SR 331/Bremen Hwy.; Classical Revival; 1926; *Architecture, Education* (694)

055 C Williard Crofoot Farm; 60500 SR 331/Bremen Hwy.; Free Classic; 1901; Bank/basement barn, pumphouse; *Agriculture, Architecture* (694) **LL**

056 N Weiss Farm; 15455 Jackson Rd.; Free Classic; 1902; English barn, transverse-frame barn; *Agriculture, Architecture* (694)

057 N Farm; 15300 Jackson Rd.; California bungalow/Craftsman; c.1920; Bank/basement barn, privy, pumphouse, sheds; *Agriculture, Architecture* (694)

058 C Jacob Lindenman Farm; 15201 Jackson Rd.; Upright-and-wing; 1873; Bank/basement barn; *Agriculture, Architecture* (694)

75036 The George Eutzler House dates to c.1865. The Italianate house is very similar to the Beers House (75029) and retains segmental-arched openings with ornate hoods, a wide frieze emphasized by scrolled brackets, and a bay window on the east side.

75054 Fulmer School was built in the Classical Revival style in 1926 and features an oversized fan light above the entry. The former school has been adaptively reused as apartments.

059 C **Barn**; 14890 Jackson Rd.; Bank/basement barn; 1885; Bank/basement barn; *Agriculture, Architecture* (694)

060 C **Barn**; 14733 Jackson Rd.; Livestock barn; c.1915; Milkhouse, silo, windmill; *Agriculture, Architecture* (694)

061 C **Barn**; 60550 Dogwood Rd.; Gothic arch barn; c.1920; *Agriculture, Architecture* (656)

062 N **Eby Farm**; 60901 Ash Rd.; Italianate; c.1880; English barn, shed; *Agriculture, Architecture* (656)

063 C **Eby House**; 10965 Kern Rd.; Lazy-T/Italianate; 1898; *Architecture* (656)

064 N **Boner School**; 11997 Kern Rd.; Classical Revival; 1926 (Willard M. Ellwood, Architect; George Moyer, Builder); *Architecture, Education* (656)

065 C **Farm**; 60900 Dogwood Rd.; Craftsman; 1880 (barn)/c.1915 (house); Bank/basement barn, silo, transverse-frame barn; *Agriculture, Architecture* (656)

066 C **Farm**; 61619 Dogwood Rd.; American foursquare; c.1915; Chicken house, English barn, garage, privy, pumphouse, shed, transverse-frame barn; *Agriculture, Architecture* (656)

067 C **House**; 60750 Elm Rd.; Dormer-front bungalow/Craftsman; c.1920; Livestock barn; *Agriculture, Architecture* (694)

068 C **Barn**; 61412 Elm Rd.; Bank/basement barn; c.1900; *Agriculture, Architecture* (694)

069 C **Barn**; 14351 Kelly Rd.; English barn; c.1910; *Agriculture, Architecture* (694)

070 C **Barn**; 15251 Kern Rd.; Sweitzer barn; c.1880; Chicken house; *Agriculture, Architecture* (694)

071 O **Henry Crofoot Farm**; 60601 SR 331; Italianate; c.1875; Bank/basement barn; *Agriculture, Architecture* (694) **LL**

072 C **House**; 61495 SR 331; Gable-front; c.1915; *Architecture* (694)

073 C **Barn**; 61024 SR 331; Bank/basement barn; c.1895; Garage; *Agriculture, Architecture* (694)

074 C **Ferrisville Cemetery**; NW corner SR 331 & Kern Rd.; c.1830; *Exploration/Settlement, Landscape Architecture, Religion* (694)

075 N **Barn**; 16519 Kern Rd.; Bank/basement barn; c.1890; Milk house, shed, Sweitzer barn; *Agriculture, Architecture* (694)

076 N **Gerry Battles Farm**; 60649 Hickory Rd.; Gabled-ell/Stick Style; 1869; Garage, grain bin, Milk house, sheds, Sweitzer barn, windmill; *Agriculture, Architecture* (694) **LL**

077 N **Farm**; 61650 Ironwood Rd.; T-plan; c.1890; Bank/basement barn, silo, windmill; *Agriculture, Architecture* (694)

078 N **Barn**; SR 331; Livestock barn; c.1930; Silos; *Agriculture, Architecture* (694) DEMOLISHED

75062 The Eby Farm is home to this Italianate house that has segmental-arched openings with stone sills and stone shields as keystones.

75064 Architect Willard M. Ellwood designed Boner School, which was built by George Moyer in 1926. Like Fulmer School (75054), it has an oversized fanlight above the entry and has been adaptively reused as a residence.

079 C **House**; 15246 Roosevelt Rd.; American foursquare; c.1915; *Architecture* (694)

080 C **Farm**; 14283 Roosevelt Rd.; English cottage; c.1940; English barn; *Agriculture, Architecture* (694)

081 C **Farm**; 61701 Elm Rd.; Upright-and-wing; c.1880; English barn; *Agriculture, Architecture* (694)

082 N **Farm**; 61590 Elm Rd.; c.1925; Granary, pumphouse, silo, transverse-frame barn; *Agriculture, Architecture* (694)

083 N **Farm**; 13801 Kline Rd.; c.1900; Bank/basement barn, milkhouse; *Agriculture, Architecture* (694)

084 N **House**; 62150 Cedar Rd.; Cross-plan; c.1895; Summer kitchen; *Architecture* (656)

085 C **House**; 62350 Cedar Rd.; American foursquare; c.1915; *Architecture* (656)

086 N **Henry Hunsberger House**; 62401 Beech Rd.; Lazy-T/Italianate; 1889; *Architecture* (656)

087 N **Jacob Berkey House**; 10555 Roosevelt Rd.; Side-gabled/Italianate; 1882; *Architecture* (656)

088 C **Farm**; 10501 Roosevelt Rd.; T-plan; c.1880; English barn, grain bins, granary, sheds; *Agriculture, Architecture* (656)

089　C　**Farm**; 17749 Layton Rd.; T-plan; c.1880; Gothic arch barn, shed; *Agriculture, Architecture* (656)

090　C　**Tamarach Methodist Episcopal Church**; 13301 Roosevelt Rd.; Side-steeple; c.1880; *Architecture, Religion* (656)

091　N　**Farm**; 61301 Cedar Rd.; American four-square; c.1920; English barn, shed; *Agriculture, Architecture* (656)

092　C　**House**; 60406 SR 331; Cape Cod; c.1930; Garage; *Architecture* (694)

093　O　**Mishawaka Reservoir Caretaker's Residence**; 16581 Chandler Blvd.; Colonial Revival; 1938; *Architecture, Community Planning, Engineering* (597) **LL, NR**; MOVED 1994

094　C　**Eutzler-Hollingshead Cemetery**; Downey Ave.; c.1831-c.1961; *Exploration/Settlement, Religion* (597) **LL**

095　C　**St. Joseph Co. Bridge No. S554**; Blackberry Rd. over Eller Ditch; Concrete slab; 1929; *Engineering, Transportation* (483)

096　C　**St. Joseph Co. Bridge No. 91**; Harrison Rd. over Woodward Ditch; Concrete slab; 1925; *Engineering, Transportation* (483)

097　C　**St. Joseph Co. Bridge No. S553**; Blackberry Rd. over Woodward Ditch; Concrete slab; 1930; *Engineering, Transportation* (483)

75084 This cross-plan house dates to c.1895 and retains original clapboard siding.

75087 The 1882 Jacob Berkey House is a classic example of a late-nineteenth century upper-middle class farmhouse.

098　N　**Twin Branch Dam and Hydroelectric Plant**; 13840 Jefferson Rd.; Art Deco; 1903/c.1925; Sanderson & Porter, Engineers; Office, screen house, substations; *Architecture, Commerce, Engineering* (597) DEMOLISHED

099　C　**Willow Creek Methodist Church**; 14000 Jefferson Rd.; Late-Gothic Revival; 1955 (Alues D. O'Keefe, Architect; Walter Eldridge, Builder); Garage, parsonage; *Architecture, Religion* (597)

100　C　**St. Joseph Co. Bridge. No. 201**; Bittersweet Rd. over St. Joseph River; Concrete; 1954/2002; *Engineering, Transportation* (483)

101　C　**Pleasant Valley Cemetery**; Jefferson Rd.; c.1831-c.1999; *Exploration/Settlement, Religion* (483) **LL**

102　C　**Chapel Hill Memorial Gardens Cemetery**; 10776 McKinley Hwy.; 1949-Present; *Religion* (483)

75093 The Mishawaka Reservoir Caretaker's Residence dates to 1938 and was built in the Colonial Revival style. In 1994, it was moved from the nearby reservoir to its present location.

103　N　**St. Joseph Co. Bridge No. 216**; Ash Rd. over St. Joseph River; Concrete open spandrel arch; 1929; William B. Moore, Engineer; Rieth-Riley Construction Co. & Edward F. Smith Co., Contractors; *Engineering, Transportation* (483) **HAER**

104　C　**Lake Shore & Michigan Southern Railroad Baugo Creek Bridge**; Lake Shore & Michigan Southern Railroad over Baugo Creek; Steel plate girder; c.1900; *Engineering, Transportation* (483)

105　C　**House**; 12889 McKinley Hwy.; California bungalow; c.1920; Garage; *Architecture* (483)

106　C　**House**; 12975 McKinley Hwy.; Pyramidal-roof cottage; c.1920; Garage; *Architecture*

107　C　**House**; 12985 McKinley Hwy.; California bungalow; c.1920; Garage; *Architecture* (483) (483)

108　C　**Byrkit Cemetery**; Cedar Dr. & Riverview Dr.; c. 1830-c. 1988; Exploration/Settlement **LL**

75103 The St. Joseph County Bridge No. 216 is a notable example of a concrete arch bridge. Engineer William B. Moore designed the 1929 bridge.

Osceola Scattered Sites (76001-021)

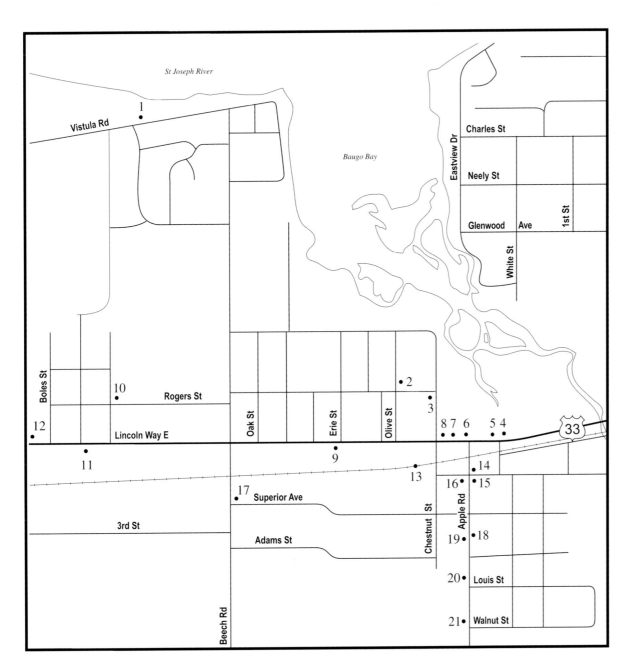

The town of Osceola is located in east-central Penn Townhip, south of the St. Joseph River, midway between Mishawaka and Elkhart.

Settlement began in the 1830s when the township was surveyed and two major routes, Vistula Road and Jefferson Road, opened. Vistula Road opened in 1832 and ran east-west from South Bend to Vistula (later Toledo), Ohio. In St. Joseph County, the road ran parallel to and south of the St. Joseph River. Jefferson Road opened in 1833 and followed the river on the north side, extending from Mishawaka to Elkhart. That same year, Osceola was divided into eight eighty-acre tracts to be sold.

Mill races were built to harness the water power of the St. Joseph River. Three are shown on the plat John A. Hendricks recorded in the Baugo Bay area. Hendricks was a prominent South Bend physician, politician, and businessman. Entrepreneurs, including early resident Zelote Bancroft, built saw mills along the races. However, the Baugo Bay area plat was voided in 1842 when growth occurred to its south.

Mid-century, the town's new location was further encouraged by the chartering of the Northern Indiana Railroad. East-west tracks were laid in 1851 through the present site of Osceola. The first depot was located at the southeast corner of Lincolnway East and Apple Roads. Finally, in 1856, William T. Thrall recorded Osceola's original plat and Milton Stokes surveyed the area. The plat occupied the core commercial area of present-day Osceola on either side of Lincolnway West, another major east-west route that was cut in 1856.

Osceola slowly grew with three more plats being recorded between 1856 and 1900. Zelote Bancroft, a nephew of Thrall's, recorded one of these and took over his father's saw mill. A grist mill was added later and the site also operated as a flour mill in 1875. Other major industries in

Osceola included maple syrup and sugar production, as well as farming. By 1885, the town boasted a general store, blacksmith shop, and post office.

The advent of the interurban railroad to Goshen via Osceola spurred the town's growth. A creamery, lumber company, garage, and coal business were among the town's start-up enterprises. Real estate development also increased between 1905 and 1924 as six new plats were recorded. In 1911, Osceola was officially incorporated and in 1915, the town received electrical service. The first road paved was in 1917, but the interurbans continued until the 1930s.

Osceola's housing stock largely reflects its rapid period of growth in the early-twentieth century. Among these is the Ivan & Irma Crull House (76003) and the Milo Hose House (76021). However, a handful of late-nineteenth century houses remain. One of the oldest homes is the c.1880 Bancroft House (76014). It is one of only a few Italianate-style houses remaining in town. The Wilber Crull House (76016) is an outstanding example of the Queen Anne style.

One of Osceola's most architecturally significant structures is the 1893 Osceola Methodist Church (76019), built by Henry A. Renner. The church began in 1851 as a circuit church pastored by Reverend Isaac Dean. The congregation constructed a church east of Osceola the same year, which was used until the new church was constructed. In 1956, the congregation moved again, selling the Gothic Revival structure. Other significant structures include the Harrison & Maude Moran House (76017), which has served as the town library since Mrs. Moran donated it in 1955, and the Bancroft Building (76005), which is one of only a few commercial buildings in town that retain original character (76005). In addition, a Craftsman-style depot stands as testament to the importance of rail transportation to Osceola (76013).

OSCEOLA SCATTERED SITES (76001-021)

No. Rtg. Description

001 N Frank Griffin Barn; 1212 Vistula Ave.; English barn; c.1870; *Agriculture, Architecture* (483)

002 C House; 202 Erie St.; Pyramidal-roof cottage; c.1940; Garage; *Architecture* (483)

003 N Ivan & Irma Crull House; 117 Olive St.; American foursquare; c.1925; Garage; *Architecture* (483)

004 C George Thrall House; 102 Lincolnway East (SR 933); American foursquare; c.1895; *Architecture* (483)

005 C Bancroft Building; 100 Lincolnway East (SR 933); Parapet-front; c.1851/1993; *Architecture, Commerce, Exploration/Settlement* (483)

006 C House; 200 Lincolnway East; Minimal traditional; c.1945; Garage; *Architecture* (483)

007 C Ray Long House; 214 Lincolnway East; Dormer-front bungalow/Craftsman; 1920; Garage; *Architecture* (483)

008 C John & Goldie Henderson House; 216 Lincolnway East; English cottage; c.1930; Garage; *Architecture* (483)

009 C Warren Eller House; 509 Lincolnway East; Dormer-front bungalow; 1901; Garage; *Architecture* (483)

010 C House; 1230 Rogers St.; English cottage; c.1930; Garage; *Architecture* (483)

011 C House; 1321 Lincolnway East; Western bungalow/Craftsman; c.1925; *Architecture* (483)

012 C Charles & Lucy Phelps Farm; 11481 Lincolnway East; T-plan; c.1895; English barn; *Agriculture, Architecture* (483)

013 N Lake Shore & Michigan Southern Railroad Depot; 350 W Washington St.; Craftsman; c.1900; *Architecture, Transportation* (483)

014 C Zelote Bancroft House; 118 Apple Rd.; Upright-and-wing/Italianate; c.1880; *Architecture* (483)

015 C Holden & Annette Doolittle House; 202 Apple Rd.; American foursquare; c.1900; *Architecture* (483)

016 O Wilber & Florence Crull House; 201 Apple Rd.; Queen Anne; 1903; *Architecture* (483)

017 N Harrison & Maude Moran House; 206 S. Beech Rd.; Dutch Colonial Revival; 1890; *Architecture* (483)

018 C House; 308 Apple Rd.; Greek Revival; c.1880; *Architecture* (483)

76003 The Ivan & Irma Crull House is a 1925 American foursquare that has overhanging eaves and a partially enclosed front porch.

76016 The Wilber Crull House dates to 1903 and is an outstanding example of the Queen Anne style. It retains its original, narrow clapboard siding and wood shingles, double-hung windows with projecting cornices, and a wood belt course demarking the first and second floors.

76017 **The Harrison & Maude Moran House** is an 1890 example of the Dutch Colonial Revival style. It features a gambrel roof with large, shed dormers on each side.

76021 **The Milo Hose House** is a 1910 American foursquare that features clapboard and wood shingle siding, a hipped dormer, and partially enclosed front porch.

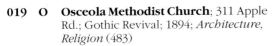

019 **O** **Osceola Methodist Church**; 311 Apple Rd.; Gothic Revival; 1894; *Architecture, Religion* (483)

020 **C** **Jacob Ocker House**; 409 Apple Rd.; Side-gabled; c.1880/1910; *Architecture* (483)

021 **N** **Milo Hose House**; 521 Apple Rd.; American foursquare; 1910; *Architecture* (483)

76019 **The Osceola Methodist Church** is an outstanding example of the Gothic Revival style applied to ecclesiastical architecture. Dating to 1894, it retains clapboard and decorative wood shingle siding, long, narrow windows with triangular heads, and a corner tower with a steep, pyramidal roof.

Madison Township (80001-106)

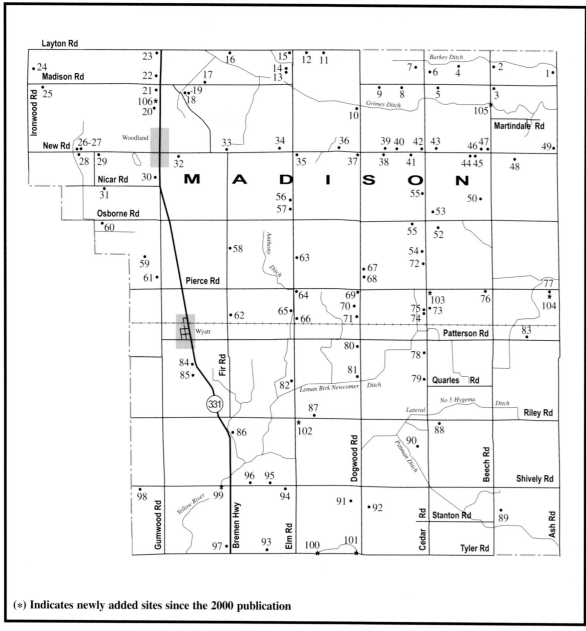

The St. Joseph County Board of Commissioners divided Penn Township in 1845 and the southern section became Madison Township. The land was heavily timbered, the soil was a strong clay, and there were many swamps and lowlands to discourage settlement. Because of this, Madison Township was settled later than other townships of St. Joseph County.

Eventually, hardy pioneers recognized the rich quality of the township's soil and they employed ditches to drain the land for tillage, resulting in valuable farmland. At the same time, sawmills converted timber into lumber, providing the settlers with a means of living while waiting for their land to become dry enough for the plow. Many of these settlers were from Pennsylvania and several Sweitzer barns in the township illustrate the Pennsylvania German influence (80006, 80025, 80051). Christian Helminger, along with Mr. Cline and Mr. Bennett, were the townships first settlers in 1840. Other settlers soon followed. The Bickell Log House is significant for its association to the settlement period, dating to c.1853 (80075).

Two small towns, Woodland in the northwest, and Wyatt in the south, developed in Madison Township. Woodland was the township's only town for most of the nineteenth century until Wyatt grew beside the Wabash Railroad, which was completed in 1893.

The township's first church building was of log construction and built in Woodland. It sheltered the Methodist congregation, who later built a more substantial structure at the same location. Other congregations who constructed churches in the township included the Evangelical Association and the United Brethrens. Extant churches include the St. Paul Lutheran Church (80032) and the Mt. Zion Methodist Church (80041).

(∗) **Indicates newly added sites since the 2000 publication**

Education was important to the wealthy farmers and lumberman of Madison Township and the township boasted the county's only rural high school for a time. The township retains a large number of historic schools compared to other parts of the county (80014, 80019, 80037, 80047).

Today, a number of farms attest to the importance of agriculture to the citizens of Madison Township. These include the Charles Geyer Farm (80074), the Enos & John Davihizar Farm (80077), and the Christian & Fredericka Eslinger Farm (80095).

MADISON TOWNSHIP SCATTERED SITES (80001-106)

No. Rtg. Description

001 C **House**; 62851 Ash Rd.; American foursquare; c.1910; *Architecture* (656)

002 C **John & Elizabeth Borhey Farm**; 62850 Beech Rd.; Greek Revival; 1867; Corn crib, English barn, garages, silo; *Agriculture, Architecture* (656)

003 N **Augustus Schalliol Farm**; 63012 Beech Rd.; Queen Anne; c.1914; English barn, shed; *Agriculture, Architecture* (656) **LL**

004 N **Farm**; 11501 Madison Rd.; Italianate; c.1870; Dairy barn, grain bins, sheds; *Agriculture, Architecture* (656)

005 C **Barn**; 11900 Madison Rd.; Sweitzer barn; c.1890; *Agriculture, Architecture* (656)

006 N **Farm**; 62840 Cedar Rd.; Italianate; c.1870; Sweitzer barn; *Agriculture, Architecture* (656)

007 C **Getz Farm**; 62801 Cedar Rd.; Gabled-ell; c.1890; Bank/basement barn, chicken house, Gothic arch barn; *Agriculture, Architecture* (656)

008 C **Emil Berger Farm**; 12470 Madison Rd.; American foursquare; 1936; Chicken house, corn crib, English barn, sheds; *Agriculture, Architecture* (656)

009 C **Roger Beehler Farm**; 12750 Madison Rd.; English cottage; c.1930; Garage, livestock barn, milk house, windmill; *Agriculture, Architecture* (656)

010 C **Harold Berger Farm**; 63363 Dogwood Rd.; Modern; c.1949; Ollie McDowell, Architect; Dairy barn, English barn, house, sweitzer barn; *Agriculture, Architecture* (656)

011 C **Farm**; 13700 Layton Rd.; Free Classic; c.1900; Granary; *Agriculture, Architecture* (694)

012 C **Farm**; 13898 Layton Rd.; American foursquare; c.1900; English barn; *Agriculture, Architecture* (694)

013 C **Farm**; 62751 Elm Rd.; Gabled-ell; c.1900; Chicken house, English barn, shed; *Agriculture, Architecture* (694)

014 C **School**; 62751 Elm Rd.; Single-pen; c.1900; *Architecture, Education* (694)

015 C **Monhout Farm**; 62535 Elm Rd.; American foursquare; c.1900; Garage, granary milk house, sheds, silo, Sweitzer barn; *Agriculture, Architecture* (694)

016 N **Derkson Farm**; 14990 Layton Rd.; American foursquare/Prairie; c.1926; English barn, garage, granary, machine shed; *Agriculture, Architecture* (694)

80003 The Augustus Schalliol Farm in Madison Township dates to c.1914 and is an example of the Queen Anne's style endurance into the 20th century. The house has stuccoed walls, a large turret, and original windows and doors.

80016 This c.1926 American foursquare house, a part of the Derkson Farm in Madison Township, has a Prairie-style influence. The brick house possesses a wrap-around porch and newer leaded-glass windows.

017 C **Laidig Farm**; 15262 Madison Rd.; Colonial Revival; c.1930; English barn, garages; *Agriculture, Architecture* (694)

018 C **Deitchley Farm**; 63200 Madison Tr.; Gabled-ell; c.1935/c.1952; English barn, garage, granary, machine shed; *Agriculture, Architecture* (694)

019 C **School**; 63200 Madison Tr.; Gable-front; c.1900; *Architecture, Education* (694)

020 C **Felton House**; 63397 SR 331; Colonial Revival; 1943; Garages; *Architecture* (694)

021 C **Charles Stuber Farm**; 63073 SR 331; Colonial Revival; 1946; English barn; *Agriculture, Architecture* (694)

022 C **Stuber House**; 62901 SR 331; Hall-and-parlor; c.1890; *Architecture* (694)

023 C **House**; 16014 Layton Rd.; American foursquare/Prairie; c.1926; Chicken house, garage, shed; *Agriculture, Architecture* (694)

024 C **Barn**; 62810 Ironwood Rd.; Sweitzer barn; c.1890; *Agriculture, Architecture* (694)

025 C **John Bartlett Farm**; 18800 Madison Rd.; Greek Revival; c.1860; Barns, English barn, sheds; *Agriculture, Architecture* (694)

026 C **House**; 17277 New Rd.; Dormer-front bungalow/Craftsman; c.1920; Chicken house, garage; *Architecture* (694)

027 C **House**; 17251 New Rd.; Tudor Revival; c.1940; *Architecture* (694)

80037 The 1889 Daugherty School is an example of vernacular Italianate architecture. The school served the community until a consolidated school was built in 1924. It was later converted to a residence.

028 **C** **House**; 17250 New Rd.; Colonial Revival; c.1930; *Architecture* (694)

029 **C** **House**; 16900 New Rd.; T-plan; c.1880/ c.1930; *Architecture* (694)

030 **C** **Mochel Farm**; 64299 Bremen Hwy.; Upright-and-wing; c.1880; English barn; *Agriculture, Architecture* (694)

031 **C** **Farm**; 16800 Nicar Rd.; Upright-and-wing; c.1900; Barn, pumphouse; *Agriculture, Architecture* (694)

032 **C** **St. Paul Lutheran Church Cemetery**; 15697 New Rd.; c.1845-present; *Exploration/Settlement, Religion* (694)

033 **N** **Jacob Kelley Farm**; 15049 New Rd.; Italianate; c.1883; English barns, garage, granary, silo, summer kitchen, transverse-frame barns; *Agriculture, Architecture* (694)

034 **C** **Phillip Beehler Farm**; 14205 New Rd.; American foursquare/Prairie; 1916; Grain bin, transverse-frame barns; *Agriculture, Architecture* (694)

035 **C** **Farm**; 13250 New Rd.; Gabled-ell; c.1900; Granary, English barn, silo; *Agriculture, Architecture* (698)

036 **C** **Fredericks Farm**; 13323 New Rd.; Upright-and-wing; c.1880/c.1910; Granary, English barn; *Agriculture, Architecture* (656)

037 **N** **Daugherty School**; 64015 Dogwood Rd.; Italianate; 1889; Barn; *Agriculture, Architecture, Education* (656)

038 **N** **James M. Culbertson/Schmeltz Farm**; 12698 New Rd.; T-plan/Italianate; c.1875; English barn, garage, machine shed, privy; *Agriculture, Architecture* (656)

039 **C** **Marker Farm**; 12667 New Rd.; T-plan; c.1893; English barn; *Agriculture, Architecture* (656)

040 **N** **Marker House**; 12499 New Rd.; Free Classic; c.1900; *Architecture* (656)

041 **N** **Mt. Zion Evangelical and Reformed Church & Parish**; 12298 New Rd.; Gothic Revival; 1868 (church), 1871 (parsonage); *Architecture, Religion* (656)

042 **C** **Rest Haven Cemetery**; New Rd.; c.1850-present; Wrought iron gate; *Exploration/Settlement, Religion* (656)

043 **C** **Barn**; 11899 New Rd.; Gothic arch barn; c.1930; Pumphouse; *Agriculture, Architecture* (656)

044 **N** **A.L. Horein Farm**; 11250 New Rd.; Bank/basement barn; 1936; *Agriculture, Architecture* (656)

80040 The c.1900 Marker House is a richly detailed example of the Free Classic style and has suffered few alterations. The frame house is topped by a complex pyramidal roof with gables having cornice returns. The side porch is supported by simple columns with dentilated trim.

80053 The Peter Beuhler House in Madison Township dates to c.1875 and is an example of Italianate architecture, featuring tall, narrow windows with segmental-arched tops.

045 **C** **House**; 11200 New Rd.; Double-pile; c.1850; Garage, summer kitchen; *Architecture* (656)

046 **N** **E.L. Meyers Farm**; 11105 New Rd.; American foursquare; 1914; English barn, privies, transverse-frame barn; *Agriculture, Architecture* (656)

047 **C** **School**; 63991 Beech Rd.; Italianate; c.1890; *Architecture, Education* (656)

048 **C** **Barn**; 10650 New Rd.; Bank/basement barn; c.1900; Silo; *Agriculture, Architecture* (656)

049 **C** **Barn**; 63895 Ash Rd.; Sweitzer barn; c.1890; *Agriculture, Architecture* (656)

050 **N** **Farm**; 64701 Beech Rd.; Italianate; c.1875; English barn, garage; *Agriculture, Architecture* (656)

051 **C** **Farm**; 11800 Osborne Rd.; Upright-and-wing; c.1850/c.1900; English barn; *Agriculture, Architecture* (656)

052 **C** **Farm**; 64900 Cedar Rd.; Gabled-ell; c.1900; English barn; *Agriculture, Architecture* (656)

053 **N** **Peter Beuhler Farm**; 64651 Cedar Rd.; Italianate; c.1875; Transverse-frame barn; *Agriculture, Architecture* (656)

054 N **Charles A. Fredericks Barn**; 65401 Cedar Rd.; Livestock barn; 1937; Barns, chicken houses, sheds, windmill; *Agriculture, Architecture* (656)

055 O **House**; 12300 Osborne Rd.; Cross-plan; c.1915; *Architecture* (656)

056 C **House**; 64673 Elm Rd.; Italianate; c.1890; Pumphouse; *Architecture* (694)

057 N **Farm**; 64777 Elm Rd.; T-plan; c.1900; English barn, garage pumphouse, shed, transverse-frame barn; *Agriculture, Architecture, Landscape Architecture* (694)

058 N **Barn**; 65450 Fir Rd.; English barn; c.1900; Silo; *Agriculture, Architecture* (694)

059 C **Barn**; 65551 Gumwood Rd.; Bank/basement barn; c.1900; *Agriculture, Architecture* (694)

060 N **Barn**; 16910 Osborne Rd.; English barn; c.1920; Pumphouse, wash house, workshop; *Agriculture, Architecture* (694)

061 N **Farm**; 65891 Gumwood Rd.; American foursquare; 1910; Garage, granary, silo; *Agriculture, Architecture* (694)

062 N **Farm**; 66390 Fir Rd.; English cottage; 1938; Bank/basement barn; *Agriculture, Architecture* (694)

063 N **House**; 65550 Elm Rd.; American foursquare; c.1915; *Architecture* (694)

80062 This 1938 English cottage has brick walls and round-arched windows and entry.

064 N **Farm**; 66048 Elm Rd.; Dairy barn; c.1940; Chicken house, garage, livestock barn, milk house, silo, transverse-frame barn; *Agriculture, Architecture* (694)

065 C **John A. & Margaret Lehman House**; 66251 Elm Rd.; Greek Revival; c.1850; *Architecture, Exploration/Settlement* (694)

066 N **Anthony & Barbara Albert House**; 66410 Elm Rd.; Italianate; c.1870; Livestock barn; *Agriculture, Architecture* (694)

067 C **Farm**; 65700 Dogwood Rd.; American foursquare; c.1930; Bank/basement barn; *Agriculture, Architecture* (656)

068 N **Farm**; 65760 Dogwood Rd.; Lazy-T/Italianate; 1888; Bank/basement barn; *Agriculture, Architecture* (656)

069 C **Commercial Building**; 66011 Dogwood Rd.; Parapet-front; c.1900; *Architecture, Commerce, Transportation* (656) DEMOLISHED

070 C **Barn**; 66201 Dogwood Rd.; Dairy barn; c.1920; Garages, granaries, shed, silo; *Agriculture, Architecture* (656)

071 N **Farm**; 66409 Dogwood Rd.; Italianate; c.1885/1880; Bank/basement barn, chicken house, corn crib, English barn, granary, pumphouse, sheds, summer kitchen; *Agriculture, Architecture, Landscape Architecture* (656)

072 C **Farm**; 65617 Cedar Rd.; T-plan; c.1890; *Architecture* (656)

073 C **Farm**; 66218 Cedar Rd.; Gable-front; c.1890; English barn; *Agriculture, Architecture* (656)

074 C **Charles Geyer Farm**; 66251 Cedar Rd.; T-plan; 1895 (Charles Geyer, Builder); Barn, English barn, shed, spring house, silo; *Agriculture, Architecture* (656) **LL**

075 N **George S. Bickell/Geyer Log House**; 66251 Cedar Rd.; Single-pen; c.1850; *Architecture, Exploration/Settlement* (656) **LL**

076 C **Farm**; 11192 Pierce Rd.; Greek Revival; c.1880/1920; Bank/basement barn; *Agriculture, Architecture* (656)

077 O **Enos L. and John Davidhizar Farm**; 10126 Pierce Rd.; American foursquare; 1918 (Enos L. Davidhizar, Builder); Bank/basement barn, barn, chicken house, house (upright-and-wing), silo; *Agriculture, Architecture, Landscape Architecture* (656)

078 N **Andrew J. Brenneman House**; 66963 Cedar Rd.; T-plan/Italianate; c.1890; *Architecture* (656) **LL**

079 C **John Weldy Farm**; 66301 Cedar Rd.; Double-pile; c.1875; Barn, English barn, house (gabled-ell), silo; *Agriculture, Architecture* (656)

080 N **House**; 66811 Dogwood Rd.; Dormer-front bungalow/Craftsman; 1920; *Architecture* (656)

80055 This outstanding example of a cross-plan house was constructed using rock-faced concrete blocks. The house has two porches, each with cast concrete columns and balustrades.

80066 The Anthony & Barbara Albert House in Madison Township has Italianate details, including segmental-arched window openings and a side porch with scrollwork, turned posts, and decorative brackets.

80068 Another example of the Italianate style in Madison Township, this house has a lazy-T plan and segmental-arched window openings.

081 N **R. Zeitwanger Barn**; 67301 Dogwood Rd.; Gothic arch barn; c.1930; *Agriculture, Architecture* (656)

082 N **House & Fox School**; 67399 Elm Rd.; T-plan (house), Gable-front (school); c.1880; *Architecture, Education* (694)

083 C **House**; 10501 Patterson Rd.; I-house; c.1880; *Architecture* (694)

084 C **House**; 67051 SR 331; Upright-and-wing; c.1880; *Architecture* (694)

085 N **House**; 67113 SR 331; Free Classic; 1914; *Architecture* (694)

086 N **Barn**; SR 331; Sweitzer barn; c.1910; *Agriculture, Architecture* (694)

087 N **Farm**; 13699 Riley Rd.; Western bungalow; c.1930; Barns, silo; *Agriculture, Architecture* (694)

088 N **Barn**; 11800 Riley Rd.; Bank/basement barn; c.1880; *Agriculture, Architecture* (656) DEMOLISHED

089 N **Oliver Pittman Farm**; 69416 Beech Rd.; American foursquare; c.1920; English barn; *Agriculture, Architecture* (444)

090 C **Barn**; 68501 Cedar Rd.; Bank/basement barn; 1881/1931; Silo; *Agriculture, Architecture* (656)

091 N **Zeiger Farm**; 69281 Dogwood Rd.; Gabled-ell; c.1880; Chicken house, English barn, granary, milk house, shed, silo; *Agriculture, Architecture* (444)

092 C **House**; 69290 Dogwood Rd.; American foursquare; 1910; *Architecutre* (444)

093 C **Garrie E. Manges Barn**; 14453 Tyler Rd.; Transverse-frame barn; 1940 (Garrie E. Manges, Builder); *Agriculture, Architecture* (065)

094 C **John Eslinger Farm**; 14116 Shively Rd.; T-plan; c.1890; Bank/basement barn, milk house; *Agriculture, Architecture* (065)

095 N **Christian & Fredericka Eslinger Farm**; 14433 Shively Rd.; T-plan; c.1880/1927; Bank/basement barn, chicken house, garages, milk houses, sheds; *Agriculture, Architecture* (065)

096 C **House**; 14665 Shively Rd.; Cross-plan/Tudor Revival; c.1890/1925; *Architecture* (065)

097 C **Farm**; 69989 Bremen Hwy.; T-plan; c.1890; Bank/basement barn, pumphouse; *Agriculture, Architecture* (065)

098 C **Farm**; 16350 Shively Rd.; Colonial Revival; c.1945; Gothic arch barn; *Agriculture, Architecture* (065)

80077 The Enos L. and John Davidhizar Farm in Madison Township is home to this grand 1918 American foursquare house. An outstanding example of the type, the house was begun in 1918 but not completed until the Depression. The farm is a Hoosier Homestead.

80080 This dormer-front bungalow is notable for its use of local cobblestone on its walls. It also features Craftsman-style elements such as the knee braces that support its overhanging eaves.

099 C **St. Joseph County Bridge No. 78**; Shively Rd. over Yellow River; Concrete slab; 1950; *Engineering, Transportation* (065)

100 C **St. Joseph County Bridge No. S531**; Tyler Rd. over Heinke Ditch; Concrete arch; 1940; *Engineering, Transportation* (065)

101 C **St. Joseph County Bridge No. 130**; Tyler Rd. over Heinke Ditch; Concrete arch; 1940; *Engineering, Transportation* (444)

102 C **Farm**; 68008 Elm Rd.; Gable-front; c.1870; Chicken house, English barn, garage, summer kitchen; *Agriculture, Architecture* (694)

103 C **Madison Union Chapel**; 66020 Cedar Rd.; Gable-front; 1906; *Architecture, Religion* (656)

104 C **John Davidhizar Farm**; 10128 Pierce Rd.; Upright-and-wing; c.1870; Bank/basement barn, chicken house, garage, milk house, windmill; *Agriculture, Architecture* (656)

105 C **St. Joseph County Bridge No. 52**; Beech Rd. over Grimes Ditch; Concrete slab; 1935; *Engineering, Transportation* (656)

106 C **William J. Felton House**; 63301 SR 331; American foursquare; 1927; Chicken house, pumphouse; *Architecture* (694)

Woodland Historic District (141-694-81001-027)

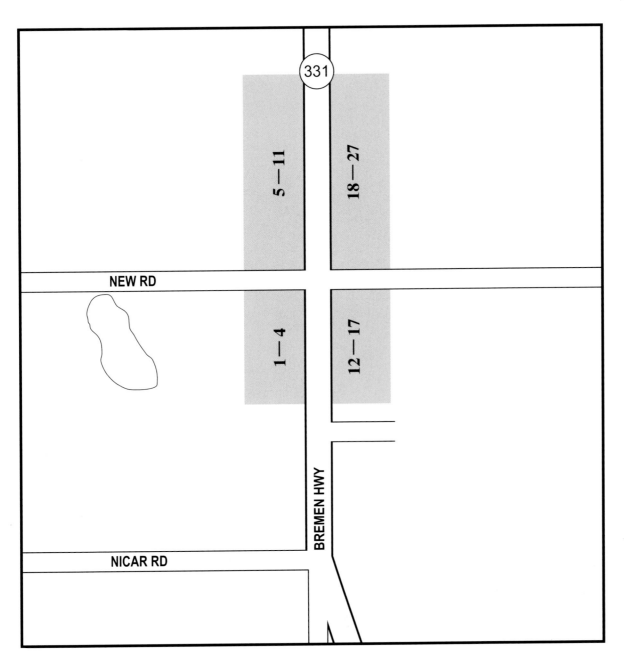

For most of the nineteenth century, Woodland was Madison Township's only town. Located in the northwest part of the township, Woodland Historic District encompasses the entire town of Woodland. Although never officially laid out as a town, Woodland was functioning as a small commercial center by 1855, at the corner of what is now New Road and Bremen Highway. At that time, Martin Rink and William Shenefield operated a store, Conrad Kelly a saloon, Philip Beehler a blacksmith shop, and Dr. Kettering a medical practice. A log church also existed on the east side of the highway.

Because Madison Township was marshy with vast hardwood forests, farming could not begin until the area had been drained and cleared. The ample wood supply was the catalyst for a number of enterprises. One such enterprise was opened by Fred Webber, a Wittenburg, Germany native, in 1870. His shop produced farm wagons and mud and snow sleds. Lang, Smith, and Company employed between four and twenty people and manufactured barrel staves. In addition, four or five sawmills operated in the area at various times. By 1874, there was a schoolhouse and post office with Webber serving as postmaster.

During the 1890s, Woodland lost commerce to the new town of Wyatt, which had been platted to the south along the Wabash Railroad. Despite this, Woodland continued to grow and in 1899 Adam and Agnes Mochel platted an addition to Woodland even though the original town had never been platted. Mochel's fifteen-lot plat was located on the east side of Bremen Highway south of New Road. During the first decade of the twentieth century, a creamery was in operation, Kelly's saloon was now the Kamm and Schellinger Brewery, and the Mochels took over and expanded Shenefield's store to also sell farm machinery (81006).

Woodland's extant architecture includes mostly vernacular structures constructed between 1860 and 1920. The collection is a good representation of a variety of vernacular types that were constructed in rural Midwestern towns. The Historic Preservation Commission of South Bend and St. Joseph County designated the 1882 Christopher Weigel House (81008) a local landmark, which is the only Italianate-style house remaining in Woodland.

WOODLAND HISTORIC DISTRICT (141-694-81001-027)

No.	Rtg.	Add.	Description

STATE ROAD 331 (*east side*)

001 C 64199 **Farm**; Double-pile; c.1860

002 C 64199 **Barn**; English barn; c.1920

003 NC 64199 **Barn**; Pole barn; c.1990

004 C 64009 **W.S. Building**; Parapet-front; c.1940

005 N 63991 **Madison Township District No. 5 School**; Craftsman; 1907

006 C 63927 **Commercial Building**; Parapet-front; c.1880 DEMOLISHED

007 NC 63921 **House**; Upright-and-wing; c.1900

008 N 63907 **Christopher Weigel Farm**; Italianate; 1882 (Christopher Weigel, Builder) **LL**

009 N 63907 **Christopher Weigel Barn**; Bank/basement barn; c.1880

010 NC 63751 **House**; Gable-front; c.1920

011 C 63695 **House**; Greek Revival; c.1860

012 N 64040 **House**; SR 331; Upright-and-wing; c.1870

013 NC 64126 **House**; Contemporary; c.1980

014 NC 64040 **House**; Massed ranch; c.1970

015 N 64058 **House**; Bungalow/Craftsman; c.1920

81005 The Madison Township District No. 5 School was built in 1907 in the Craftsman style. It has brick and stucco walls, a hipped roof, and multi-light windows.

016 C 64070 **House**; T-plan; c.1890

017 NC 64052 **House**; Dutch Colonial Revival; c.1900

018 C 63992 **Commercial Building**; Parapet-front; c.1920

019 NC 63982 **House**; Minimal traditional; c.1940

020 C 63942 **House**; Gabled-ell; c.1900

021 C 63924 **House**; Gabled-ell; c.1880

022 C 63912 **House**; Dormer-front bungalow; 1915

81008 The Christopher Weigel House is an 1882 example of the Italianate style. It has a square plan, shiplap siding, and a pyramidal roof with projecting cornice. The full porch has turned posts. It is a designated local landmark.

81012 This c.1870 upright-and-wing has six-over-six windows, a front porch with scrollwork, and an original paneled door.

023 N 63850 **St. John's Cemetery**; c.1895

024 C 63850 **St. John's United Church of Christ**; Gothic Revival; 1892

025 N 63822 **House**; Cross-plan; c.1885/1880

026 N 63800 **Barn**; English barn; c.1900

027 C 63800 **House**; T-plan; c.1880

81015 This bungalow exhibits Craftsman features, including knee braces beneath the overhanging eaves and tapered wood porch posts.

Wyatt Scattered Sites (82001-013)

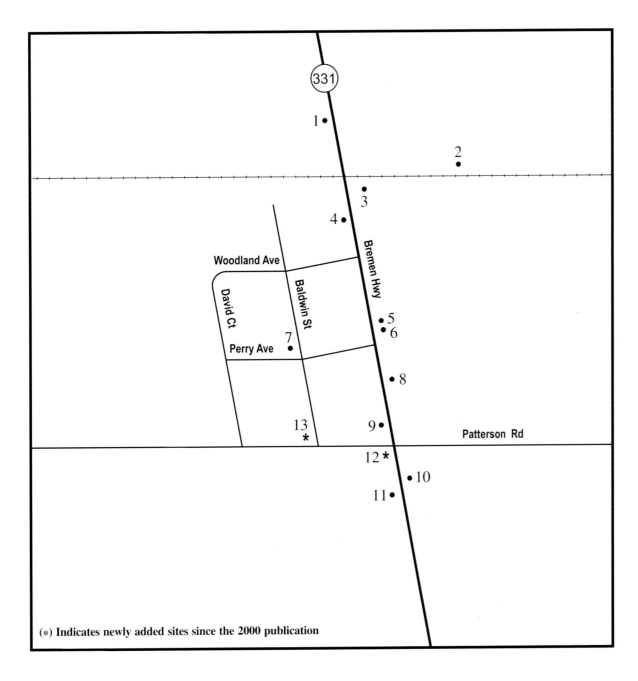

(∗) **Indicates newly added sites since the 2000 publication**

Wyatt is located in the west-central portion of Madison Township. Samuel Shearer was the first settler in what would become the town of Wyatt in 1851. By 1875, the Enders, Hetzel, and Berger families also lived in the area.

In 1893, the Wabash Railroad was completed through the area and Wyatt began to thrive. The new line extended from Cleveland and Toledo to Chicago and provided a means for farmers to ship their crops to new markets. That year, Daniel Goheen platted an area surveyed by W. E. Groves that was located north of the railroad and west of Bremen Highway. The following year, Jeremiah and Louisa Bechtel recorded the original plat of the town of Wyatt. During the next decade, three more plats were recorded. By 1900, the upstart town boasted 100 residents, some who had moved from nearby Woodland. Wyatt's primary occupations were timber, lumber, and agriculture.

Wyatt's built environment coincides with the railroad boom, having a number of twentieth-century bungalows (82004, 82007, 82009). The Wyatt Christian Church is the town's only extant church, which is a good example of a vernacular, small-town place of worship (82012).

WYATT SCATTERED SITES (82001-013)

No. Rtg. Description

001 N House; 66479 Bremen Hwy.; Tudor Revival; 1924; Garage; *Architecture* (694)

002 N Grain Elevator; 66500 Bremen Hwy.; 20th century functional; c.1950; *Agriculture, Architecture, Commerce* (694)

003 C Grain Elevator; 66500 Bremen Hwy.; 20th century functional; c.1910; *Agriculture, Architecture, Commerce* (694)

004 N House; 66547 Bremen Hwy.; Dormer-front bungalow/Craftsman; c.1920; *Architecture* (694)

005 C Commercial Building; 66650 Bremen Hwy.; 1-part commercial block; c.1940; *Architecture, Commerce* (694)

006 C House; 66666 Bremen Hwy.; Western bungalow; c.1925; *Architecture* (694)

007 N House; 15695 Perry Ave.; Western bungalow; c.1910; *Architecture* (694)

008 N Commercial Building; 66720 Bremen Hwy.; Parapet-front; c.1900; *Architecture, Commerce* (694)

82004 This dormer-front bungalow dates to c.1920 and possesses elements of the Craftsman style, including knee braces beneath overhanging eaves and a full-width integral porch with paired, square columns that slightly taper.

82008 Surviving framed commercial buildings are becoming more and more rare. This well-preserved and unaltered example has shiplap siding and a parapet wall.

009 C House; 66761 Bremen Hwy.; Dormer-front bungalow/Craftsman; c.1920; Garage; *Architecture* (694)

010 C House; 66828 Bremen Hwy.; Dormer-front bungalow/Craftsman; c.1920; Garage; *Architecture* (694)

011 C Commercial Building; 66841 Bremen Hwy.; 20th century functional; c.1940; *Architecture, Commerce* (694)

012 C Wyatt Christian Church; 66801 SR 331; Gable-front; c.1900; *Architecture, Religion* (694)

013 N House; 15697 Patterson Rd.; Bungalow/Craftsman; c.1920; Chicken house, wood shed; *Architecture* (694)

82001 This 1924 house is a modest example of the Tudor Revival style. It has brick walls, a steeply-pitched slate roof with cornice returns, and a recessed door behind a round-arched opening.

82007 This house in Wyatt is a notable example of a western bungalow. Western bungalows have hipped roofs, most often with dormers. This example has gabled dormers with cornice returns and an integral front porch.

Union Township (85001-102)

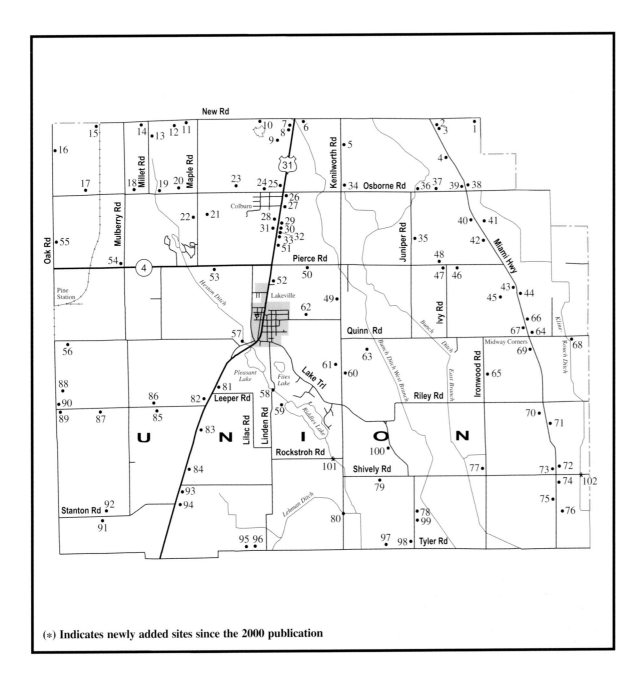

(∗) Indicates newly added sites since the 2000 publication

The St. Joseph County commissioners formed Union Township in 1837. The township consisted of heavily timbered clay and marsh lands, which were not favorable to pioneers. However, with drainage the land was well-suited to agricultural pursuits. Numerous small lakes dot the landscape, including Riddle's Lake and Pleasant Lake.

The first settlements in the township occurred near the Michigan Road. Elijah Lineback, John Henderson, John Gardner, and the Rector family arrived in 1833. Other early settlers included the Henderson, Moon, Annis, Hupp, Mills, Robertson, Hardy, Lamb, Glenn Heston, Riddle, Watson, Shively, Hughes, Morris, Nickelson, Whitinger, and Long families.

The village of Lakeville developed near the banks of Riddle's Lake. Initially dependent upon the Michigan Road, the town prospered after the coming of two railroads, the Vandalia and the Wabash. The wooden trestle over Heston Ditch is a reminder of the township's railroad heritage (85057).

The Methodist Episcopal Society, which organized in 1839, built the township's first church north of Lakeville in 1858. The Lakeville United Methodist Church is an outstanding example of the late-Gothic Revival style (85052). The first school was built in 1836 of log construction. The c.1902 Pleasant View School (85026) and the 1931 consolidated high school in Lakeville (86001) demonstrate the progress of public education in the township.

Extant resources significant to the township's early development include the c.1830 Union Cemetery (85004), the c.1853 Conrad Schafer Farm (85002), and the c.1863 Mangus Farm (85093). In addition, Union Township is home to an outstanding round barn, a rare resource in the state of Indiana (85078).

UNION TOWNSHIP SCATTERED SITES (85001-102)

No. Rtg. Description

001 C Farm; 18098 New Rd.; T-plan; c.1890; Barn, garage, granary; *Agriculture, Architecture* (694)

002 O Conrad Schafer Farm; 65154 Miami Rd.; Double-pile; 1853; Bank/basement barn, barn, garage, pumphouse, silo; *Agriculture, Architecture, Exploration/Settlement* (694)

003 C House; 64204 Miami Rd.; Free Classic; c.1916; Garage; *Architecture* (694)

004 C Union Cemetery; Miami Rd.; c.1830; *Exploration/Settlement, Landscape Architecture, Religion* (694)

005 C House; 64500 Kenilworth Rd.; Colonial Revival; 1939; *Architecture, Education* (339)

006 C Farm; 20390 New Rd.; Colonial Revival; c.1915; Bank/basement barn, pumphouse; *Agriculture, Architecture* (339)

007 C House; 64087 US 31; California bungalow; 1924; Garage; *Architecture* (339)

008 C House; 64109 US 31; 1 1/2 I-house; c.1890; *Architecture* (339)

009 N D.F. Bailey Barn; 64347 US 31; Transverse-frame barn; 1940 (Andrew S. Toth, Architect); Barn; *Agriculture, Architecture* (339)

85013 The William & Elnora Geyer House has a T-plan with Queen Anne embellishments, including cutaway corner bays and a side porch with turned posts, scroll work, and pendants.

85026 The Union Township District No. 2 School, also known as the Pleasant View School, has a T-plan with Romanesque Revival details, like the round-arched openings.

010 N Farm; 21140 New Rd.; I-house; c.1870; Bank/basement barn, English barn, livestock barn, privy, shed; *Agriculture, Architecture* (339)

011 C Barn; 22166 New Rd.; Bank/basement barn; c.1910; *Agriculture, Architecture* (339)

012 N Barn; 22300 New Rd.; Bank/basement barn; c.1910; Granary; *Agriculture, Architecture* (339)

013 N William & Elnora Geyer Farm; 64172 Mulberry Rd.; Queen Anne; 1885; Bank/basement barn, sheds, smokehouses; *Agriculture, Architecture* (339)

014 C Barn; 23100 New Rd.; Bank/basement barn; c.1900; *Agriculture, Architecture* (339)

015 C Farm; 23350 New Rd.; T-plan; c.1900; Bank/basement barn, barn, tenant house; *Agriculture, Architecture* (339)

016 C Barn; 64350 Oak Rd.; Bank/basement barn; c.1890; *Agriculture, Architecture* (339)

017 C House; 23597 Osborne Rd.; Colonial Revival; c.1910; *Architecture* (339)

018 C House; 22793 Osborne Rd.; Gable-front; c.1900; Barn, privy; *Agriculture, Architecture* (339)

019 C House; 22533 Osborne Rd.; Gabled-ell; c.1890; *Architecture* (339)

020 C House; 22261 Osborne Rd.; Greek Revival; c.1890; *Architecture* (339)

021 C Charles Schafer Farm; 65300 Maple Rd.; Free Classic; c.1902; Bank/basement barn, privy, shed; *Agriculture, Architecture* (339)

022 N Farm; 65345 Maple Rd.; Dormer-front bungalow/Craftsman; c.1920; Bank/basement barn, barn, garage; *Agriculture, Architecture* (339)

023 C House; 21447 Osborne Rd.; Upright-and-wing; c.1880; *Architecture* (339)

024 C House; 21099 Osborne Rd.; Free Classic; c.1905; Silo; *Agriculture, Architecture* (339)

025 C House; 64757 US 31; Western bungalow; c.1925; Garage; *Architecture* (339)

026 O Pleasant View/Union Township District No. 2 School; 65014 US 31; T-plan/Romanesque Revival; 1903; Windmill; *Architecture, Education* (339) **LL**

027 C House; 65204 US 31; Dormer-front bungalow/Craftsman; c.1920; Garage, shed; *Architecture* (339)

028 C House; 65351 US 31; English cottage; c.1945; *Architecture* (339)

029 C House; 65406 US 31; English cottage; c.1945; *Architecture* (339)

85051 This English cottage is believed to have been built by a returning war veteran c.1950. A notable example of an English cottage, it exhibits an extended side wall and steep roof slope.

030 C Lakeville Cemetery; US 31; c.1850; *Exploration/Settlement, Landscape Architecture, Religion* (339)

031 O Barn; 65465 US 31; English barn; c.1880; *Agriculture, Architecture* (339) DEMOLISHED

032 C Commercial Building; 65504 US 31; Parapet-front; 1946; *Architecture, Commerce* (339)

033 N Italianate; 65558 US 31; Italianate; c.1880; *Architecture* (339)

034 C House; 64910 Kenilworth Rd.; Free Classic cottage; c.1910; *Architecture* (339)

035 C Barn; 65582 Juniper Rd.; Bank/basement barn; c.1910; *Agriculture, Architecture* (694)

85052 Architect Kenneth Williams designed the 1959 Lakeville United Methodist Church, executed in the late-Gothic Revival style. A striking bell tower is topped by a spire and metal cross.

85053 This American foursquare is constructed from concrete blocks. It has a pyramidal roof and wrap-around porch that has been enclosed.

036 C Farm; 18901 Osborne Rd.; Midwest box; c.1905; English barn, garages, silo; *Agriculture, Architecture* (694)

037 N Farm; 18681 Osborne Rd.; T-plan; 1875; Gothic arch barn, shed, silos; *Agriculture, Architecture* (694)

038 C M.E. Zeiger Barn; 64955 Miami Rd.; Bank/basement barn; c.1915; *Agriculture, Architecture* (694)

039 C House; 64955 Miami Rd.; Gabled-ell; c.1875; Shed; *Architecture* (694) DEMOLISHED

040 C Barn; 65391 Miami Rd.; Bank/basement barn; c.1900; *Agriculture, Architecture* (694)

041 C Barn; 65434 Miami Rd.; Sweitzer barn; c.1880; *Agriculture, Architecture* (694)

042 N Barn; 65737 Miami Rd.; Bank/basement barn; c.1900; Chicken house, silos; *Agriculture, Architecture* (694)

043 C Farm; 66363 Miami Rd.; American foursquare; 1928; Bank/basement barn; *Agriculture, Architecture* (694)

044 C Barn; 66501 Miami Rd.; Bank/basement barn; c.1900; *Agriculture, Architecture* (694)

045 N Farm; 66523 Miami Rd.; Pyramidal roof cottage; c.1939; Bank/basement barn, chicken houses, milk house, shed; *Agriculture, Architecture* (694)

046 N John & Sophia Walz Farm; 18318 Pierce Rd.; Lazy-T; c.1880; Bank/basement barn, pumphouse; *Agriculture, Architecture* (694)

047 N Isaac Sells Farm; 18518 Pierce Rd.; Gabled-ell; c.1890; Privy, shed, Sweitzer barn; *Agriculture, Architecture* (694)

048 C Barn; 18601 Pierce Rd.; Sweitzer barn; c.1900; Silo; *Agriculture, Architecture* (694)

049 C House; 66447 Kenilworth Rd.; Gable-front; c.1915; *Architecture* (339)

050 N Americus & Sarah O. Bunch Farm; 20538 Pierce Rd.; Gabled-ell; 1881 (Americus Bunch, Builder); Bank/basement barn, granary, pumphouse, sheds; *Agriculture, Architecture* (339)

051 N House; 65676 US 31; English cottage; c.1950; Garage; *Architecture* (339)

052 O Lakeville United Methodist Church; 502 N Michigan St.; Late-Gothic Revival; 1959 (Kenneth Williams, Architect); *Architecture, Religion* (339) IN LAKEVILLE

053 N Farm; 21700 Pierce Rd.; American foursquare; c.1915; Garage, Gothic arch barn, summer kitchen; *Agriculture, Architecture* (339)

054 C Huggard Settlement Historical Marker; Pierce Rd. and Mulberry Rd.; 1998; *Agriculture, Ethnic Heritage* (339)

055 C Barn; 65620 Oak Rd.; Bank/basement barn; c.1904; *Agriculture, Architecture* (339)

85071 The John Seifer House dates to the late-19th century. The cross-plan house has two porches with turned posts, spindle work, and scrolled brackets.

85075 Robert Shafer designed the 1928 George Shafer House. The impressive Colonial Revival displays cornice returns and half-fanlights on the sides, and a front porch with tapered posts.

056 C **Barn**; 23850 Quinn Rd.; Bank/basement barn; c.1920; *Agriculture, Architecture* (339)

057 C **Terre Haute & Logansport Railroad Bridge**; Over Heston Ditch; Wood trestle; c.1900; *Engineering, Transportation* (339)

058 C **St. Joseph County Bridge No. 71**; Linden Rd. over Heston Creek; Concrete slab; 1935; *Engineering, Transportation* (339)

059 C **Farm**; 67998 Linden Rd.; Gabled-ell; 1894; Bank/basement barn, chicken house, milk house; *Agriculture, Architecture* (339)

060 C **House**; 67518 Kenilworth Rd.; T-plan; c.1890; Stone wall; *Architecture* (339)

061 C **Barn**; 67475 Kenilworth Rd.; Gothic arch barn; c.1945; *Agriculture, Architecture* (339)

062 C **Barn**; 20483 Patterson Rd.; Bank/basement barn; c.1930; Garage; *Agriculture, Architecture* (339)

063 C **Farm**; 19682 Quinn Rd.; Minimal traditional; c.1948; Chicken house, dairy barn, garage, milk house, pumphouse, shed

064 C **House**; 17251 Quinn Rd.; T-plan; c.1915; *Architecture* (694)

065 N **Farm**; 67450 Ironwood Rd.; T-plan; c.1900; Bank/basement barn, chicken house, pumphouse, shed, workshop; *Agriculture, Architecture* (694)

066 N **Barn**; 66690 Miami Rd.; Gothic arch barn; c.1925; Corn crib, sheds; *Agriculture, Architecture* (694)

067 N **Schrader Barn**; 66867 Miami Rd.; Bank/basement barn; c.1890; *Agriculture, Architecture* (694)

068 C **House**; 16718 Quinn Rd.; English cottage; c.1930; *Architecture* (694)

069 C **Barn**; 67191 Miami Rd.; Bank/basement barn; 1922; *Agriculture, Architecture* (694)

070 C **Barn**; 68105 Miami Rd.; Bank/basement barn; c.1920; Granary; *Agriculture, Architecture* (694) DEMOLISHED

071 N **John Seifer Farm**; 68286 Miami Rd.; Cross-plan; c.1890; Garage, shed; *Architecture* (694) **LL**

072 N **Farm**; 68906 Miami Rd.; American foursquare; c.1915; Bank/basement barn, garage; *Agriculture, Architecture* (065)

073 C **House**; 68937 Miami Rd.; English cottage; c.1948; Garage; *Architecture* (065)

074 N **Edward Seifer Farm**; 69062 Miami Rd.; Free Classic; c.1900; Bank/basement barn, garage, silo; *Agriculture, Architecture* (065)

075 N **George Shafer House**; 69351 Miami Rd.; Colonial Revival; 1928 (Robert Shafer, Architect); Garage, milk house; *Architecture* (065)

076 C **Farm**; 69488 Miami Rd.; Upright-and-wing; 1876; Dairy barn, garage, milk house, silo; *Agriculture, Architecture* (065)

077 N **Farm**; 68901 Ironwood Rd.; Cross-plan; c.1890; Bank/basement barn, barn, chicken house, garage, granary, milk house, privy, sheds, silo, summer kitchen; *Agriculture, Architecture* (065)

078 O **John & Susie Rouch Farm**; 69490 Juniper Rd.; American foursquare; c.1910; Garage, round barn; *Agriculture, Architecture* (065)

079 N **Barn**; 19528 Shively Rd.; Gothic arch bank/basement barn; c.1950; Silo; *Agriculture, Architecture* (065)

080 C **St. Joseph County Bridge No. S537**; Kenworth Rd. over Lehman Ditch; Concrete slab; 1958; *Engineering, Transportation* (342)

85078 The Rouch Round Barn has narrow vertical board siding with a belt course at the first ceiling line. The roof blends from round to slightly segmented at the peak. A round monitor with regularly spaced vents completes the barn.

081 C **House**; 67650 US 31; American foursquare; c.1915; *Architecture* (339)

082 C **Barn**; 67935 US 31; Bank/basement barn; c.1918; *Agriculture, Architecture* (339)

083 N **House**; 68294 US 31; Queen Anne; c.1895; Pool; *Architecture* (339)

084 C **Farm**; 68790 US 31; American foursquare; c.1900; Bank/basement barn, shed; *Agriculture, Architecture* (342)

085 C **House**; 22590 Riley Rd.; T-plan; c.1890; *Architecture* (339)

086 N **Jonathan Knepp Farm**; 22651 Riley Rd.; Italianate Cube; 1873; Barn, privy, pumphouse, sheds, Sweitzer barn, windmill; *Agriculture, Architecture* (339)

087 C **Barn**; 23338 Riley Rd.; Bank/basement barn; c.1920; *Agriculture, Architecture* (339)

088 C **Jacob & Sarah Smith Farm**; 23901 Riley Rd.; T-plan; c.1890; Bank/basement barn; *Agriculture, Architecture* (339)

089 C **Farm**; 23954 Riley Rd.; T-plan; c.1880; Bank/basement barn, summer kitchen; *Agriculture, Architecture* (339)

090 C **Dice Cemetery**; Riley Rd. & Oak Rd.; c.1850; *Exploration/Settlement, Religion* (339)

85079 This barn combines elements of English, bank, and Gothic arch barns to create a functional and attractive agricultural resource.

091 N Barn; 23408 Stanton Rd.; English barn; c.1935; Sears, Roebuck & Co. catalog barn; *Agriculture* (342)

092 C Farm; 23391 Stanton Rd.; Dormer-front bungalow; c.1935; Bank/basement barn, silo; *Agriculture, Architecture* (342)

093 C George Folk/Mangus Farm; 69084 US 31; Gabled-ell; 1863; Shed; *Agriculture, Architecture, Politics/Government* (342)

094 C High View Egg Farm; 69282 US 31; Colonial Revival; c.1925; Brooder house, chicken house; *Agriculture, Architecture* (342)

095 C Barn; 21421 Tyler Rd.; Sweitzer barn; c.1910; Corn crib, garage, pumphouse, wall; *Agriculture, Architecture* (342)

096 C Farm; 21151 Tyler Rd.; American foursquare; c.1905; Barn, garage, pumphouse; *Agriculture, Architecture* (342)

097 C House; 19467 Tyler Rd.; Gable-front; c.1900; Barn, garage, pumphouse; *Agriculture, Architecture* (065)

098 C Farm; 69891 Juniper Rd.; Free Classic; c.1910; Bank/basement barn; *Agriculture, Architecture* (065)

099 C House; 69682 Juniper Rd.; Upright-and-wing; c.1895; Summer kitchen; *Architecture* (065)

100 C Barn; 68645 Lake Tr.; Bank/basement barn; c.1900; Garage, hog house; *Agriculture, Architecture* (065)

101 C St. Joseph County Bridge No. 68; Rockstrah Rd. over Heston Creek; Concrete slab; 1950; *Engineering, Transportation* (342)

102 C St. Joseph County Bridge No. 77; Shively Rd. over Kline Ditch; Concrete slab; 1935; *Engineering, Transportation* (065)

Lakeville Scattered Sites (86001-021)

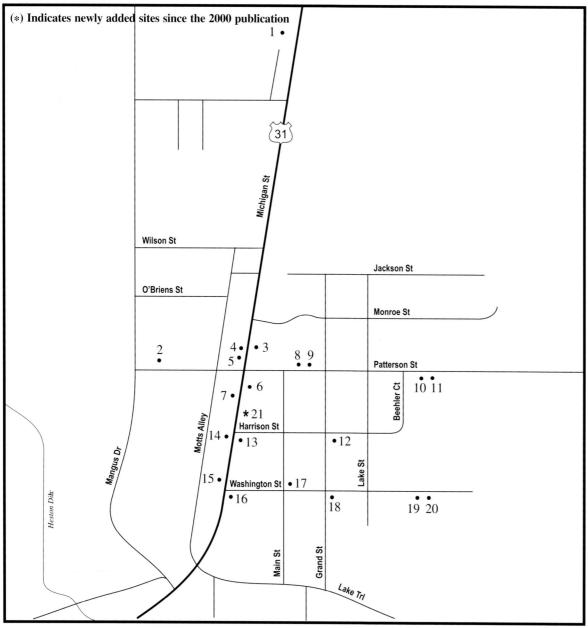

(∗) **Indicates newly added sites since the 2000 publication**

Situated along the former Michigan Road, Lakeville is located in the central part of Union Township. The town is named in honor of the small lakes that dot the area's landscape. Typical types of timber found in the area included walnut, ash, oak, hickory, and white trees.

One of Indiana's earliest over-land transportation routes, the Michigan Road, was built in 1830 and extended from Madison, Indiana to what is now Michigan City. Initially constructed with planks, the road was built on land secured from the Potawatomis in 1826. Lakeville served as a resting place for travelers along the road and early settlers included Elijah Linebach, Hubbard Henderson, John Moon, Michael Hupp, and Henry Hardy.

The first election was held in Lakeville in 1836, at which John Henderson and Jacob Rector were elected justices of the peace. Eleven years later, family members of South Bend founder Alexis Coquillard recorded a plat in the area and in 1859, Lakeville's original plat was recorded adjoining the Coquillard Addition.

Lumbering and milling became principal industries in the area and by 1880 there was a saw mill and gristmill. Other businesses included drug and hardware stores, a hotel, shoe shops, blacksmiths, and doctor's offices. The town also boasted two churches and a school.

Lakeville grew steadily, with two plats recorded in 1873 and another in 1893. The construction of two railroad lines contributed to Lakeville's development. The Vandalia extended from Logansport to South Bend, reaching Lakeville in 1884, and the Wabash Railroad ran from Cleveland and Toledo to Chicago, reaching Lakeville in 1893. Lakeville incorporated in 1902 with a population of 350.

Despite its early history, most of Lakeville's existing historic architecture dates to the early-twentieth century. One of the oldest surviving buildings is a c.1880 I-house (86002). Other buildings of note include the 1910 Lincoln & Sarah Fisher House (86009), which is sheathed in clay tile, and the 1931 Lakeville High School (86001), built in the Collegiate Gothic style.

LAKEVILLE SCATTERED SITES (86001-021)

No. Rtg. Description

001 O **Lakeville High School**; 601 N Michigan St.; Collegiate Gothic; 1931; *Architecture, Education* (339) **NR**

002 N **House**; 307 W Jefferson St.; I-house; c.1880; *Architecture* (339)

003 C **House**; 112 N Michigan St.; California bungalow; c.1920; *Architecture* (339)

004 N **House**; 109 N Michigan St.; American foursquare; 1910; *Architecture* (339)

005 C **House**; 103 N Michigan St.; 1 1/2 I-house; c.1910; Garage; *Architecture* (339)

006 C **Commercial Building**; 106 S Michigan St.; Parapet-front; 1950; *Architecture, Commerce* (339)

007 C **House**; 111 S Michigan St.; Upright-and-wing; c.1915; *Architecture* (339)

008 C **House**; 109 E Patterson St.; Dormer-front bungalow/Craftsman; c.1920; *Architecture* (339)

009 N **Annis/Fisher House**; 113 E Patterson St.; American foursquare; 1927; Garage; *Architecture* (339)

010 C **House**; 412 E Patterson St.; English cottage; c.1925; Garage; *Architecture* (339)

011 C **House**; 502 E Patterson St.; Western bungalow; c.1920; *Architecture* (339)

012 C **House**; 202 E Harrison St.; English cottage; c.1930; *Architecture* (339)

013 C **House**; 202 S Michigan St.; Gable-front; 1910; *Architecture* (339)

014 C **Commercial Building**; 201-203 S Michigan St.; 2-part commercial block; 1920; *Architecture, Commerce* (339)

015 C **House**; 221 S Michigan St.; T-plan; c.1900; *Architecture* (339)

016 C **Commercial Building**; 302 S Michigan St.; Art Moderne; 1939; *Architecture, Commerce, Transportation* (339)

017 C **Christian Church Rectory**; 109 W Washington St.; Free Classic; 1913; *Architecture, Religion* (339)

018 C **House**; 202 E Washington St.; Gable-front; c.1905; Garage; *Architecture* (339)

019 C **House**; 406 E Washington St.; Gable-front; c.1900; Garage; *Architecture* (339)

020 C **House**; 410 E Washington St.; Shotgun; c.1920; Privy; *Architecture* (339)

021 C **Lakeville Waterworks**; 118 S Michigan St.; 20th century functional; 1938 (John W. Toyne, Engineer; Works Progress Administration, Builder); *Architecture, Community Planning* (339)

86004 This 1910 American foursquare is constructed of rock-faced concrete blocks and features a full-width porch with three concrete block columns.

86010 This English cottage has wood shingle walls, a round-arched opening in the entry bay, original windows, and a mahogany paneled door.

Liberty Township (90001-068)

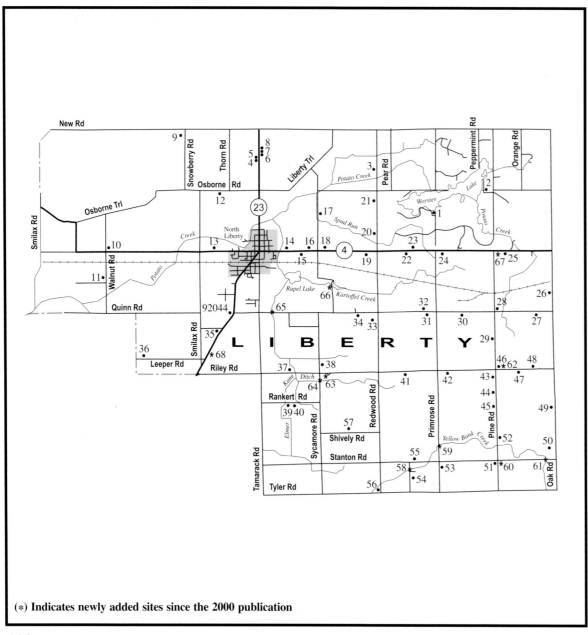

The St. Joseph County Commissioners formed Liberty Township in 1837. Located along the Kankakee River, the township largely consists of heavily-timbered lowlands. In addition, several small lakes have been reclaimed by drainage. The township's uplands are exceedingly fertile, with gravel and sandy soils found in some areas. Settlements were first made by John Kane, Isaac Townsend, and Jacob and John Earhart in 1833, near present-day North Liberty.

The town of North Liberty is located in the northwest portion of the township. Situated along the junction of two railroads, the Wabash and the Three I's, North Liberty prospered.

The Methodist Society built Liberty Township's first church in North Liberty in 1851. It was replaced in 1878. The first log-constructed school opened in 1838. It was followed by other schools as education in the township improved, including the 1868 high school in North Liberty. Today, only three one-room schools survive in the township (90010, 90028, 90051).

Outside North Liberty, Liberty Township's primary occupation was agriculture, as evidenced by its many historic farms. These include the Solomon Knepp (90011), Allen McEndarfer (90030), Paul Mangus (90032), Zachariah Sheneman (90044), and Opal & Louis Kranitz (90053) farms.

(*) **Indicates newly added sites since the 2000 publication**

LIBERTY TOWNSHIP SCATTERED SITES (90001-068)

No.	Rtg.	Description

001 C Barn; 25601 SR 4; Bank/basement barn; c.1900; *Agriculture, Architecture* (339)

002 C Porter Rea Cemetery; 25601 SR 4; c.1854-Present; *Ethnic Heritage, Exploration/Settlement, Religion* (339)

003 N House; 64701 Redwood Rd.; Dormer-front bungalow/Craftsman; c.1920; *Architecture* (468)

004 C House; 64509 SR 23; Cape Cod; c.1949; *Architecture* (468)

005 C House; 64489 SR 23; Cape Cod; c.1950; *Architecture* (468)

006 C House; 64428 SR 23; California bungalow; 1936; Garage; *Architecture* (468)

007 C House; 64416 SR 23; Bungalow/Craftsman; c.1925 (Adams, Builder); *Architecture* (468)

008 C House; 64406 SR 23; Bungalow/Craftsman; c.1925 (Adams, Builder); *Architecture* (468)

009 C Earl Eldred House; 64101 Snowberry Rd.; California bungalow/Craftsman; 1926; *Architecture* (468)

010 N Liberty Township District No. 11 School; 31491 SR 4; T-plan/Romanesque Revival; 1905; *Architecture, Education* (468)

90010 The Liberty Township District No. 11 School was built in 1905 of cast concrete blocks in the Romanesque Revival style. The school has been converted into a residence.

90011 The 1869 Solomon J. Knepp Farm is a notable example of the Italianate style, having a cornice with paired, scrolled brackets, segmental-arched window openings, and decorated porches. It is a designated local landmark.

011 N Rosebaugh/Solomon J. Knepp Farm; 66441 Walnut Rd.; Italianate; 1869; English barn, milk house; *Agriculture, Architecture* (468) **LL**

012 C House; 29700 Osborne Rd.; Upright-and-wing; c.1900; *Architecture* (468)

013 C Westlawn Cemetery; SR 4; c.1850; *Exploration/Settlement, Landscape Architecture, Religion* (468)

014 C House; 28543 SR 4; American foursquare; c.1910; *Architecture* (468)

015 C House; 28250 SR 4; English cottage; c.1950; *Architecture* (468)

016 C Barn; 28101 SR 4; English barn; 1909; Chicken house, shed; *Agriculture, Architecture* (468)

017 C Farm; 65336 Sycamore Rd.; T-plan; 1905; English barn, garage, granary, shed; *Agriculture, Architecture* (468)

018 N Farm; 27817 SR 4; Dormer-front bungalow/Craftsman; c.1920; English barn, garage; *Agriculture, Architecture* (468)

019 N Farm; 27118 SR 4; T-plan; c.1900; Barn, corn crib, summer kitchen, sheds; *Agriculture, Architecture* (468)

020 C House; 65733 Redwood Rd.; Gabled-ell; c.1900; Barn, garage; *Agriculture, Architecture* (468)

90018 This dormer-front bungalow in Liberty Township has narrow clapboard siding, original windows with carved surrounds, exposed rafter tails, and an integral concrete block porch with tripled square posts.

021 N Levi & Sarah W. Mangus House; 65150 Redwood Rd.; Italianate; 1878 (Levi Mangus, Builder); *Architecture* (468) **LL**

022 N Farm; 26568 SR 4; Italianate; c.1882; Bank/basement barn, granary; *Agriculture, Architecture* (468)

023 C Farm; 26419 SR 4; American foursquare; c.1910; Livestock barn; *Agriculture, Architecture* (468)

024 C Barn; 25838 SR 4; Sweitzer barn; c.1900; Garage, sheds; *Agriculture, Architecture* (339)

90019 This T-plan house retains original clapboard siding with cornerboards, a wrap-around porch with concrete block piers topped by round posts, and three paneled doors.

90021 Levi Mangus built his house in 1878 in the Italianate style. Situated into the side of a hill, the notable house is a designated local landmark.

025　C　**Farm**; 24800 SR 4; Double-pile; c.1850; Chicken houses; *Agriculture, Architecture* (339)

026　C　**House**; 66711 Oak Rd.; Upright-and-wing; c.1880; Shed; *Architecture* (339) DEMOLISHED

027　C　**Barn**; 24238 Quinn Rd.; Bank/basement barn; c.1920; Silo; *Agriculture, Architecture* (339)

028　N　**McEndarfer/Liberty Township District No. 7 School**; 66984 Pine Rd.; T-plan; 1901; *Architecture, Education* (339) **LL**

029　N　**Eli McEndarfer Barn**; 67521 Pine Rd.; Sweitzer barn; c.1870; *Agriculture, Architecture* (339)

030　O　**Allen McEndarfer Farm**; 25618 Quinn Rd.; Italianate; c.1850/1890; English barn, hall-and-parlor house; *Agriculture, Architecture, Exploration/Settlement* (339) **LL**

031　C　**Barn**; 26190 Quinn Rd.; Bank/basement barn; c.1910; *Agriculture, Architecture* (339)

032　O　**Paul Mangus Farm**; 26205 Quinn Rd.; Italianate; 1870; Bank/basement barn, garage, granary, log house, privy, pumphouse; *Agriculture, Architecture* (339)

033　C　**Farm**; 67117 Redwood Rd.; American foursquare; c.1903; Sweitzer barn; *Agriculture, Architecture* (468)

034　C　**Barn**; 27350 Quinn Rd.; Bank/basement barn; c.1920; *Agriculture* (483)

035　C　**House**; 67315 SR 23; c.1880; *Architecture* (468)

036　C　**Farm**; 30809 Leeper Rd.; Free Classic; c.1905; Garage, livestock barn; *Agriculture, Architecture* (468)

037　C　**Farm**; 28489 Riley Rd.; T-plan; c.1920; Bank/basement barn, chicken house, garages, granary; *Agriculture, Architecture* (468)

038　C　**House**; 67850 Sycamore Rd.; T-plan; c.1880; *Architecture* (468)

039　C　**House**; 28518 Rankert Rd.; American foursquare; c.1915; Privy; *Architecture* (658)

040　C　**Farm**; 28450 Rankert Rd.; American foursquare; c.1905; Livestock barn; *Agriculture, Architecture* (658)

041　N　**House**; 26520 Riley Rd.; T-plan; c.1895; *Architecture* (468)

042　C　**Farm**; 25800 Riley Rd.; T-plan; c.1897; Chicken house, garage, transverse-frame barn, shed; *Agriculture, Architecture* (339)

043　C　**House**; 68137 Pine Rd.; Gabled-ell; c.1880; Shed; *Architecture* (339)

044　O　**Zachariah & Sarah L. Sheneman Farm**; 68437 Pine Rd.; Lazy-T/Italianate; 1891; Barns, garage, milk house, privy, smoke house, summer kitchen, Sweitzer barn; *Agriculture, Architecture* (339) **LL**

045　N　**John Long House**; 68737 Pine Rd.; Double-pile/Greek Revival; c.1840; Pumphouse; *Architecture, Exploration/Settlement* (342)

90022 The Italianate style was obviously very popular in Liberty Township during the 1860s and 70s. This outstanding example has wide eaves with a boxed cornice and scrolled brackets. The segmental-arched window openings have stone shield-medallion keystones. The flanking side porches have square posts and decorative scrollwork.

90028 The T-plan Liberty Township District No. 7 School, also known as McEndarfer School, was built in 1901. After closing as a school, the building was later converted to a residence.

046　C　**St. John's Lutheran Cemetery**; 24955 Riley Rd.; c.1870-Present; *Exploration/ Settlement, Religion* (339)

047　N　**Farm**; 24550 Riley Rd.; Italianate; c.1870; English barn, garage, granary, pumphouse, sheds; *Agriculture, Architecture* (339)

048　N　**Farm**; 24319 Riley Rd.; Italianate; c.1875; Barns, chicken house, English barn, granary, milk house, sheds; *Agriculture, Architecture* (339)

90032 The 1870 Paul Mangus House is a framed example of the Italianate style that retains its original clapboard siding. It features a boxed cornice with scrolled brackets, front and side porches with turned posts and lattice work, and window openings with projecting cornices.

049 N Farm; 68651 Oak Rd.; Italianate; c.1880; English barn, summer kitchen; *Agriculture, Architecture* (342)

050 C Fair Cemetery; Oak Rd.; c.1860; *Exploration/Settlement, Religion* (342)

051 C Yellow Bank/Liberty Township District No. 5 School; Pine Rd.; Gable-front; 1883; *Architecture, Education* (342)

052 C Farm; 69150 Pine Rd.; Gabled-ell; c.1890; Bank/basement barn, tenant house, sheds, summer kitchen; *Agriculture, Architecture* (342)

053 C Opal & Louis Kranitz Farm; 69594 Primrose Rd.; Colonial Revival; c.1945; Dairy barn, garage, grain elevator, granary, milk house, sheds; *Agriculture, Architecture* (342)

054 C Ulrich J. & Metheny Burkholder House; 69750 Quinn Rd.; Italianate; 1880; *Architecture* (658)

055 C House; 26419 Stanton Rd.; Italianate; c.1880; Privy; *Architecture* (342)

056 C Farm; 27045 Tyler Rd.; Gable-front; c.1850; Chicken house, English barn, transverse-frame barn; *Agriculture, Architecture* (658)

057 C Farm; 27439 Shively Rd.; Gable-front; c.1880; Barns, chicken house, corn crib, garage, kennel, milk house, privy, pumphouse, transverse-frame barn, shed, summer kitchen; *Agriculture, Architecture* (658)

90041 This c.1895 T-plan house has a rubblestone foundation and retains a slate roof. Its rectangular window openings have rusticated stone sills and lintels.

90044 Another outstanding Italianate home in Liberty Township is the 1891 Zachariah & Sarah L. Sheneman Farm. At the time of the survey in 2000, the farm had been owned by just two families.

058 C St. Joseph County Bridge No. 129; Quince Rd. over Yellow Bank Creek; Concrete slab; 1915; *Engineering, Transportation* (658)

059 C St. Joseph County Bridge No. S506; Primrose Rd. over Yellow Bank Creek; Concrete slab; 1925; *Engineering, Transportation* (342)

060 C Pine Creek Church of the Brethren Historical Marker; Stanton Rd. and Pine Rd.; *Religion* (342)

061 C St. Joseph County Bridge No. S541; Stanton Rd. over Yellow Bank Creek; Concrete slab; 1925; *Engineering, Transportation* (342)

062 C St. John's Lutheran Church; 24955 Riley Rd.; Gable-front/Greek Revival; 1865/1936/1954; *Architecture, Exploration/Settlement, Religion* (339)

063 N Farm; 27828 Riley Rd.; 1 1/2 I-house; c.1850; Bank/basement barn; *Agriculture, Architecture, Exploration/Settlement* (468)

064 C St. Joseph County Bridge No. S546; Sycamore Rd. over Elmer Kane Ditch; Concrete arch; 1960; *Engineering, Transportation* (468)

90047 This notable Italiante house retains its original clapboard siding with cornerboards, rectangular window openings with carved surrounds and projecting cornices, and original paneled front door with double glazing.

065 C St. Joseph County Bridge No. 128; Quinn Rd. over Elmer Kane Ditch; Concrete arch; 1940; *Engineering, Transportation* (468)

066 C St. Joseph County Bridge No. S568; Rosewood Rd. over Kartoffel Creek; Concrete slab; 1940; *Engineering, Transportation* (468)

067 C Tabor Evangelical United Brethren Church; 66066 Pine Rd.; Gable-front; c.1880; *Architecture, Religion* (339)

068 C Farm; 67588 SR 23; Cross-plan; c.1890; English barn, shed, silo, stable, summer kitchen; *Agriculture, Architecture* (468)

90049 This brick Italianate house has wide, overhanging eaves with a plain, wide frieze, and segmental-arched window openings with medallions as keystones.

North Liberty Historic District (141-468-91001-019)

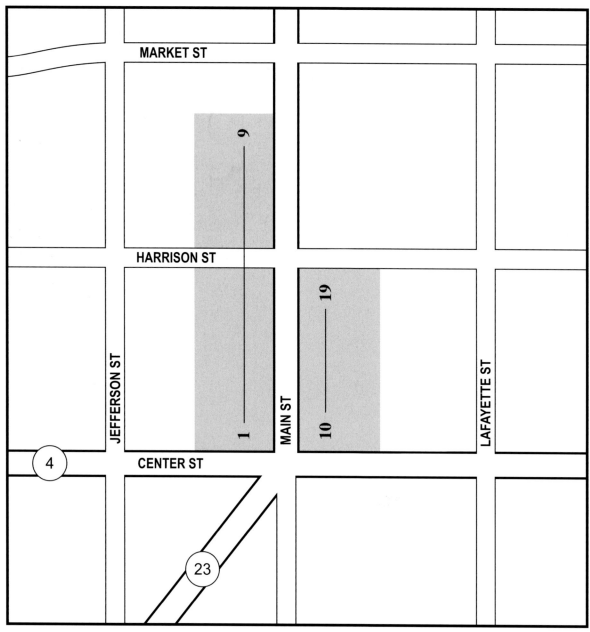

The North Liberty Historic District encompasses the downtown commercial district of the town of North Liberty. Platted in 1836 by Daniel and James Antrim, the town grew slowly until the 1890s, when two railroads arrived, bringing with them a time of economic prosperity.

The Wabash Railroad, which extended from Cleveland and Toledo, Ohio to Chicago reached North Liberty in 1893. The following year, the Indiana, Illinois, and Iowa reached North Liberty and the town incorporated. Situated at the junction of two railroads, the town prospered. Four plats were recorded in the 1890s, compared to only three during the previous fifty years. By the 1920s, North Liberty was bustling with a number of major industries and commercial firms.

Most of the historic structures in the North Liberty Historic District date to the town's boom of the 1890s. One of the most significant commercial buildings is the Hoffman Block building (91014). Built in the Italianate style, the Hoffman Block building served as a furniture store and an undertaker at the beginning of the century.

NORTH LIBERTY HISTORIC DISTRICT (141-468-91001-019)

No. Rtg. Add.   Description

NORTH MAIN STREET (*west side*)

001 C   101   **Commercial Building**; Art Moderne; c.1935

002 NC 103   **Commercial Building**; Contemporary; c.1970

003 NC 119   **Commercial Building**; 2-part commercial block; c.1890

004 N   125   **Commercial Building**; Italianate; c.1890

005 NC 127   **House**; Pyramidal-roof cottage; c.1920

006 C   129-131 **Pearse Block**; 2-part commercial block; 1913

91014-015 The Hoffman Block dates to c.1890 and exhibits Italianate elements such as a projecting cornice decorated with brackets and tall, narrow windows with decorated heads and stone sills.

91017 The North Liberty City Hall was built in 1915 and still houses governmental offices.

91004 This Italianate-style commercial building has a projecting pressed-metal cornice with brackets. Its window openings are accentuated by stone sills.

007 C   135   **Commercial Building**; 2-part commercial block; c.1900

008 C   137   **Commercial Building**; Italianate; c.1900

009 C   139   **Commercial Building**; Italianate; c.1890

NORTH MAIN STREET (*east side*)

010 C   100   **Commercial Building**; 2-part commercial block; c.1900

011 C   102   **Commercial Building**; 2-part commercial block; c.1900

012 C   104   **Commercial Building**; 2-part commercial block; c.1900

013 C   106   **Commercial Building**; 2-part commercial block; c.1900

014 N   108   **Hoffman Block**; Italianate; c.1890

015 N   110   **Hoffman Block**; Italianate; c.1890

016 N   114   **L.W. Pommert Building**; 2-part commercial block; 1920

017 N   120   **North Liberty City Hall**; 2-part commercial block; 1915

018 NC 124   **Commercial Building**; 1-part commercial block; 1990

019 C   202   **Commercial Building**; 1-part commercial block; 1911

North Liberty Scattered Sites (92001-047)

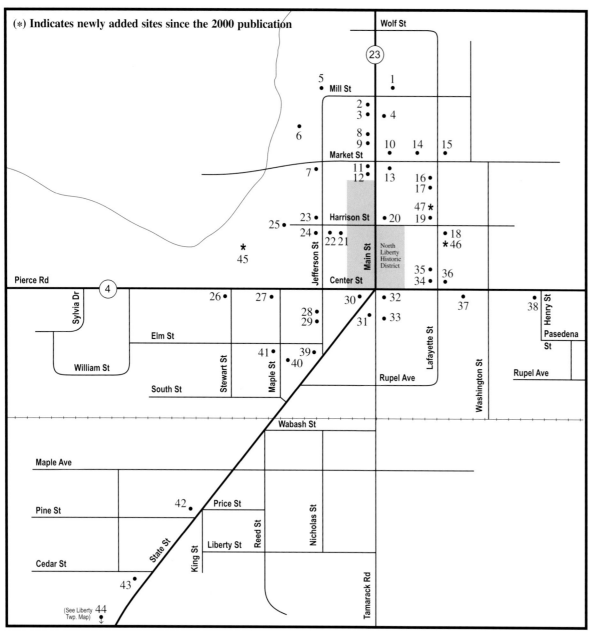

(∗) Indicates newly added sites since the 2000 publication

Wolf St

23

5
Mill St

1

2
3
8
9

4

6

10 14 15

Market St

7

11
12

13

16
17

47 ∗

25 23

Harrison St

20

19

24

18

∗ 46

22 21

North Liberty Historic District

45

Jefferson St

Main St

35
34

36

Pierce Rd

4

Center St

26

27

30

32

28
29

31

33

37

38

Henry St

Sylvia Dr

Elm St

Pasedena St

William St

41
39
40

Stewart St

Maple St

Rupel Ave

Lafayette St

Washington St

Rupel Ave

South St

Maple Ave

Wabash St

Pine St

42

Price St

Reed St

Nicholas St

Cedar St

43

State St

King St

Liberty St

(See Liberty Twp. Map)

44

Tamarack Rd

The town of North Liberty is located in the northwest portion of Liberty Township. Settlers John Kane, Isaac Townsend, and John and Jacob Earhart came to the area as early as 1833. The area was heavily forested, but other settlers followed, including Daniel Ross, F. Pearse, and Rheinhart Cripe. Early settlers were chiefly Pennsylvania Germans.

Daniel and James Antrim laid out North Liberty in 1836. Tyra Bray, an engineer and county surveyor, surveyed the town plat. Bray later became the St. Joseph County auditor. James Downey owned the first house in town and Daniel Antrim operated a store. Antrim's brother James built a grist mill and by 1837, there were four houses in town. That year an election was held and residents elected James Antrim as justice of the peace. Alonzo Hill and Hiram Bean built a saw mill in 1839; because the area was heavily timbered, clearing needed to be accomplished before the land could be farmed. Eventually there were five saw mills in Liberty Township and agriculture and lumbering were its primary occupations. Successful North Liberty merchants included the Houser brothers, the Cole brothers, Norman Miller, and House & Knepp.

Gowth was slow until the last decade of the nineteenth century. The Wabash Railroad, which extended from Cleveland and Toledo, Ohio to Chicago, reached North Liberty in 1893. The following year, the Indiana, Illinois, and Iowa Railroad reached North Liberty and the town incorporated. Situated at the junction of two railroads, the town prospered. Four plats were recorded in the 1890s, compared to only three during the previous fifty years. The town's first newspaper, the *North Liberty Herald*, began in 1892, followed by the *North Liberty News* in 1895 and the *North West Indianian* in 1903.

By the 1920s, North Liberty was bustling with a number of major industries and commercial firms, including the Pure Food Bakers, O'Conner Electrical Shop, North Liberty Lumber and Coal Company, and North Liberty Silo and Concrete Shop. Will Hass established the Lumber and Coal Company, which was operated by R. J. Holman. The company delivered seven trucks of lumber daily to South Bend. M. C. Clark was president of the Silo and Concrete Company, which manufactured building materials including silos and chimney and concrete blocks. In addition, there were five garages to service automobiles, four restaurants and ice cream parlors, a bank, and various other stores. Besides the two railroads, the South Bend-Bremen Motor Bus Company ran three buses daily through North Liberty.

Most of North Liberty's historic buildings date from the boom of the 1890s through the 1920s. One example is the 1911 late-Gothic Revival North Liberty Methodist Episcopal Church (92031). A later notable public building includes the 1936 North Liberty City Park, built by the Works Progress Administration (92006). Outstanding residences include the 1917 Dr. Fish House, a dormer-front bungalow with Craftsman details (92004), the 1928 Clem & Edna DeCoudres House, built in the Tudor Revival style (92010), and the 1903 Stephen & Grace Pearse House, which has Stick Style influences (92019).

NORTH LIBERTY SCATTERED SITES (92001-047)

No. Rtg. Description

001 N Dell Pearse House; 400 N Main St.; Double-pile/Colonial Revival; 1937; Garage; *Architecture* (468)

002 C House; 311 N Main St.; American foursquare; c.1910; Garage; *Architecture* (468)

003 C Heim House; 309 N Main St.; American foursquare; 1913; *Architecture* (468)

004 O Dr. Fish House; N Main St.; Dormer-front bungalow/Craftsman; 1917; *Architecture* (468)

005 N Daniel R. & Elizabeth T. McKenzie House; 109 W Mill St.; Italianate; c.1861; *Architecture* (468)

006 O North Liberty City Park; 309 N Jefferson St.; Rustic; 1936 (Works Progress Administration, Builder); Bathhouse, bridges, platform, stone entry markers, stone piers, stone steps, stone walks; *Architecture, Entertainment/Recreation, Landscape Architecture* (468)

007 C House; N Jefferson St.; L-plan; c.1890; Garage; *Architecture* (468)

008 C House; 305 N Main St.; English cottage; c.1940; Garage; *Architecture* (468)

009 C House; 303 N Main St.; Dormer-front bungalow/Colonial Revival; c.1920; Garage; *Architecture* (468)

010 O Clem & Edna DeCoudres House; 304 N Main St.; Tudor Revival; 1928; Garage; *Architecture* (468)

011 C Bill Haas House; 211 N Main St.; Dormer-front bungalow; c.1920; Garage; *Architecture* (468)

012 C House; 209 N Main St.; Italianate; c.1880; Garage; *Architecture* (468)

013 C George S. Collins House; 210 N Main St.; T-plan/Stick Style; 1893; Cottage; *Architecture* (468)

014 O Michael Becker House; 107 E Market St.; Upright-and-wing/Eastlake; 1894; *Architecture* (468)

92006 Features of the 1936 North Liberty Park were constructed by the Works Progress Administration, part of President Roosevelt's New Deal. The stone bath house pictured here is typical of the WPA's work.

015 C North Liberty Church of the Brethren; 201 E Market St.; Gothic Revival; c.1890; *Architecture, Religion* (468)

016 C Adams House; 207 N Lafayette St.; American foursquare; 1916; *Architecture* (468)

92004 The Dr. Fish House, as it appeared in 2000. The Craftsman-style dormer-front bungalow features a cobblestone porch and shed dormer.

92010 Clem DeCoudres was the editor of the *North Liberty Herald*. His Tudor Revival home, built between 1926 and 1928, replaced an earlier 1880s house.

121

017 C **House**; 205 N Lafayette St.; Colonial Revival; c.1920; *Architecture* (468)

018 C **House**; 112 N Lafayette St.; Side-gable bungalow/Craftsman; c.1915; *Architecture* (468)

019 O **Stephen & Grace H. Pearse House**; 201 N Lafayette St.; T-plan/Stick Style; 1903; Garage; *Architecture* (468)

020 N **House**; 101 E Harrison St.; American foursquare; c.1920; *Architecture* (468)

021 C **House**; 104 W Harrison St.; Gable-front/Craftsman; 1915; *Architecture* (468)

022 N **North Liberty Christian Church**; 110 W Harrison St.; Late-Gothic Revival; 1916; *Architecture, Religion* (468)

023 C **Charles Keck House**; 201 N Jefferson St.; Stick Style; c.1895; *Architecture* (468)

024 C **Britton Smith House**; 111 N Jefferson St.; Eastlake; 1898; *Architecture* (468)

025 C **House**; 206 W Harrison St.; Italianate; c.1880; *Architecture* (468)

026 C **House**; 101 S Stewart St.; Upright-and-wing; c.1880/1920; *Architecture* (468)

027 N **First Brethren Church**; 101 S Maple St.; Late-Gothic Revival; 1904; *Architecture, Religion* (468)

028 C **House**; 107 S Jefferson St.; Gable-front; c.1890; *Architecture* (468)

92014 The 1894 Michael W. Becker House is a well-preserved example of an upright-and-wing house having Eastlake ornamentation, including fishscale shingles on the gable ends and an intricate porch with turned posts.

92019 The Stephen Pearse House dates to 1903 and is an example of a T-plan house with Stick-style elements. Stephen Pearse and his father Wakefield operated a store in the Pearse Block (91006).

029 C **House**; 109 S Jefferson St.; T-plan; c.1890; *Architecture* (468)

030 N **John & Connie Hoffman House**; 101 State St.; American foursquare/Prairie; 1910; *Architecture* (468)

031 O **North Liberty Methodist Episcopal Church**; 100 State St.; Late-Gothic Revival; 1911; *Architecture, Religion* (468)

032 N **House**; 102 S Main St.; American foursquare; c.1915; *Architecture* (468)

033 C **House**; 106 S Main St.; Colonial Revival; c.1945; *Architecture* (468)

034 C **House**; 109 E Center St.; Stick Style; c.1890; *Architecture* (468)

035 N **Melvin & Vida Summers House**; 103 N Lafayette St.; Dormer-front bungalow/Craftsman; 1926; *Architecture* (468)

036 C **Henry & Maggie Worster House**; 201 E Center St.; Gabled-ell; 1892; *Architecture* (468)

037 C **House**; 208 E Center St.; T-plan; c.1895; *Architecture* (468)

038 C **Sam & Daisy Finch House**; 306 E Center St.; Lazy-T; c.1895; *Architecture* (468)

039 N **Levi Yonser House**; 201 S Jefferson St.; T-plan/Stick Style; 1890; *Architecture* (468)

040 C **House**; 202 S Maple St.; Gabled-ell; c.1890; *Architecture* (468)

041 N **Edwin Steele House**; 201 S Maple St.; T-plan; 1900; *Architecture* (468)

042 N **House**; 405 S State St.; Ranch; c.1945; *Architecture* (468)

043 C **House**; S State St.; Cape Cod; c.1945; Garage; *Architecture* (468)

044 C **Farm**; 811 S State St.; Dormer-front bungalow/Craftsman; c.1920; Livestock barn; *Agriculture, Architecture* (468)

045 C **Eastlawn Cemetery**; W Center St.; 1842-Present; *Exploration/Settlement, Religion* (468)

046 C **House**; 110 N Lafayette St.; Dutch Colonial Revival; c.1920; Workshop; *Architecture* (468)

047 C **House**; 203 N Lafayette St.; American foursquare; c.1920; Garage; *Architecture* (468)

92031 The 1911 North Liberty Methodist Episcopal Church replaced an earlier 1878 church located on the same site. Designed in the late-Gothic Revival style, the church has a fortress-like appearance thanks to its crenellated square towers.

Lincoln Township (95001-023)

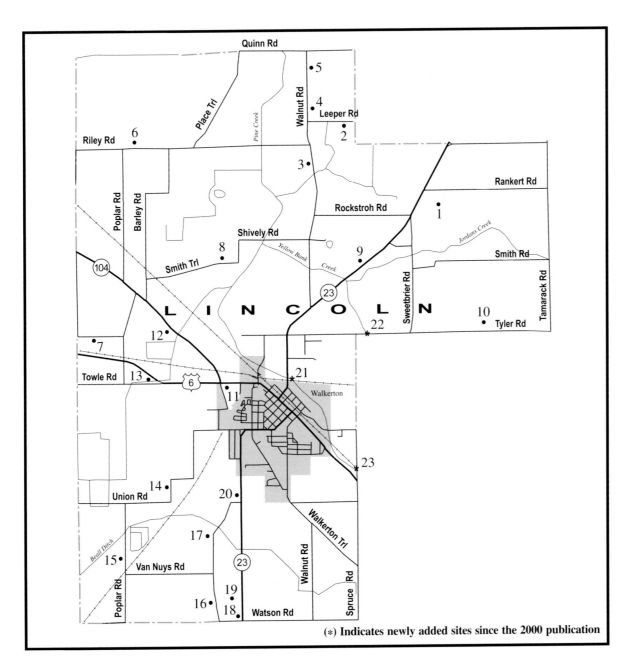

Lincoln Township was formed in 1866, when Liberty Township was divided. Like other parts of St. Joseph County, the lands of Lincoln Township became valuable for agricultural pursuits after being drained. The dredging and straightening of the Kankakee River and the construction of river drains through St. Joseph, LaPorte, and Starke Counties transformed rich, water-covered river bottoms into meadows and corn fields.

The first settlements in the area were made as early as 1835 when Christian Fulmer arrived. He was soon followed by other pioneers including Thomas Wiley, Philo Ruggles, Joshua Cole, Washington Fuson, Thomas Barton, Archibalk Goit, Samuel Lorens, Ebenezer Jones, Charles Havens, Morris Frost, and Charles and Jackson Usher.

Walkerton is the township's only town. The Methodist Episcopals, also known as the West York Mission Church, erected the township's first church in 1859. Other places of worship followed, including an 1870 Baptist church and an 1876 Catholic church. Presbyterian, United Brethren, and Seventh Day Adventist congregations also built churches in the township. The first school was built in 1858 about one mile from present-day Walkerton. It was removed to Walkerton in 1876.

Many of Lincoln Township's remaining historic structures date to the 1910s and 1920s. These include examples of American foursquares (95007), period revivals (95018), and Craftsman bungalows (95016).

LINCOLN TOWNSHIP SCATTERED SITES
(95001-023)

No. Rtg. Description

001 C Farm; 30240 Rankert Rd.; Greek Revival; 1869; English barn; *Agriculture, Architecture* (658)

002 C Barn; 30950 Leeper Rd.; Livestock barn; c.1930; Granary; *Agriculture, Architecture* (468)

003 C Farm; 68173 Walnut Rd.; Upright-and-wing; c.1880; Bank/basement barn, garage, Gothic arch barn, milk house, pumphouse, smoke house; *Agriculture, Architecture* (468)

004 C Farm; 67614 Walnut Rd.; Dormer-front bungalow/Craftsman; c.1925; Chicken house, garage, granaries, quonset barn; *Agriculture, Architecture* (468)

005 C House; 67208 Walnut Rd.; Cross-gable; c.1915; *Architecture* (468)

006 C Farm; 33427 Riley Rd.; Upright-and-wing; c.1920; Granary; *Agriculture, Architecture* (610)

95006 This granary in Lincoln Township is an interesting agricultural resource. Dating to about 1920, it has open, horizontal siding and a gabled "penthouse" with windows.

95011 North Woodlawn Cemetery contains burials dating from about 1870 and a memorial to those killed during World War II.

007 C Farm; 33800 Tyler Rd.; American foursquare; c.1915; English barn; *Agriculture, Architecture* (260)

008 C Farm; 32501 Smith Tr.; Upright-and-wing; c.1860; *Architecture* (658)

009 N Tree Nursery Office; 69241 SR 23; Craftsman; c.1930; *Architecture, Commerce* (658)

010 C Barn; 29995 Tyler Rd.; English barn; c.1920; Garage, transverse-frame barn, windmill, workshop; *Agriculture, Architecture* (658)

011 N North Woodlawn Cemetery; SR 6; c.1870; *Exploration/Settlement, Landscape Architecture, Religion* (658)

012 C House; 69990 SR 104; Craftsman; c.1930; *Architecture* (260)

013 C Commercial Building; US 6; Craftsman; c.1925; *Architecture, Commerce, Transportation* (260) DEMOLISHED

014 C Joseph Malstaff Barn; 71561 Timothy Tr.; English barn; 1924; Silo; *Agriculture, Architecture* (260)

015 C House; 72447 Poplar Rd.; California bungalow; c.1932; *Architecture* (260)

016 C House; 72863 Willow Trace; Western bungalow; c.1930; *Architecture* (658)

017 N Linnwood Farm; 72133 Willow Trace; English barn; 1885; Granaries, hog house, pumphouse, silos; *Agriculture, Architecture* (658)

95018 This 1933 Tudor Revival house is believed to be one of three built between St. Joseph County and Chicago by Sears as a demonstration house to showcase their product to visitors of the lake area.

018 N House; 72983 SR 23; Tudor Revival; 1933 (Sears, Roebuck & Co. catalog house); Garage; *Architecture* (658)

019 C Gjemre House; 72707 SR 23; International; c.1955; *Architecture* (658)

020 C Barn; 71707 SR 23; Bank/basement barn; c.1915; *Agriculture, Architecture* (658)

021 C Baltimore & Ohio Railroad Pine Creek Bridge; Over Pine Creek; Steel plate girder; c.1920; *Engineering, Transportation* (658)

022 C St. Joseph County Bridge No. 65; Tyler Road over Yellow Bank Creek; Steel plate girder; 1930; *Engineering, Transportation* (658)

023 C St. Joseph County Bridge No. 57; Spruce Road over Pine Creek; Steel plate girder; 1960; *Engineering, Transportation* (658)

95019 The Gjemre House is an excellent example of the International style applied to residential architecture. The interior features redwood ceilings.

Walkerton Historic District (141-658-96001-030)

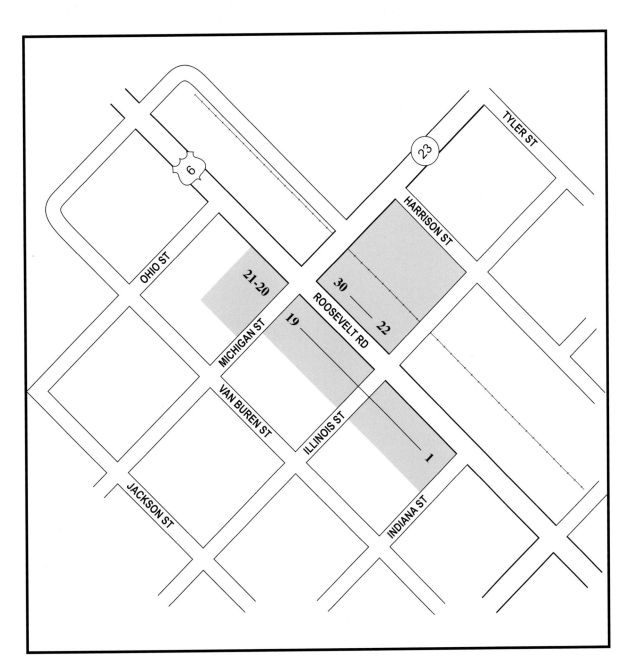

The Walkerton Historic District encompasses the downtown commercial district of Walkerton. Walkerton experienced rapid growth during the last half of the nineteenth century with the arrival of three rail lines. The first, the Indianapolis, Peru, and Chicago Railroad, was in place by 1854. It was followed in 1873 by the Baltimore and Ohio and the Indiana, Illinois, and Iowa in 1894. In addition to the railroad, John Miller established a stage coach route to South Bend in 1871.

Early commerce took place surrounding the railroad tracks. Some of the earliest businesses were located north of the railroad on Tyler and Harrison Streets, but over the years these businesses relocated to the south side of the tracks and Roosevelt Road became the main street.

Like many communities, Walkerton was plagued by fires, damaging or destroying downtown areas. The 600 block of Roosevelt Road experienced multiple fires in 1889 and 1891. The Queen Anne commercial building at 600 Roosevelt Road replaced Arlington's Drug Store, which was destroyed in an 1891 fire (96019). Likewise, the Endly Brady Block (96015) was the site of Tuttle's Barber Shop and Broden's Saloon before an 1891 fire. One of the few structures to survive the late-nineteenth century fires is the 1887 Rensberger Block, owned by Noah Rensberger who operated a general store there (96014).

WALKERTON HISTORIC DISTRICT (141-658-96001-030)

No. Rtg. Add. Description

ROOSEVELT ROAD (*west side*)

001 C 726 **Commercial Building**; Queen Anne; c.1890

002 N 724 **Commercial Building**; Italianate; c.1890

003 C 720 **Daniel Beall Building**; Italianate; c.1894

004 C 716-18 **Commercial Building**; Italian Renaissance Revival; c.1900

005 NC 714 **Masonic Lodge**; 2-part commercial block; c.1900

006 NC 712 **Commercial Building**; 1-part commercial block; c.1920

007 C 710 **Commercial Building**; Art Moderne; 1948

008 N 708 **Farmers State Bank**; Classical Revival; c.1915

009 N 706 **Commercial Building**; Queen Anne; c.1915

010 NC NA **Parking Lot**

011 NC 626 **Commercial Building**; Contemporary; c.1960

012 C 622 **Commercial Building**; Romanesque Revival; c.1890

013 NC 618 **Commercial Building**; 1-part commercial block; c.1980

014 O 614-16 **Rensberger Block**; Italianate; 1887

015 N 610-12 **Endly Brady Block**; Italianate/Queen Anne; 1891

016 C 608 **Commercial Building**; Italianate; 1892

017 C 606 **Commercial Building**; Italianate; c.1890

018 C 602-04 **Commercial Building**; Italianate; c.1890

019 C 600 **Commercial Building**; Italianate; 1891

020 C 510 **Commercial Building**; Classical Revival; 1915

021 C 508 **Commercial Building**; Parapet-front; c.1940

ROOSEVELT ROAD (*east side*)

022 C NA **Harold C. Urey Historical Marker**; c.1920

023 C 627 **Commercial Building**; 2-part commercial block; 1910

024 NC 623 **Vacant Lot**

96001 This commercial building dates to c.1890 and is an example of how the Queen Anne style was sometimes applied to commercial architecture. It features a projecting, rounded tower on the second story.

96002 Despite blocked-in windows on the second story, this commercial building is a notable example of the Italianate style. It features a storefront with an intact wood cornice, cast iron piers, and full-light display windows.

96008 The 1918 Farmers State Bank was built in the Classical Revival style and boasts terra cotta trim.

96009 This c.1915 commercial building carries a three-sided oriel window that projects from the second story.

96014 The 1887 Rensberger Block features segmental-arched window openings and a three-sided oriel window, a bracketed cornice, and decorative parapet showing the building's name.

96026 The 1890 Bose & Thompson Building exhibits a corbelled brick cornice, segmental-arched windows, and two storefronts, one of which is historically intact with cast iron columns, original entry, and full display windows.

025	C	619-21	Commercial Building; Italianate; c.1900
026	N	615-17	Bose & Thompson Building; Italianate; 1890
027	NC	611-13	Commercial Building; 2-part commercial block; c.1890
028	C	607-09	Commercial Building; 1-part commercial block; 1900
029	NC	605	Commercial Building; 1-part commercial block; c.1980
030	C	601-03	Commercial Building; 2-part commercial block; c.1905

96015 The 1891 Endly Brady block has both Italianate and Queen Anne characteristics. It possesses a bracketed cornice, two oriel windows on the second story with a segmental-arched window in between, and modern storefronts.

96020 This 1915 commercial building is nearly symmetrical, and possesses an unusual concrete block finish with a decorative oriel window.
Courtesy of Historic Preservation Commission of South Bend and St. Joseph County.

Walkerton Scattered Sites (97001-049)

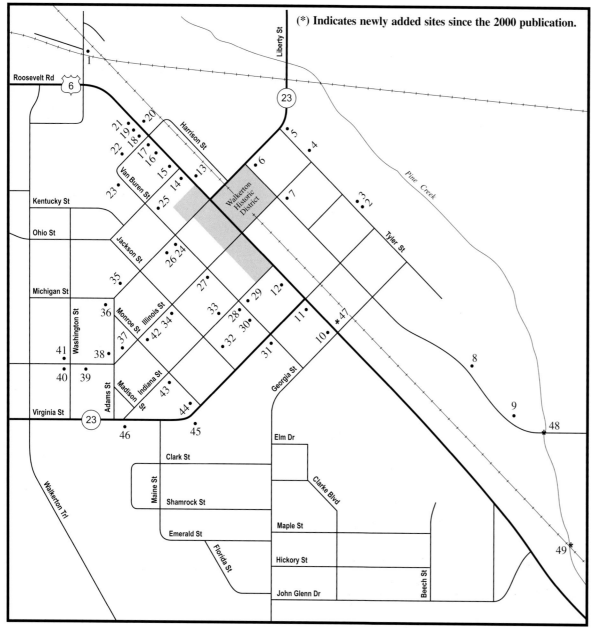

(*) Indicates newly added sites since the 2000 publication.

Walkerton is located in the southern portion of Lincoln Township and is the township's only town. Although settlement in the area began in the 1830s, Walkerton did not experience much growth until the arrival of the railroads mid-century. West Troy, which was later incorporated into Walkerton, was the earliest plat recorded in 1854 by Elias D. Jones. The plat shows the Indianapolis, Peru, and Chicago Railroad (later the Norfolk and Western), which extended southeast from Michigan City to Indianapolis. In 1873, the Baltimore and Ohio connected the area to the east, and in 1894, the Indiana, Illinois, and Iowa was laid out. In addition to the railroad lines, John Miller established a stage coach route to South Bend in 1871.

William C. Hannah recorded Walkerton's original plat in 1856. At its center was the depot grounds and tracks. The name of the town is believed to come from LaPorte resident John Walker, who promoted the first railroad. The perceived importance of the railroad is visible even in how the town was laid out. Instead of having streets that followed a north-south axis, Walkerton's original plat and several early additions were laid out in a northwest/southwest direction to follow the course of the railroad. Walkerton continued to grow and incorporated as a town in 1876. By the 1920s, Walkerton was the third largest municipality in St. Joseph County after South Bend and Mishawaka.

Agriculture and manufacturing became the primary occupations of Walkerton residents. By 1880, wheat was the number one crop. Later, marshlands around Walkerton were drained for fertile farmland. Cucumbers grown for pickles also became an important crop; the H.J. Heinz Company operated a salting station and pickle factory in Walkerton. In 1887, 70,000 bushels of pickles passed through the plant. At the turn of the twentieth century, two other crops, onions and peppermint, became prominent. The Walkerton and Koontz Lake area was unofficially known as the "Peppermint Capital of the World."

By the 1880s, Walkerton boasted a town hall, school, three churches, two railroad depots, two saloons, two hotels and restaurants, and about twenty other shops selling a variety of items. Henry Mintle operated the town's first newspaper, *The Walkerton Visitor*, between 1875 until 1886. James Endly established *The Republican* in 1879, which lasted until 1886 when he purchased *The Walkerton Visitor* for his son William to operate. They changed the paper's name to *the St. Joseph County Independent* and in 1919, consolidated with the *North Liberty News* to become the *Independent News*, which continues today.

After 1900, several factories and other industries provided employment opportunities in Walkerton. The Cut Glass Factory began in 1910 and employed about 100 skilled workers. In 1916, the C. R. Folsom Iron Works was established to build oil tanks. The Walkerton Ladder Works began in 1928, producing extension ladders. Other businesses included the Walkerton Lumber Company and the Walkerton Banking Company. The popularity of corn, oats, wheat, and rye in the 1930s and 40s led to the demise of mint and onion as important crops.

Most of Walkerton's existing historic structures date from the 1880s through the 1930s. One of the earliest buildings is the c.1875 Francis Gable House (97029). Walkerton retains a number of Queen Anne (97013, 97014, 97019, 97045), American foursquare (97004, 97009, 97016, 97020, 97036, 97041), and Craftsman bungalow (97021, 97031, 97037, 97044) houses. In addition, several outstanding churches attest to Walkerton's religious heritage. These include the c.1903 United Brethren in Christ Church (97024), the c.1904 First Presbyterian Church (97028), and the c.1937 United Methodist Church (97027).

WALKERTON SCATTERED SITES (97001-050)

No.	Rtg.	Description
001	C	**Baltimore & Ohio Railroad Interlocking Tower**; 303 Adams St.; Italianate; c.1880; *Architecture, Transportation* (658)
002	N	**St. Patrick School**; 811 Tyler St.; Art Moderne; 1956; *Architecture, Education* (658)
003	C	**St. Patrick Church**; 805 Tyler St.; Gothic Revival; c.1870; *Architecture, Religion* (658)
004	N	**House**; 609 Tyler St.; American foursquare; c.1930; *Architecture* (658)
005	C	**House**; 601 Tyler St.; Ranch; c.1945; *Architecture* (658)
006	C	**House**; 601 Harrison St.; American foursquare; c.1905; *Architecture* (658)
007	C	**House**; 701 Harrison St.; L-plan; c.1880; *Architecture* (658)
008	C	**House**; 1115 Harrison St.; Hall-and-parlor; c.1900; *Architecture* (658)
009	N	**House**; 1135 Harrison St.; American foursquare; c.1905; *Architecture* (658)
010	C	**House**; 908 Roosevelt Rd.; Upright-and-wing; c.1900; *Architecture* (658)
011	C	**House**; 900 Roosevelt Rd.; T-plan; c.1890; *Architecture* (658)
012	N	**House**; 806 Roosevelt Rd.; Queen Anne; c.1890; *Architecture* (658)

97014 This c.1900 Queen Anne house retains original clapboard siding, a combination hipped and gabled roof, and a wrap-around porch with brick piers supporting Ionic columns.

97018 This English cottage dates to the 1920s and features a steeply-pitched, cross-gabled roof, a segmental-arched entry, and diamond-paned windows.

No.	Rtg.	Description
013	N	**William A. Endly House**; 505 Roosevelt Rd.; Queen Anne; c.1890; *Architecture* (658)
014	O	**House**; 500 Roosevelt Rd.; Queen Anne; c.1900; *Architecture* (658)
015	C	**House**; 406 Roosevelt Rd.; American foursquare; c.1910; *Architecture* (658)
016	N	**Hudelmeyer House**; 402 Roosevelt Rd.; American foursquare; c.1910; *Architecture* (658)
017	C	**House**; 400 Roosevelt Rd.; Dormer-front bungalow/Craftsman; c.1920; *Architecture* (658)
018	N	**House**; 316 Roosevelt Rd.; English cottage; c.1925; *Architecture* (658)
019	N	**Furman Brady House**; 314 Roosevelt Rd.; Queen Anne; c.1890; *Architecture* (658)
020	N	**House**; 323 Roosevelt Rd.; American foursquare; c.1905; *Architecture* (658)
021	N	**House**; 312 Roosevelt Rd.; Dormer-front bungalow/Craftsman; c.1920; *Architecture* (658)
022	C	**House**; 407 Kentucky St.; Gabled-ell; c.1900; *Architecture* (658)
023	C	**House**; 404 Van Buren St.; L-plan; c.1890; *Architecture* (658)

97019 The c.1890 Furman Brady House is an example of the Queen Anne style. The T-plan house features a front-facing gable with cutaways and decorative embellishments.

97028 The First Presbyterian Church in Walkerton is an outstanding example of the late-Gothic Revival style. The L-plan church is constructed from rock-faced concrete block and has a corner tower with a steep, pyramidal roof. In addition, the church boasts pointed-arched openings with stained glass windows with stone trim.

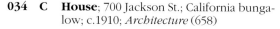

97029 The Francis Gable House dates to the 1870s and has a lazy-T plan. It exhibits a decorated boxed cornice and plain frieze, suggestive of the Greek Revival style.

024 O **United Brethren in Christ Church**; 600 Van Buren St.; Romanesque Revival; 1903 (W.H. Bost, Architect, Ernest Liebole, Builder); *Architecture, Religion* (658)

025 C **House**; 503 Michigan St.; American foursquare; c.1925; *Architecture* (658)

026 C **House**; 503 Van Buren St.; Upright-and-wing; 1905; *Architecture* (658)

027 O **Walkerton Methodist Church**; 702 Van Buren St.; Late-Gothic Revival; 1937 (LeRoy Bradley, Architect; Heim Construction Company, Builder); *Architecture, Religion* (658)

028 O **First Presbyterian Church**; 800 Van Buren St.; Late-Gothic Revival; 1904; *Architecture, Religion* (658)

029 O **Francis Gable House**; 413 Indiana St.; Lazy-T; c.1875; *Architecture* (658)

030 C **House**; 804 Van Buren St.; American foursquare; c.1900; Garage; *Architecture* (658)

031 N **House**; 501 Virginia St.; Craftsman; c.1920; Garage; *Architecture* (658)

032 C **House**; 804 Jackson St.; 1 1/2 I-house; c.1880; *Architecture* (658)

033 C **House**; 504 Indiana St.; Dutch Colonial Revival; c.1915; *Architecture* (658)

034 C **House**; 700 Jackson St.; California bungalow; c.1910; *Architecture* (658)

035 C **House**; 604 Michigan St.; California bungalow/Craftsman; 1915; Garage; *Architecture* (658)

036 N **Herman Roseen House**; 600 Monroe St.; American foursquare; c.1913; *Architecture* (658)

037 N **Harley & Ida McKeeson House**; 702 Illinois St.; Dormer-front bungalow/Craftsman; 1921; Garage; *Architecture* (658)

038 N **John E. & Hannah McCarthy House**; 800 Illinois St.; Craftsman; 1920; Garage; *Architecture* (658)

039 C **House**; 807 Illinois St.; Dormer-front bungalow/Craftsman; c.1920; Garage; *Architecture* (658)

040 C **House**; 901 Illinois St.; Dormer-front bungalow/Craftsman; c.1920; *Architecture* (658)

041 N **House**; 900 Illinois St.; American foursquare; c.1910; Garage; *Architecture* (658)

042 C **House**; 701 Monroe St.; Prairie; c.1920; Garage; *Architecture* (658)

043 C **House**; 701 Indiana St.; Cross-plan/Stick Style; c.1895; Garage; *Architecture* (658)

044 N **Milo Slick House**; 804 Monroe St.; Dormer-front bungalow/Craftsman; 1916; *Architecture* (658)

045 N **House**; 701 Virginia St.; Queen Anne; c.1900; *Architecture* (658)

046 N **House**; 715 Virginia St.; T-plan; c.1900; *Architecture* (658)

047 C **Gas Station**; 909 Roosevelt Rd.; Contemporary; c.1960; *Architecture, Commerce, Transportation* (658)

048 C **St. Joseph County Bridge No. 185**; Underwood Rd. over Pine Creek; T-beam; 1925; *Engineering, Transportation* (658)

049 N **Lake Erie & Western Railroad Pine Creek Trestle**; Over Pine Creek; Wood trestle; c.1900; *Engineering, Transportation* (658)

Conclusion

Where to go for Help

The Inventory as a Tool

The Indiana Historic Sites and Structures Inventory can serve as a starting place for encouraging historic preservation in St. Joseph County. Individuals or organizations interested in nominating properties to the National Register of Historic Places can use the survey ratings as a guide in determining which properties should be nominated. Local governments and planning organizations can use the survey results as a planning tool, so that the county's unique cultural resources can be incorporated into long-range development planning. The survey can also awaken general awareness among citizens of the importance of protecting their heritage for the benefit of future generations.

Forming Community Groups

Although preservation efforts on the part of the private individual may at times be successful, a group of citizens acting together can often achieve their preservation objectives more effectively.

Neighborhood associations and preservation committees can work with local and state agencies to encourage projects beneficial to preservation. They can also initiate projects on their own to increase awareness and appreciation of historic and architectural resources. Such activities can include walking tours, publications, exhibitions, site markings, lectures and programs, and lobbying for preservation legislation. Coverage by local newspapers of preservation-related issues or events can also be a very effective means of increasing public awareness and support.

Legally incorporated, nonprofit organizations can become even more actively involved in the financial and technical aspects of preservation. Establishing such a group involves securing a charter, obtaining a 501(c)(3) Internal Revenue Service classification and defining an organizational structure. The group can then become directly involved with redevelopment through buying, marketing, and selling historic properties; establishing a revolving fund for making loans; seeking government or private grants; securing preservation covenants and facade easements; or actually restoring specific buildings. In many localities, existing organizations such as improvement associations or historical societies can conduct these programs.

Private Organizations

There are numerous organizations already in existence that can assist with specific projects or in setting up the kinds of organizations discussed above. Membership in some of the private organizations can provide a way to learn about publications and programs that are available.

Local Organizations

Historic Preservation Commission of South Bend & St. Joseph County

125 South Lafayette Boulevard
South Bend, Ind. 46601
(574) 235-9798
www.stjosephcountyindiana.com/sjchp/index.html

Established by the common councils of St. Joseph County and South Bend in 1973, the Historic Preservation Commission of South Bend & St. Joseph County identifies historically and architecturally significant sites, drafts preservation plans, and advises the county on preservation issues. Since inception over six thousand sites have been identified throughout the county by the organization.

Statewide Organizations

Historic Landmarks Foundation of Indiana

340 West Michigan Street
Indianapolis, Ind. 46202-3204
(317) 639-4534 or (800) 450-4534
www.historiclandmarks.org

Historic Landmarks Foundation of Indiana (HLFI) is a statewide, private, nonprofit, membership-supported organization established to promote the preservation and restoration of Indiana's architectural and historic heritage. HLFI sponsors several programs on a statewide basis. The Indiana Historic Sites and Structures Inventory (county surveys), a program administered by the Indiana Division of Historic Preservation & Archaeology (DHPA), is undertaken by the DHPA in cooperation with HLFI. A revolving loan fund assists local non-profit organizations in saving, protecting, and reselling significant properties. HLFI also accepts facade easements and other property donations and arranges for covenants to protect buildings from undesirable change or demolition. In addition, the Foundation publishes a newsletter, *Indiana Preservationist*, and maintains a library of preservation publications available to members of HLFI. Regional offices in South Bend, Gary, Wabash, Jeffersonville, Aurora, Evansville,

---

Opposite: The circa 1870 St. Patrick Church (97004) is designed in the Gothic Revival style. *Courtesy of Historic Preservation Commision of South Bend and St. Joseph County.*

Cambridge City, Terre Haute, and Indianapolis provide consulting services for its members and coordinate activities on a statewide basis.

Affiliate Council

Historic Landmarks Foundation of Indiana
340 West Michigan Street
Indianapolis, Ind. 46202-3204
(317) 639-4534 or (800) 450-4534
www.historiclandmarks.org

In 1978, Historic Landmarks Foundation of Indiana (HLFI) established an affiliate program to provide local preservation organizations around the state a close link with HLFI and each other. Historic Landmarks' affiliated organizations benefit from direct access to the professional expertise of Historic Landmarks' staff, priority for interest-free and low-interest loans from Historic Landmarks' statewide revolving fund, and supplemental funding assistance grants for organizational development. Each member of an affiliate group receives all of Historic Landmarks' publications. Through the Affiliate Council, composed of delegates from each affiliate organization, a forum facilitates the regular exchange of information and experience of Historic Landmarks' staff and affiliate members. The affiliates have also undertaken joint projects such as the sponsorship of annual statewide workshops.

Indiana Alliance of Historic District Commissions

402 West Washington Street
South Bend, Ind. 46601
(574) 232-4534
north@historiclandmarks.org
http://pages.prodigy.net/hlfinro/

The Indiana Alliance of Historic District Commissions began in 1984, and membership is open to historic district commissions, preservation non-profits, and individuals. The Alliance sponsors regional workshops dealing with common problems of historic district commissions and how to form such a commission. The Alliance plans to initiate other services, including a quarterly

newsletter, production of a training manual for commission members, establishment of a speakers' bureau, and a library of reference materials for use by members.

Indiana Historical Society

450 West Ohio Street
Indianapolis, Ind. 46202
(317) 232-1882
www.indianahistory.org

The Indiana Historical Society is a private, non-profit membership organization chartered by the Indiana General Assembly. The Society provides several publications for its members, works with local historical groups, sponsors various historical and cultural programs and activities, and maintains a library at its Ohio Street address. It is also sponsor of the Indiana Junior Historical Society.

National Organizations

National Trust for Historic Preservation

1785 Massachusetts Avenue, N.W.
Washington, D.C. 20036
(202) 673-4000
www.nationaltrust.org

The National Trust for Historic Preservation is a private, nonprofit, nationwide organization chartered by Congress to encourage public participation in historic preservation. Dues from members, contributions from donors and matching grants from the National Park Service of the U.S. Department of the Interior support the programs of the National Trust. The Preservation Services Fund offers grants on a matching basis to nonprofit, membership-supported organizations to help pay for consultant services on preservation issues. A National Preservation Loan Fund provides low-interest loans to nonprofit organizations to establish revolving funds for improving significant properties. Maritime Preservation Grants provide 50-percent matching grants for a wide range of maritime projects. The Endangered Properties

Fund is a $1-million fund to protect properties of national significance faced with serious threats.

American Association for State and Local History (AASLH)

1717 Church Street
Nashville, Tenn. 37203
(615) 320-3203
www.aaslh.org

The AASLH is a nonprofit educational organization dedicated to advancing knowledge and appreciation of local history in the United States and Canada, providing help and materials on all aspects of local history. Membership benefits include the monthly *History News*, educational programs, job placement, audio-visual training programs, and discounts on books.

Preservation Action

1054 31st Street N.W.
Suite 526
Washington, D.C. 20007
(202) 298-6180
www.preservationaction.org

A national nonprofit lobbying organization for preservation, Preservation Action carries out lobbying activity at the national level, monitors administrative and legislative action, disseminates information, and coordinates grass-roots lobbying

Entrance gates to the Sumption Prairie Cemetery (66014) established around 1830 in Green Township. *Courtesy of Historic Preservation Commission of South Bend and St. Joseph County.*

activities through a system of statewide lobbying coordinators and preservation organizations. The organization regularly produces a series of "alerts" to maintain awareness of pending issues and motivate local lobbying efforts.

Government Programs and Agencies

State and federal governments, as well as some local governments, have established programs that can be beneficial to historic properties. Some of these programs benefit properties included in the National Register of Historic Places or locally designated districts; others are generally available for any qualified properties, whether or not they are historic.

Local Programs and Agencies

Since 1977, local governments in Indiana have been authorized by Indiana state law (I.C. 36-7-11) to enact ordinances creating historic district commissions, which may then designate historic districts and monitor changes affecting the districts' visual character. For further information, contact Historic Landmarks Foundation of Indiana or the Division of Historic Preservation and Archaeology.

The state also authorizes deductions or abatements in local property taxes if assessments have increased because of a rehabilitation (I.C.6-1.1-12). Property owners should contact their local township assessor for more information.

State Programs and Agencies

Division of Historic Preservation and Archaeology

402 W. Washington Street
Room W274
Indianapolis, Ind. 46204
(317) 232-1646
www.in.gov/dnr/historic

Indiana's State Historic Preservation Officer (SHPO) is the director of the Department of Natural Resources. Through the Division of Historic Preservation and Archaeology (DHPA), the SHPO administers state and federal government preservation programs. State programs include the Indiana Register of Historic Sites and Structures, which parallels the National Register program of the federal government, and the Indiana Historic Sites and Structures Inventory program, of which this *St. Joseph County Interim Report* is a part.

The Indiana Residential Historic Rehabilitation Tax Credit is a program that allows owner-occupants to take a credit against state income tax liability equal to 20 percent of "qualified" preservation or rehab expenses. Interested property owners must receive approval from the DHPA prior to beginning work.

The DHPA also reviews state and federal government actions for their impacts on historic

This image captures the Collegiate Gothic details found in the pointed-arch windows of Notre Dame's South Dining Hall (13035) built in 1927. *Courtesy of Historic Preservation Commission of South Bend and St. Joseph County.*

resources and administers the preservation programs offered by the National Park Service. These include the National Register, tax certification, and grants. The DHPA also provides technical assistance to the public and information on all aspects of historic preservation.

Indiana Office of Rural Affairs

One North Capitol, Suite 600
Indianapolis, Ind. 46204
Community Economic Development:
(317) 232-1703
Indiana Main Street Program:
(317) 232-8912
www.state.in.us/

The Indiana Office of Rural Affairs assists rural communities in community development projects through its technical assistance and grant programs. The office also administers the **Indiana Main Street** program, a downtown economic revitalization program accomplished through merchant organization, economic restructuring, facade rehabilitation, and downtown promotion.

Indiana Historical Bureau

140 North Senate Avenue
Indianapolis, Ind. 46204
(317) 232-2535
http://www.statelib.lib.in.us/www/ihb/ihb.html
The Indiana Library and Historical Department Act established and governs the Bureau as a state agency. Among its programs are aiding local historical organizations, providing free materials to teachers of Indiana history, and publishing the *Indiana Historian* and the *Indiana History Bulletin*. The Bureau is in charge of the Governors' Portraits Collection and the Indiana Historical Marker program.

Indiana State Library

Indiana Division
140 North Senate Avenue
Indianapolis, Ind. 46204
(317) 232-3675
www.statelib.in.us

The Indiana Division of the State Library contains county and town histories, newspaper indices, historic photos, maps of Indiana, and special primary and secondary research resources dealing with Indiana's history and histories of most communities.

Federal Programs and Agencies

National Park Service

1100 L Street, N.W.
Washington, D.C. 20240
www.cr.nps.gov/nr

The National Park Service, U.S. Department of the Interior, administers the federal government's historic preservation programs. Foremost among these is the **National Register of Historic Places**, the nation's official list of its cultural resources worthy of preservation. The criteria for the National Register appear on page 9. Listing in the National Register provides recognition of a property's cultural significance and offers protection from the impact of state or federal projects by requiring review and comment by the State Historic Preservation Officer and the National Advisory Council on Historic Preservation. It does not, however, prevent a private owner from altering or disposing of the property as he or she wishes. The National Register is usually the first step in qualifying a property for the other federal programs encouraging preservation, such as the federal tax credit.

Substantial rehabilitation of income-producing buildings can qualify for an investment tax credit under the tax provisions of the Tax Act of 1986, which allows a 10-percent credit for structures at least 50 years old and 20-percent credit for certified historic structures. Structures must be listed in the National Register or located in a certified historic district to qualify for the 20-percent credit and must have the rehabilitation work reviewed for compliance with the Secretary

This 1912 photo depicts the northeast corner of Main and Second streets in Michiwaka. *Courtesy of Historic Preservation Commission of South Bend and St. Joseph County.*

of the Interior's Standards for Rehabilitation. The Park Service uses Historic Preservation Certification applications to identify eligible buildings and certify their rehabilitation.

The Park Service also administers Federal historic preservation grants-in-aid, which are available if appropriated by Congress. Amounts and eligibility requirements vary from year to year. In recent years, the Park Service has allotted funds for survey and planning projects, such as this St. Joseph County Inventory, archaeological projects, and rehabilitation/acquisition projects.

The Historic American Buildings Survey (HABS) began in 1933 as a Civil Works Administration project. It provided funds for unemployed architects and draftsmen to record and document historic structures throughout the United States. The Library of Congress' Division of Prints and Photographs cares for this architectural data. A related program is the **Historic American Engineering Record (HAER)**, which records and documents structures significant in the history of American engineering and technology.

No longer extant, this barn from Harris Township featured unusual paired round-arched window openings. *Courtesy of Historic Preservation Commission of South Bend and St. Joseph County.*

135

Bibliography

Local References

An Illustrated Historical Atlas of St. Joseph County, Indiana. Chicago: Higgins, Beldon & Co., 1875.

Atlas & Plat Book of St. Joseph County, Indiana. Rockford, IL: The Thrift Press, 1929.

Baker, George. The St. Joseph-Kankakee Portage. South Bend, IN: Northern Indiana Historical Society, 1958.

Sister Bernadette Marie. St. Mary's College Archives, College Archivist. Interview. Notre Dame, IN, n.d.

Sister Campion. St. Mary's College Archives, Campus Archivist. Interview. Notre Dame, IN, n.d.

Chapman, Charles C. History of St. Joseph County, Indiana. Chicago: Charless C. Chapman & Co., 1880.

City of South Bend Summary Report: Indiana Historic Sites and Structures Inventory. South Bend: Historic Preservation Commission of South Bend and St. Joseph County, 1993.

"Civic Column." The Michigan News and Dispatch (Michigan City, IN). July 1925.

Creek, Helen (Sister Mary Immaculate). A Panorama: 1844-1977, St. Mary's College, Notre Dame, Indiana. Notre Dame, IN: Congregation of the Sisters of the Holy Cross, 1977.

Crockett, Harrison H. Roseland 1916-1967. Roseland, IN, 1967.

Department of Commerce, Bureau of Census. County Data Book: A Supplement to and Statistical Abstract of the U.S. Washington, DC: GPO, 1947.

Dixon, Lori. RP3 Agricultural Context for St. Joseph County, In. June, 1990

Duvall, David. Brick Streets in South Bend, Indiana. Historic Preservation Commission of South Bend & St. Joseph County, 1997.

Eisen, David. Biographical Index to St. Joseph County, Ind. Histories. South Bend, IN: The Northern Indiana Historical Society, Inc., 1978.

Goff, Germain. The History of Harris Township. n.p., 1980.

Greiff, Glory June. The New Deal in St. Joseph County, Indiana. Historic Preservation Commission of South Bend & St. Joseph County, 1997.

_____. "New Carlisle Historic District." National Register Nomination. Indiana Division of Historic Preservation and Archaeology, 1992.

Left: Whimsical architecture found in this 1940s A&W Root Beer road-side stand is a rarity today. *Courtesy of Historic Preservation Commission of South Bend and St. Joseph County.*

Howard, Timothy Edward. *A History of St. Joseph County, Indiana, Vol. 1.* Chicago: Lewis Publishing Co., 1907.

Hurcomb, Florence. "Woodland, A Crossroads Community." *The Old Courthouse News* 14.2 (summer 1980).

Independent News. Walkerton, IN: n.p., n.d.

International Teamster. September 1949. Northern Indiana Historical Society ephemeral file.

Kankakee Valley Drilling Company. 1871. Northern Indiana Historical Society, Map #350, flat, M41.

Kiracofe, J. Harold. *100th Anniversary: A History of Osceola Methodist Church from 1851-1951.* Osceola, IN: n.p.

_____. "A History of Ocseola and the Eastern Portion of Penn Township, St. Joseph County, Indiana." Unpublished paper, n.d.

Lyons, John Joseph. "The Pioneer Farmer and the Settlement of St. Joseph County, Indiana 1830-1851." Ph.D. diss., University of Notre Dame, 1955.

Milliken, Ronald. "Modern Day Trends Sidetrack Lydick Born of Railroads." *The South Bend Tribune.* 25 August 1974.

McCandless, Kenneth William. "The Endangered Domain: A Review and Analysis of Campus Planning and Design at the University of Notre Dame." Masters thesis, University of Notre Dame, 1974.

McCandless, Marion. *Family Portraits: A History of the Holy Cross Alumnae Association of St. Mary's College, Notre Dame, Indiana, 1879-1949.* Notre Dame, IN: St. Mary's College Press, 1952.

Moore, W. S. *Standard Atlas of St. Joseph County, Indiana, 1909-1910.* South Bend, IN: George A. Ogle & Company, 1911.

Notre Dame Scholastic Magazine (25 August 1885).

Osceola & Rural Directory. Osceola, IN: Osceola Volunteer Fire Dept., 1947.

The Osceola Owl. Osceola, IN: n.p., n.d.

Richard, Karen. "Granger Heyday Reminders Few." *The South Bend Tribune.* 5 September 1982.

St. Joseph County Interim Report. South Bend: Historic Preservation Commission of South Bend & St. Joseph County, 2000.

St. Patrick's Church Today. n.p. 1956.

Schlereth, Thomas J. *The University of Notre Dame: A Portrait of It's History and Campus.* Notre Dame, IN: University of Notre Dame Press, 1976.

Sisters of the Holy Cross. *Superior Generals: Centenary Chronicles of the Sisters of the Holy Cross, St. Mary's of the Immaculate Conception, Notre Dame, Holy Cross, Indiana, Vol. 11.* Peterson, NJ: St. Anthony Guild Press, c.1947.

South Bend Tribune Clipping Files. South Bend Public Library.

South Bend Recorder's Office. Plat Books & Deed Records of St. Joseph County.

Souvenir Program: Centennial Celebration for Walkerton, Indiana & Community. Walkerton: n.p., 31 July, 1-5 August 1956.

Stoll, John B., ed. *An Account of St. Joseph County from Its Organization, Vol. 3.* Dayton: National Historical Association, 1923-1928.

The 12th Census of the United States Taken in the Year 1900. Washington, DC: U.S. Census Office, 1901. Vols. III, VI, VIII.

The 14th Census of the United States Taken in the Year 1920. Washington, DC: GPO, 1923. Vols. III, VI, VIII.

The 15th Census of the United States. Washington, DC: GPO, 1932. Vols. II, III.

General References

Baker, Ronald L. *From Needmore to Prosperity.* Bloomington: Indiana University Press, 1995.

Blumenson, John J. G. *Identifying American Architecture: A Pictorial Guide to Styles and Times 1600-1945,* 2nd ed. Nashville American Association for State and Local History, 1981.

Cooper, James L. *Artistry and Ingenuity in Artificial Stone.* Greencastle, IN: DePauw University, 1997.

_____. *Iron Monuments to Distant Posterity.* Greencastle, IN: DePauw University, 1997.

Derry, Anne et. al. *Guidelines for Local Surveys: A Basis for Preservation Planning.* Washington: National Register of Historic Places, 1985.

Dunn, Jacob Piatt, Jr. *Indiana, A Redemption From Slavery.* Boston: Houghton, Mifflin, 1888.

Fitch, James Marston. *Historic Preservation: Curatorial Management of the Built Environment.* Charlottesville: University Press of Virginia, 1990.

Glassie, Henry. *Vernacular Architecture.* Bloomington, IN: Indiana University Press, 2000.

Glenn, Elizabeth, and Stewart Rafert. "Native Americans." *Peopling Indiana: The Ethnic Experience.* Indianapolis: Indiana Historical Society, 1996: 392-418.

Harris, Cyril M. *Historic Architecture Sourcebook.* NY: McGraw-Hill, 1977.

Illustrated Historical Atlas of the State of Indiana. Chicago: Baskin, Forster & Company, 1876. Reprinted, Indianapolis: Indiana Historical Society, 1968.

McAlester, Virginia & Lee. *A Field Guide to American Houses.* NY: Alfred A. Knopf, 1984.

McClelland, Linda. *National Register Bulletin: How to Complete the National Register Form.* Washington: National Park Service, 1997.

McCord, Shirley S., ed. "Father Louis Hennepin's Account of 1679." *Travel Accounts of Indiana, 1679-1961.* Indiana Historical Collections, Vol XLVIII. Indiana Historical Bureau, 1970, p.1-4.

Montague, Wilbert Holland. *The Rise and Progress of the Standard Oil Co.* New York: Harper and Bros., 1903.

Noble, Allen. *Wood, Brick and Stone, The North American Settlement Landscape, Volumes I and II.* Amherst: University of Massachusetts Press, 1984.

Noble, Allen G. and Hubert G.H. Wilhelm, eds. *Barns of the Midwest.* Athens, OH: Ohio University Press, 1995.

Peat, Wilbur D. *Indiana Houses of the Nineteenth Century.* Indianapolis: Indiana Historical Society, 1962.

Pence, Gregory, and Nellie C. Armstrong. *Indiana Boundaries.* Indianapolis: Indiana Historical Bureau, 1933.

Poppeliers, John and S. Allen Chambers, Jr. *What Style Is It?* Washington: John Wiley & Sons/The Preservation Press, 2003.

Roberts, Warren E. *Log Buildings of Southern Indiana.* Bloomington, IN: Trickster Press, 1996.

Rifkind, Carole. *A Field Guide to American Architecture.* New York: New Library, 1980.

Schuler, Stanley. *American Barns, In a Class by Themselves.* Exton, PA: Schiffer, 1985.

Schweitzer, Robert, and Michael W.R. Davis. *America's Favorite Homes: Mail Order Catalogues as a Guide to Early 20th C. Houses.* Detroit: Wayne State Press, 1990.

Scully, Vincent. *American Architecture and Urbanism* (Revised Edition). New York: Henry Holt and Company, 1988.

Simons, Richard S. *Rivers of Indiana.* Bloomington: Indiana University Press, 1985.

Simons, Richard S. and Francis H. Parker. *Railroads of Indiana.* Bloomington: Indiana University Press, 1997.

Stevenson, Katherine Cole and H. Ward Jandl. *Houses by Mail.* Washington, DC: The Preservation Press, 1986.

Strausberg, Stephen F. "Indiana and the Swamp Land Act." *Indiana Magazine of History,* LXXII, No. 3 (Sep. 1977): 191-203.

Taylor, Robert M., Jr., ed. *The Northwest Ordinance 1787.* Indianapolis: Indiana Historical Society, 1987.

Walker, H. Jesse and Randall A. Detro. *Cultural Diffusion and Landscapes: Selections by Fred B. Kniffen.* Baton Rouge: Louisiana State University, 1990.

Whiffen, Marcus. *American Architecture Since 1790: A Guide to Styles.* Cambridge: The M.I.T. Press, 1969.

Index

This project received federal funds from the National Park Service. Regulations of the U.S. Department of the Interior strictly prohibit unlawful discrimination in the Department's federally assisted programs on the basis of race, color, national origin, age or handicap. Any person who believes he or she has been discriminated against in any program, activity, or facility operated by a recipient of federal assistance should write to: Director, Equal Opportunity Program, U.S. Department of the Interior, National Park Service, 1849 C Street NW, Washington, D.C. 20240.

Federal funds from the National Park Service, Department of the Interior, have partially financed this county interim report. However, the contents and opinions do not necessarily reflect the views and policies of the Department of the Interior, nor does the mention of trade names or commercial products constitute endorsement or recommendation by the Department of the Interior.

Printed on recycled paper.

Please submit revisions or corrections to the information in this interim report to the Division of Historic Preservation and Archaeology, 402 W. Washington Street, Room W-274, Indianapolis, Ind. 46204.

Call (317) 232-1646 for more information.

Additional copies of this report may be available. Contact Historic Landmarks Foundation of Indiana, 340 W. Michigan Street, Indianapolis, Ind. 46202, (800) 450-4534, www.historiclandmarks.org for information.

Index of Places

Left: The Interurban and its overhead wires were once a common sight in St. Joseph County. *Courtesy of Historic Preservation Commission of South Bend and St. Joseph County.*

E

F

G

H

**Undated historical photograph of the Italianate
Sheneman House (90117) in a snowy setting.**
*Courtesy of Historic Preservation Commission of
South Bend and St. Joseph County.*

S

Sacred Heart Basilica (13023), 62, **62**
Sacred Heart Cemetery (11017), 55
Sacred Heart of Jesus Church (70046), 89
Sacred Heart Shrine (12020), 59
Sacred Heart Statue (13061), 63
St. Bridget's Convent (12006), 58
St. Edward Statue (13055), 63, **64**
St. Edward's Hall (13015), 62
St. Francis of Assisi Statue (13059), 63
St. John the Evangelist Sculpture (13062), 63

Touted in its day as more efficient, round barns like the Rouch Barn (85078) in Union Township, built in the early 1900s, are extremely rare in Indiana. *Courtesy of Historic Preservation Commission of South Bend and St. Joseph County.*

St. John's Cemetery (81023), 104
St. John's Hall (12044), 59
St. John's Lutheran Cemetery (90046), 116
St. John's Lutheran Church (90062), 117
St. John's United Church of Christ (81024), 104
St. Joseph County Bridge No. 5/Darden Road Bridge (05037), 47
St. Joseph County Bridge No. 12 (62040), 75
St. Joseph County Bridge No. 52 (80107), 102
St. Joseph County Bridge No. 57 (95023), 124
St. Joseph County Bridge No. 65 (95022), 124
St. Joseph County Bridge No. 68 (85101), 111
St. Joseph County Bridge No. 71 (85058), 110
St. Joseph County Bridge No. 77 (85102), 111
St. Joseph County Bridge No. 78 (80099), 102
St. Joseph County Bridge No. 91 (75096), 94
St. Joseph County Bridge No. 128 (90065), 117
St. Joseph County Bridge No. 129 (90058), 117
St. Joseph County Bridge No. 130 (80101), 102
St. Joseph County Bridge No. 185 (97048), 130
St. Joseph County Bridge No. 201 (75100), 94
St. Joseph County Bridge No. 214 (05051), 47
St. Joseph County Bridge No. 216 (75103), 94, **94**
St. Joseph County Bridge No. S506 (90059), 117
St. Joseph County Bridge No. S531 (80100), 102
St. Joseph County Bridge No. S537 (85080), 110
St. Joseph County Bridge No. S541 (90061), 117
St. Joseph County Bridge No. S546 (90064), 117
St. Joseph County Bridge No. S553 (75097), 94
St. Joseph County Bridge No. S554 (75095), 94
St. Joseph County Bridge No. S557 (00027), 44
St. Joseph County Bridge No. S564 (05043), 47
St. Joseph County Bridge No. S568 (90066), 117
St. Joseph County Bridge No. S580 (62041), 75
St. Joseph County Bridge No. S581 (62042), 76
St. Joseph County Bridge No. S583 (62043), 76
St. Joseph County Bridge No. S589 (05011), 46
St. Joseph County Farm Bureau Co-Op Grain Elevator (62045), 76
St. Joseph County Tuberculosis Sanitarium (05036), 47, **47**
St. Joseph Hospital, **40**
St. Joseph's Cemetery (11018), 55, **56**
St. Joseph's Farm (00026), *33*, 44
St. Joseph's Hall (12043), 59
St. Jude Statue (13057), 63
St. Luke the Evangelist Sculpture (13064), 63
St. Mary's Convent (12037), 59

St. Michael's Hall (12045), 59
St. Michael's Laundry (13012), 62
St. Michael's Shrine (12030), 59
St. Patrick Church (97003), 129
St. Patrick School (97002), 30
St. Patrick's Farm (05009), 46
St. Paul Lutheran Church Cemetery (80032), 100
St. Stanislaus Kostka Church (62024), 75, **76**
Salem Church of the Evangelical Association (00002), 43, **43**
Salem Church of the Evangelical Association Cemetery (00001), **36**, 43
Savidge, Robert House (05028), 47, **47**
Schafer, Charles Farm (85021), 108
Schafer, Conrad Farm (85002), 108
Schafer, George & Elizabeth Farm (70027), 88, **89**
Schafer, George F. Farm (70029), 88
Schafer, Peter Farm (70026), 88
Schalliol, Augustus Farm (80003), 99, **99**
Schmeitz/James M. Culbertson Farm (80040), 100
Schrader Barn (85067), 110
Schrader House (70042), 89
Science Hall/LaFortune Student Center (13026), 28
Sculpture Studio (13043), 63
Seifer, Edward, Farm (85074), 110
Seifer, John Farm (85071), **109**, 110
Sellers, Henry & Mary Jane House (58006), 68, **68**, **69**
Sells, Isaac Farm (85047), 109
Service, George H. House (63048), 79, **80**
Shady Lane/Mathys Farm (58025), 69
Shafer Farm (70021), 88
Shafer, George Farm (85075), 110, **110**
Shaheen-Mestrovic Memorial Park (13040), 63
Sheneman, Zachariah & Sarah L. Farm (90044), 116, **117**
Slick, Milo House (97044), 130
Smith, Adam House (75010), 91
Smith, Britton House (92024), 122
Smith, Catherine & John House (00003), 43
Smith, Henry F. House (05042), 47
Smith, Jacob & Sarah Farm (85088), 110
Smith, Jobe House (62030), 75
Smith, John House (66049), 86
Smith, Mary A. House (63084), 80, **80**
Smith, Michael House (00005), 43
Smith, Morgan & Mary S./William Trowbridge House (63085), 80

This unusual Dutch Colonial house in Walkerton (97034) is sided in pressed concrete block, which was a popular choice among cost-conscious home builders in the early 1900s. *Courtesy of Historic Preservation Commission of South Bend and St. Joseph County.*

Index of Streets with Inventoried Sites

Street Name	Range	Twp(s)/SS(s)/HD(s)	Page No.
32nd St	NA	Clay Twp SS	45-47
Ada St	Bray St-Timothy Rd	New Carlisle SS	81-82
Adams Rd	Gumwood Rd-Ash Rd	Harris Twp	42-44
	Ironwood Rd-Gumwood Rd	Clay Twp SS	45-47
	NA	German Twp SS	51-52
Adams St	NA	Walkerton SS	128-130
Alden Rd	NA	Warren Twp SS	67-70
Alice St	NA	Harris Twp	42-44
Apple Rd	Edison Rd-Ireland Rd	Penn Twp SS	90-94
	US 33-Walnut St	Osceola SS	95-97
Anderson Rd	Chestnut Rd-Ash Rd	Harris Twp	42-44
Arch St	Front St-Ada St	New Carlisle HD	77-80
Ardmore Tr	US 31-Hartzer Rd	Portage Twp SS	53-56
Ash Rd	NA	Harris Twp	42-44
	Douglas Rd-Roosevelt Rd	Penn Twp SS	90-94
	Madison Rd-Shively Rd	Madison Twp SS	98-102
Auten Rd	St. Joseph River-Hickory Rd	Clay Twp SS	45-47
	Portage Ave-St. Joseph River	German Twp SS	51-52
Basswood Rd	Harrison Rd-Dragoon Trl	Penn Twp SS	90-94
Baughman Ct	NA	Centre Township SS	87-89
Beckley St	NA	Harris Twp	42-44
Beech Rd	Douglas Rd-Roosevelt Rd	Penn Twp SS	90-94
	Vistula Rd-Adams St	Osceola SS	95-97
	Madison Rd-Tyler Rd	Madison Twp SS	98-102
Birch Rd	US 20-Jefferson Rd	Penn Twp SS	90-94
Bittersweet Rd	NA	Harris Twp	42-44
	Douglas Rd-SR 33	Penn Twp SS	90-94
Blackberry Rd	US 33-Dragoon Trl	Penn Twp SS	90-94
Bremen Hwy	Layton Rd-Tyler Rd	Madison Twp SS	98-102
	Woodland Ave-Patterson Rd	Wyatt SS	105-106
Brick Rd	Gumwood Rd-Cherry Rd	Harris Twp	42-44
	NA	Clay Twp SS	45-47
	NA	Warren Twp SS	67-70
Bulla Rd	NA	Notre Dame SS	65-66
Butternut Rd	Western Rd-Grant Rd	Portage Twp SS	53-56
Carroll Dr	NA	Notre Dame SS	65-66
Cavanaugh Dr	NA	Notre Dame HD	60-64
Cedar Rd	Dragoon Trl-Roosevelt Rd	Penn Twp SS	90-94
	Madison Rd-Tyler Rd	Madison Twp SS	98-102
Center St	NA	North Liberty SS	120-122
Chain-O-Lakes Dr	NA	Lydick SS	71-72
Chandler Blvd	NA	Penn Twp SS	90-94
Cherry St	Front St-Chestnut St	New Carlisle HD	77-80
Chestnut Rd	NA	Harris Twp	42-44
Chestnut St	Bray St-Arch St	New Carlisle HD	77-80
Chicago Tr	NA	Warren Twp SS	67-70
	County Line Rd-Tamarack Rd	Olive Twp SS	73-76
Chippewa St	NA	Centre Township SS	87-89
Cleveland Rd	St. Joseph River-Gumwood Rd	Clay Twp SS	45-47
	NA	Roseland SS	49-50
	NA	German Twp SS	51-52
Clover Rd	NA	Harris Twp	42-44
	Dragoon Trl-Jackson Rd	Penn Twp SS	90-94
Country Club Rd	NA	Warren Twp SS	67-70
County Line Rd	Gordon Rd-US 80/90	Olive Twp SS	73-76
Cowles Ave	NA	Clay Twp SS	45-47
Cripe St	McCombs St-Dixieway S	Roseland SS	49-50
Crumstown Rd	Western Rd-Grant Rd	Portage Twp SS	53-56
	NA	Warren Twp SS	67-70
Crumstown Tr	Willow Rd-Tulip Rd	Olive Twp SS	73-76
Currant Rd	SR 23-Cleveland Rd	Harris Twp	42-44

Street Name	Range	Twp(s)/SS(s)/HD(s)	Page No.
	Day Rd-US 20	Penn Twp SS	90-94
Darden Rd	St. Joseph River-Juniper Rd	Clay Twp SS	45-47
	NA	Olive Twp SS	73-76
David St	US 93-Myrtle St	Roseland SS	49-50
Day Rd	SR 331-Ash Rd	Penn Twp SS	90-94
Detroit Ave	NA	Centre Township SS	87-89
Dice St	NA	Centre Township SS	87-89
Dixie Way N	Cleveland Rd-Pendle St	Roseland SS	49-50
Dogwood Rd	Dragoon Trl-Layton Rd	Penn Twp SS	90-94
	Layton Rd-Tyler Rd	Madison Twp SS	98-102
Douglas Rd	SR 331-Ash Rd	Penn Twp SS	90-94
Douglas Rd Ext.	NA	St. Mary's College HD	57-59
Downey Ave	NA	Penn Twp SS	90-94
Dragoon Tr	Ironwood Rd-Beech Rd	Penn Twp SS	90-94
Early Rd	NA	Warren Twp SS	67-70
	County Line Rd-Spruce Rd	Olive Twp SS	73-76
Eaton Rd	Tulip Rd-Sage Rd	Olive Twp SS	73-76
Edison Rd	NA	German Twp SS	51-52
	US 31-Hartzer Rd	Portage Twp SS	53-56
	Pear Rd-Davenport Rd	Lydick SS	71-72
	Bittersweet Rd-Ash Rd	Penn Twp SS	90-94
Elm Rd	Douglas Rd-Layton Rd	Penn Twp SS	90-94
	Layton Rd-Tyler Rd	Madison Twp SS	98-102
Elm St	Jon St-College St	New Carlisle SS	81-82
Erie St	Beech Rd-Chestnut St	Osceola SS	95-97
Evergreen Rd	NA	Harris Twp	42-44
Filbert St	Front St-Ada St	New Carlisle HD	77-80
	Front St-Chapman Dr	New Carlisle SS	81-82
	Day Rd-US 20	Penn Twp SS	90-94
Fillmore Rd	US 31-Mayflower Rd	Portage Twp SS	53-56
Fir Rd	Douglas Rd-Kelly Rd	Penn Twp SS	90-94
	New Rd-SR 331	Madison Twp SS	98-102
Front St	Bray St-Arch St	New Carlisle HD	77-80
	Jon St-Arch St	New Carlisle SS	81-82
Gordon Rd	NA	Olive Twp SS	73-76
Grape Rd	Adams Rd-Edison Rd	Clay Twp SS	45-47
Grandview Ave	NA	Portage Twp SS	53-56
Grass Rd	Ireland Rd-Hickory Rd	Penn Twp SS	90-94
Gumwood Rd	NA	Harris Twp	42-44
	SR 331-Tyler Rd	Madison Twp SS	98-102
Harrison Rd	SR 331-Ash Rd	Penn Twp SS	90-94
Harrison St	US 31-Beehler Ct	Lakeville SS	112-113

Street Name	Range	Twp(s)/SS(s)/HD(s)	Page No.
	Jefferson St-Washington St	North Liberty SS	120-122
	Kentucky St-Michigan St	Walkerton SS	128-130
Hartzer Rd	NA	Portage Twp SS	53-56
Harvest St	NA	Clay Twp SS	45-47
Henry Rd	Willow Rd-Strawberry Rd	Olive Twp SS	73-76
Hickory Rd	Adams Rd-SR 23	Clay Twp SS	45-47
	Grass Rd-Kern Rd	Penn Twp SS	90-94
Holy Cross Dr	NA	Notre Dame HD	60-64
Hollyhock Rd	State Line Rd-Cleveland Rd	Clay Twp SS	45-47
Hollywood Blvd	Western Rd-Grant Rd	Portage Twp SS	53-56
Ice Tr	NA	Greene Twp SS	83-86
Illinois St	Walkerton Trl-Tyler St	Walkerton SS	128-130
Indiana St	NA	Walkerton SS	128-130
Inwood Rd	NA	Warren Twp SS	67-70
	Willow Rd-Tulip Rd	Olive Twp SS	73-76

Now demolished, this house in Walkerton exhibited nice Italianate features like paired carved bracketing at the cornice, narrow windows, and original clapboard. *Courtesy of Historic Preservation Commission of South Bend and St. Joseph County.*

Street Name	Range	Twp(s)/SS(s)/HD(s)	Page No.	Street Name	Range	Twp(s)/SS(s)/HD(s)	Page No.
Ireland Rd	NA	Greene Twp SS	83-86	Madison Tr	Madison Rd-New Rd	Madison Twp SS	98-102
	Locust Rd-Ironwood Rd	Centre Township SS	87-89	Magnolia Rd	NA	Portage Twp SS	53-56
Ironwood Rd	State Line Rd-Edison Rd	Clay Twp SS	45-47	Main Ave	NA	St. Mary's College HD	57-59
	US 33-Layton Rd	Penn Twp SS	90-94	Main St	Market St-Center St	North Liberty HD	118-119
	Layton Rd-New Rd	Madison Twp SS	98-102		Wolf St-Center St	North Liberty SS	120-122
	Quinn Rd-Tyler Rd	Union Twp SS	107-111	Maple Rd	New Rd-SR 4	Union Twp SS	107-111
Island Ave	NA	Penn Twp SS	90-94	Maple St	SR 4-South St	North Liberty SS	120-122
Jackson Rd	Ironwood Rd-Ash Rd	Penn Twp SS	90-94	Market St	Jefferson St-Lafayette St	North Liberty SS	120-122
Jackson St	Ohio St-SR 23	Walkerton SS	128-130	Mayflower Rd	Edison Rd-US 31	Portage Twp SS	53-56
Jefferson Rd	NA	Penn Twp SS	90-94		NA	Greene Twp SS	83-86
Jefferson St	Mangus Dr-US 31	Lakeville SS	112-113	McKinley Hwy	SR 331-Ash Rd	Penn Twp SS	90-94
	Mill St-SR 23	North Liberty SS	120-122	Miami Hwy	New Rd-Tyler Rd	Union Twp SS	107-111
Jewell Ave	NA	Centre Township SS	87-89	Michigan St	Bray St-Arch St	New Carlisle HD	77-80
Johnson Rd	Willow Rd-Tulip Rd	Olive Twp SS	73-76		NA	New Carlisle SS	81-82
	Laurel Rd-Miami Hwy	Centre Township SS	87-89		NA	Union Twp SS	107-111
Juniper Rd	State Line Rd-Edison Rd	Clay Twp SS	45-47		NA	Lakeville SS	112-113
	NA	Indian Village SS	48		NA	Walkerton SS	128-130
	Douglas Rd-Edison Rd	Notre Dame SS	65-66	Mill St	Jefferson St-Lafayette St	North Liberty SS	120-122
	Osborne Rd-Quinn Rd	Union Twp SS	107-111				
Kelly Rd	NA	Greene Twp SS	83-86				
	Bremen Rd-Elm Rd	Penn Twp SS	90-94				
Kenilworth Rd	New Rd-Tyler Rd	Union Twp SS	107-111				
Kentucky St	Harrison St-Van Buren St	Walkerton SS	128-130				
Keria Tr	Inwood Rd-Ireland Rd	Centre Township SS	87-89				
Kern Rd	NA	Greene Twp SS	83-86				
	Locust Rd-Ironwood Rd	Centre Township SS	87-89				
	Ironwood Rd-Ash Rd	Penn Twp SS	90-94				
Kline Rd	Elm Rd-Ash Rd	Penn Twp SS	90-94				
Lafayette St	Wolf St-Rupel Ave	North Liberty SS	120-122				
Lake Tr	US 31-Tyler Rd	Union Twp SS	107-111				
Lath Tr	NA	Greene Twp SS	83-86				
Laurel Rd	State Line Rd-Darden Rd	Clay Twp SS	45-47				
Layton Rd	Poppy Rd-Oak Rd	Greene Twp SS	83-86				
	Ironwood Rd-Dogwood Rd	Penn Twp SS	90-94				
	Gumwood Rd-Beech Rd	Madison Twp SS	98-102				
Leeper Rd	NA	Liberty Twp SS	114-117				
	NA	Lincoln Twp SS	123-124				
Lincoln Way E	NA	Osceola SS	95-97				
Lincoln Way W	NA	Osceola SS	95-97				
Linden Rd	NA	German Twp SS	51-52				
	Lake Trl-Tyler Rd	Union Twp SS	107-111				
Locust Rd	US 20-Madison Rd	Centre Township SS	87-89				
Madison Rd	NA	Greene Twp SS	83-86				
	Ironwood Rd-Ash Rd	Madison Twp SS	98-102				

This English barn is part of the oustanding Rupel Farm (70002) in Centre Township. *Courtesy of Historic Preservation Commission of South Bend and St. Joseph County.*

Street Name	Range	Twp(s)/SS(s)/HD(s)	Page No.
Monroe St	Adams St-SR 23	Walkerton SS	128-130
Moss Rd	NA	Portage Twp SS	53-56
Mulberry Rd	Roosevelt Rd-New Rd	Greene Twp SS	83-86
	New Rd-Stanton Rd	Union Twp SS	107-111
Myrtle Rd	NA	Clay Twp SS	45-47
	SR 23-Kern Rd	Greene Twp SS	83-86
New Rd	NA	Greene Twp SS	83-86
	Maple Rd-Ironwood Rd	Centre Township SS	87-89
	Ironwood Rd-Ash Rd	Madison Twp SS	98-102
	Mulberry Rd-Miami Hwy	Union Twp SS	107-111
Nicar Rd	NA	Madison Twp SS	98-102
Northern Ave	NA	Clay Twp SS	45-47
Notre Dame Ave	NA	Notre Dame SS	65-66
Oak Rd	SR 23-New Rd	Greene Twp SS	83-86
	Osborne Rd-Tyler Rd	Union Twp SS	107-111
	New Rd-Tyler Rd	Liberty Twp SS	114-117
Olive Rd	Brick Rd-Lincoln Way W	German Twp SS	51-52
Olive St	NA	Osceola SS	95-97
Orange Rd	NA	German Twp SS	51-52
	SR 23-New Rd	Greene Twp SS	83-86
Osborne Rd	Gumwood Rd-Ash Rd	Madison Twp SS	98-102
	Oak Rd-Miami Hwy	Union Twp SS	107-111
	Snowberry Rd-Liberty Trl	Liberty Twp SS	114-117
Patterson Rd	Gumwood Rd-Ash Rd	Madison Twp SS	98-102
	NA	Wyatt SS	105-106
	US 31-Kenilworth Rd	Union Twp SS	107-111
Patterson St	US 31-Beehler Ct	Lakeville SS	112-113
Paxson Dr	NA	Clay Twp SS	45-47
Pear Rd	NA	Lydick SS	71-72
Pendel St	McCombs St-Myrtle St	Roseland SS	49-50
Peppermint Rd	NA	Warren Twp SS	67-70
Perry Ave	David Ct-SR 331	Wyatt SS	105-106
Pierce Rd	Gumwood Rd-Ash Rd	Madison Twp SS	98-102
	Oak Rd-Miami Hwy	Union Twp SS	107-111
Pine Rd	Lincoln Way W-Edison Rd	German Twp SS	51-52
	US 20-SR 223	Warren Twp SS	67-70
	Roosevelt Rd-New Rd	Greene Twp SS	83-86
	SR 4-Tyler Rd	Liberty Twp SS	114-117
Pine St	NA	Portage Twp SS	53-56
Poplar Rd	Riley Rd-Watson Rd	Lincoln Twp SS	123-124
Poppy Rd	Cleveland Rd-US 20	Warren Twp SS	67-70
Portage Ave	NA	German Twp SS	51-52
Prairie Ave	NA	Portage Twp SS	53-56
Primrose Rd	New Rd-Tyler Rd	Liberty Twp SS	114-117
Quince Rd	Auten Rd-SR 2	Warren Twp SS	67-70
	Stroup St-Early Rd	Lydick SS	71-72
Quinn Rd	Oak Rd-Miami Hwy	Union Twp SS	107-111
	Walnut Rd-Oak Rd	Liberty Twp SS	114-117
Rankert Rd	Tamarack Rd-Sycamore Rd	Liberty Twp SS	114-117
	SR 23-Tamarack Rd	Lincoln Twp SS	123-124
Redwood Rd	NA	Warren Twp SS	67-70
	SR 23-New Rd	Greene Twp SS	83-86
	New Rd-Tyler Rd	Liberty Twp SS	114-117
Riley Rd	Gumwood Rd-Ash Rd	Madison Twp SS	98-102
	Oak Rd-Miami Hwy	Union Twp SS	107-111
	SR 23-Oak Rd	Liberty Twp SS	114-117
	Poplar Rd-Walnut Rd	Lincoln Twp SS	123-124
Rockstroh Rd	Linden Rd-Kenilworth Rd	Union Twp SS	107-111
Rogers St	Boles St-Beech Rd	Osceola SS	95-97
Roosevelt Rd	SR 23-Myrtle Tr	Greene Twp SS	83-86
	Locust Rd-Ironwood Rd	Centre Township SS	87-89
	Ohio St-Indiana St	Walkerton HD	125-127
	Walkerton Trl-John Glenn Dr	Walkerton SS	128-130
Rose Rd	NA	Warren Twp SS	67-70
Rosewood Rd	Liberty Trl-Quinn Rd	Liberty Twp SS	114-117
Ruth Ave	NA	Centre Township SS	87-89
Sage Rd	SR 2-US 20	Olive Twp SS	73-76
Southland Ave	NA	Centre Township SS	87-89
St. Joseph's Dr	Douglas Rd-Moose Krause Cir	Notre Dame SS	65-66
St. Mary's Rd	US 31-Holy Cross Dr	Notre Dame SS	65-66
St. Thomas St	NA	Harris Twp	42-44
Shively Rd	Gumwood Rd-Ash Rd	Madison Twp SS	98-102
	Sycamore Rd-Redwood Rd	Liberty Twp SS	114-117
Smith Tr	Barley Rd-Shively Rd	Lincoln Twp SS	123-124
Snowberry Rd	New Rd-Osborne Trl	Liberty Twp SS	114-117
Spruce Rd	US 6-Watson Rd	Lincoln Twp SS	123-124
Stanton Rd	Oak Rd-US 31	Union Twp SS	107-111
	Tamarack Rd-Oak Rd	Liberty Twp SS	114-117
State Line Rd	St. Joseph River-Ironwood Rd	Clay Twp SS	45-47
SR 2	US 31-Mayflower Rd	Portage Twp SS	53-56
	NA	Warren Twp SS	67-70
	County Line Rd-Sage Rd	Olive Twp SS	73-76
SR 4	Smilax Rd-Oak Rd	Liberty Twp SS	114-117
SR 23	Gumwood Rd-Adams Rd	Harris Twp	42-49

Street Name	Range	Twp(s)/SS(s)/HD(s)	Page No.
	Ice Tr-New Rd	Greene Twp SS	83-86
	New Rd-Riley Rd	Liberty Twp SS	114-117
	Riley Rd-US 6	Lincoln Twp SS	123-124
SR 933	State Line Rd-Douglas Rd	Clay Twp SS	45-47
SR 104	NA	Lincoln Twp SS	123-124
SR 331	Day Rd-Layton Rd	Penn Twp SS	90-94
	Layton Rd-Tyler Rd	Madison Twp SS	98-102
	NA	Woodland HD	103-104
State St	Center St-Cedar St	North Liberty SS	120-122
Stewart St	SR 4-South St	North Liberty SS	120-122
Sumption Tr	SR 23-Kern Rd	Greene Twp SS	83-86
Sunnybrook St	US 93-Myrtle St	Roseland SS	49-50
Sycamore Rd	Liberty Trl-Tyler Rd	Liberty Twp SS	114-117

Street Name	Range	Twp(s)/SS(s)/HD(s)	Page No.
Tamarack Rd	NA	Olive Twp SS	73-76
Taylor Rd	NA	St. Mary's College HD	57-59
Timothy Rd	Gordon Rd-US 80/90	Olive Twp SS	73-76
	Marvel Ln-Chapman Dr	New Carlisle SS	81-82
Timothy Tr	NA	Lincoln Twp SS	123-124
Tulip Rd	Hurd Rd-US 20	Olive Twp SS	73-76
Turkey Tr	Roosevelt Rd-Miller Rd	Centre Township SS	87-89
Tyler Rd	Gumwood Rd-Beech Rd	Madison Twp SS	98-102
	NA	Lincoln Twp SS	123-124
Tyler St	SR 23-Georgia St	Walkerton SS	128-130
Underwood Rd	NA	Walkerton SS	128-130
US 6	NA	Lincoln Twp SS	123-124
US 20	NA	Warren Twp SS	67-70
	County Line Rd-Sage Rd	Olive Twp SS	73-76
	County Line Rd-Marvel Ln	New Carlisle SS	81-82
	NA	Centre Twp SS	87-89
	Ironwood Rd-Ash Rd	Penn Twp SS	90-94
US 31	State Line Rd-Douglas Rd	Clay Twp SS	45-47
	Cleveland Rd-Douglas Rd	Roseland SS	49-50
	Clereland Rd-New Rd	Centre Township SS	87-89
	New Rd-Tyler Rd	Union Twp SS	107-111
US 33	Ironwood Rd-Ash Rd	Penn Twp SS	90-94
University Drive Ct	Gumwood Rd-Fir Rd	Harris Twp	42-44
Van Buren St	Kentucky St-Georgia St	Walkerton SS	128-130
Virgiia St	Tyler St-Walkerton Trl	Walkerton SS	128-130
Vistula Rd	NA	Penn Twp SS	90-94
	NA	Osceola SS	95-97
Walnut Rd	Fillmore Rd-Chicago Tr	Olive Twp SS	73-76
	Osborne Trl-Quinn Rd	Liberty Twp SS	114-117
	Quinn Rd-Watson Rd	Lincoln Twp SS	123-124
Washington St	NA	Osceola SS	95-97
	US 31-Lake St	Lakeville SS	112-133
Welworth Ave	Juniper Rd-Palmer St	Indian Village SS	48
Willow St	US 93-Myrtle St	Roseland SS	49-50
Willow Trace	SR 23-Watson Rd	Lincoln Twp SS	123-124
Zigler St	Arch St-Michigan St	New Carlisle SS	81-82

Though home to cities like South Bend and Mishawaka, St. Joseph County is predominately rural in character. *Courtesy of Historic Preservation Commission of South Bend and St. Joseph County.*

Glossary of Terms

Applied ornamentation   Any decorative feature added to a surface.

Architrave   The lower horizontal member of a classical *entablature* that also includes the *frieze* and *cornice*.

Bay   A repetitive division of a wall's surface, such as window and door openings.

Board-and-batten An exterior wall covering composed of vertical boards separated by gaps covered with thin boards called battens.

Boxed eave   An enclosed *eave*.

Bracket   An angled support member placed between a wall and an *eave*; mostly ornamental.

Camelback truss   A type of *Pratt truss* bridge having five slopes, with the top chord parallel to the bottom chord.

Casement window   A type of window whose hinge is located along its vertical edge and swings in or out.

Character   The distinctive qualities that make a building or structure what it is.

Chevron   An ornamental pattern shaped like a V. Also called a *zigzag*. Commonly found on Art Deco architecture.

Chord   An important component of a *truss bridge's* construction. Usually paired and horizontally-placed.

Cohesive   Describes the unity formed by the similarities of many distinct parts.

Contextual   A way of understanding a smaller segment by comparing it to a larger segment.

Continuity   An unbroken sequence, correlation, or bond.

Corner post   A vertical board that finishes a corner of a wood-sided building.

Cornice   A decorative *molding* that projects from the top of a wall where it meets the roofline. Also, the upper member of a classical *entablature* that also includes a *frieze* and *architrave*.

Cornice return   Found on a *gable* end where the *cornice* turns horizontally for a short segment. Common in Greek Revival architecture.

Covenant   A restrictive order attached to a property's deed that serves to protect the property from changes that would diminish its historical, architectural, or natural *character*.

Crib   Typically a small, wood-*frame* agricultural building used to store grain or corn.

Cultural resources   Human-made buildings, structures, works of art, memorials, etc., that a community has deemed significant for its age, beauty, innovation, or impact.

Density   The concentration of buildings within a certain area.

Dormer window   A window that protrudes from the *slope* of a roof that has side walls and a *hipped*, *gabled*, *shed*, or rounded roof.

Double-hung window   A type of window that has two vertically moving *sashes* that work independently and slide past each other.

Drip molding   Any *molding* that has the appearance of a drip. First designed to guide rainwater away from the structure.

Easement   A legal agreement that grants a partial interest in a historic property to a nonprofit organization in order to protect the property from changes that would compromise its historical, architectural, or natural *character*. An easement is permanently attached to a property's title and is binding on all future owners.

Eave   The portion of the roof that extends beyond the wall. Sometimes called an *overhang*.

Economic restructuring   A strategy of strengthening and encouraging business in downtown areas or historic commercial districts by identifying and meeting consumer demand.

Elevation   An exterior wall of a building.

Ell   A side wing of a building that is situated at a right angle to the main wing forming an "L" shape.

Entablature   A term derived from classical architecture to describe the *molding* that includes an *architrave*, *frieze*, and *cornice*, often spanning the expanse between columns.

Extant   Something that still exists.

Fabric   The materials that make up a community, place, or building.

Façade   The principal "face" or *elevation* of a building.

Fenestration   The arrangement of window openings in a building.

Finial   An ornamental object that tops architectural elements like *gables* or archways.

Folk   Designs derived from local building traditions that may or may not be executed by trained professionals.

Footprint   The shape of a building as seen from above.

Frame construction   A method of building in which the supporting structure is made of cut lumber.

Frieze   The middle member of a classical *entablature* that also includes an *architrave* and *cornice*.

Frontage   The portion of a building that faces the principal right-of-way, usually a street.

Gable roof   A roof having two *slopes* downward from a central ridge, forming a triangle on each end wall called a gable end. Common on gable-front structures.

Gambrel roof   A roof having a central ridge with a steeply-pitched slope paired with a low-pitched slope on each side of the ridge. Common in barns and Dutch Colonial Revival architecture.

HABS   An acronym for the Historic American Building Survey, a nationwide project that measures, draws, researches, and photographs historic buildings. Began in 1933 as a New Deal Project, the program was revived in 1966. HABS records are archived at the Library of Congress.

HAER   An acronym for Historic American Engineering Record, a nationwide project that measures, draws, researches, and photographs historic engineering structures such as bridges and dams. The program began in 1969. HAER records are archived at the Library of Congress.

High-style   Implies a design created by an architect or other trained professional and executed in an exemplary fashion.

Hipped roof   A roof having four slopes downward from a central ridge. Common on western bungalows.

Historical resources   A type of *cultural resource* that is significant for its age or contribution to local, state, or national history.

Hood   A molding that projects from the wall above a door or window opening used to deflect rainwater, but often decorative.

Integral   A portion of a building located beneath the roof line, such as a porch that does not extend beyond the roof line.

Integrity   The amount of authentic or original *fabric* that remains with a historic building or structure during its period of significance. Buildings with high integrity have few alterations.

Knee brace   A short piece of support lumber placed at an angle between a wall and an *eave*; usually decorative.

Linear-plan   A term used to describe a building having rooms or spaces laid out in a straight line. Such buildings have rectangular footprints.

Macadam   A type of early road invented by John Loudon McAdam that used broken stones laid in tight, symmetrical patterns and covered with small stones to create hard surfaces.

Mansard roof   A type of *hipped roof* having a steeply-pitched slope paired with a low-pitched or flat slope on each side of the building. Common in Second Empire architecture.

Massed-plan   A term used to describe a building that is more deep than wide. Such buildings usually have short *frontages* and extend deep into the lot.

Molding   A decorative element used to finish surfaces where two points meet, such as where a wall meets the roof or window and door openings.

Mullion   A *molding* that connects individual panes of glass within a window *sash*.

National Register of Historic Places   A list of properties maintained by the National Park Service that are significant at a local, state, or national level in areas of history, architecture, archeology, engineering, and/or culture.

Non-contributing   A property that is not historically significant based on National Register criteria.

Overhang   The portion of the roof that extends beyond the wall. Usually called an *eave*.

Parapet   A wall that extends above the roofline.

Parker truss   A type of *Pratt truss* bridge having an inclined top *chord* of more than five *slopes*.

Pediment   A triangular-shaped *molding* that sometimes caps doorways, windows, and *gable* ends. Common in Neoclassical and Colonial Revival architecture.

Plan   The shape of a building or structure as viewed from above; plans may be simple or complex depending on the building's shape and depth. Plan types include *linear, rectangular,* and *massed*.

Portico   A covered porch supported by a series of columns. Common in Neoclassical architecture.

Pratt truss   A metal *truss bridge* having horizontal and parallel *chords* whose strength relies on a series of interlocking triangles.

Pressed metal   Metal that is molded into shapes and used for *cornices*, window *hoods*, and other decorative *moldings*.

Primary research   Research that involves consulting information that has not been filtered through an interpretive source; examples include diaries, autobiographies, letters, newspaper articles, and census records.

Prism glass   A type of glass cut in small squares that deflect light and create prisms of color; commonly found in commercial building *transoms* and used as an additional light source.

Rectangular plan   A *plan* that is rectangular in shape; it may stand alone (simple) or be combined with other shapes to formed complex *plans*.

Revolving loan fund   A program by which an organization such as Historic Landmarks Foundation of Indiana loans money to a nonprofit organization to buy and/or rehabilitate endangered historic properties. Protective *covenants* are attached to the property's deed.

Ribbon window   A horizontal band of windows grouped together. Common in Prairie style architecture.

Rubble stone   Remnants of larger stones used for construction. Edges are not finished. May be used as a veneer or to construct fences or paths.

Sash   The moveable part of a window that holds the glass.

Section 106   A part of the National Historic Preservation Act of 1966 requiring federal agencies that fund any project that might affect *National Register*-eligible properties to evaluate that project's impact on said properties in conjunction with the State Historic Preservation Officer (SHPO), other interested individuals or organizations (called consulting parties), and occasionally with the Advisory Council on Historic Preservation. The agency must give the SHPO and the Advisory Council a reasonable opportunity to comment on the project in an effort to minimize any negative impacts on eligible properties. A type of environmental review.

Secondary research   Research that involves consulting information that has been filtered through an interpretive source; examples include textbooks, encyclopedias, biographies, and documentaries.

Shed roof   A roof having one *slope*.

Slope   A slanted roof surface.

Surround   A border, usually made of *molding*, that frames a panel, door, or window.

Tracery   Interlaced window *mullions* in the Gothic Revival style.

Transom   A short window located above a door or display window.

Truss bridge   A type of metal bridge that consists of parallel top and bottom *chords*, connected by a series of diagonal beams spanning the bridge's length that add strength.

Vernacular   A common way of building that is not designed by an architect. Often constructed by local carpenters who may or may not have consulted pattern books.

Warren truss   A type of *truss bridge* composed of parallel, flat top and bottom *chords*, with inclined end posts and diagonal interior posts.

Zigzag   Another term for *chevron*. Commonly found on Art Deco architecture.

Log cabins at Camp Crosswick, date unknown. *Courtesy of Historic Preservation Commission of South Bend and St. Joseph County.*